The Token Economy

The Token Economy

Why Everything Is Becoming a Digital Asset

Arjun Malhotra

Mindful Pages

Published in 2026

ISBN: 9789374596999 (PB)
ISBN: 9789374597002 (eBook)

Published by

Mindful Pages
Imprint of Alpha Editions LLC
312 W. 2nd St #1834
Casper, WY 82601, USA

This book was developed using advanced writing tools to support the drafting and ideation process. All content has been thoughtfully curated, refined, and reviewed to ensure quality and relevance.

Content

Introduction
The New Grammar of Ownership

On a rainy afternoon in Manchester, a teenager uploads a song she has written in her bedroom to a digital marketplace. Within hours, the track is not merely streamed or downloaded but *minted*: turned into a token that allows strangers to buy slivers of its future royalties. A museum in Florence, meanwhile, issues time-bound digital passes that behave like living assets—tradable, time-limited, and programmable. In Berlin, a cooperative of local traders fractionalises a warehouse, letting each participant own a digital certificate representing their share of space and rent. None of these actors sees themselves as financiers. Yet each is now, in a subtle but profound way, participating in an economy where ownership behaves like software. The world is learning to programme value.

The term *tokenisation* may sound technical, but its implications are cultural before they are financial. Tokens are not just a new format for money—they are a new grammar for how we hold, share, and signify ownership. The difference is as great as the move from handwriting to word processing, or from postal mail to email. We no longer merely *possess*; we encode, we grant, we trace. To own something now can mean holding a cryptographic key rather than a physical deed. And yet, in this exhilarating shift, a dangerous confusion has emerged: not everything that can be tokenised *should* be. The future of property may depend less on what we can programme, and more on what we *choose* not to.

The story of ownership is one of civilisation's oldest scripts. Ancient Mesopotamians used clay tablets to record claims on grain stores and land parcels. Roman law codified possession, use, and transfer—the triptych of rights that still defines modern property. The feudal manor, the joint-stock company, the modern nation-state—all are architectures of ownership. But today, that architecture is being rewritten not by kings or legislators, but by code. Ledgers, once physical or institutional, are becoming public and decentralised. Instead of a single registry guarded by a sovereign, we now have global, transparent databases that anyone can verify. The shift is subtle but seismic: *trust* moves from hierarchy to network, from paper to protocol.

Yet technology alone does not explain why tokenisation has seized the imagination. It speaks to something deeper—a collective desire to reimagine participation, to make ownership more inclusive, fluid, and programmable. For centuries, property has been bound by friction: borders, bureaucracy, and inequality of access. A token promises to dissolve those walls. It can turn a single painting into a thousand shares, a membership card into a dynamic credential, a song into a living instrument of revenue. For the first time, the infrastructure of ownership is as malleable as software. That is both liberation and temptation.

This book begins with a conviction: that tokenisation is neither a fad nor a panacea, but a structural transformation in how societies record and express value. It will not, as many breathless advocates claim, replace existing institutions overnight. But nor can it be dismissed as a passing crypto craze. It is the next logical evolution in our centuries-long effort to align trust with technology. At its best, it can democratise access, increase transparency, and give creators, communities, and consumers new forms of agency. At its worst, it can trivialise meaning, commodify intimacy, and replace understanding with speculation.

The urgency lies precisely in that tension. We are witnessing the rise of a new kind of economic language—one capable of encoding loyalty, authorship, and belonging as easily as cash flow. When everything from a concert ticket to a carbon credit becomes tokenised, society faces a crucial question: how do we ensure that *meaning* is not lost amid markets? Ownership is not only a mechanism for exchange; it is a mirror of what we value as human beings. A careless approach to tokenisation risks confusing what is *meant* to be shared with what is *fit* to be traded.

Historically, every major transformation in property has been accompanied by both opportunity and crisis. The invention of the joint-stock company in the seventeenth century unlocked global trade but also fuelled speculation and exploitation. The rise of digital platforms promised empowerment but concentrated control.

Tokenisation now stands at a similar threshold. Its pioneers frame it as a revolution in decentralisation, yet many of its early experiments have recreated the same hierarchies of attention and inequality. Tokens promise to free us from middlemen, but can just as easily bind us to opaque code and volatile markets. The challenge is to distinguish structural value from speculative noise.

This book's task is to explain tokenisation without mystique—to strip away the jargon and reveal what genuinely changes when ownership becomes programmable. Each chapter traces one dimension of this new order: from the philosophical roots of property to the practical mechanics of tokens, from the promise of fractional investment to the ethics of what should never be tokenised. It is a map for decision-makers, designers, regulators, and citizens alike: a framework for asking *what* to tokenise, *how* to do it responsibly, and *why* it matters.

The essence of tokenisation lies in its paradox. On one hand, it offers clarity: every transaction traceable, every rule encoded, every claim auditable. On the other, it introduces new forms of opacity: hidden algorithms, technical asymmetries, and the illusion of decentralisation where power still concentrates. It promises frictionless ownership but risks frictionless speculation. The same tool that can empower artists to earn fairly can also inflate worthless hype into fortunes. The question, then, is not merely how tokens work, but *what kind of world they build.*

To explore this, we must begin with the fundamentals of ownership itself. Property, as legal scholars have long noted, is not a thing but a *bundle of rights*: to use, to enjoy, to transfer. Tokens make that bundle programmable. They allow us to separate and recombine access, income, and governance in ways previously impossible. A museum might let patrons earn discounts for attendance. A cooperative might issue digital shares that track both labour and capital contribution. These are not abstractions—they are prototypes of a broader economic imagination in which value is participatory, contextual, and dynamic.

But while code can make property more fluid, it cannot replace the social contracts that give property legitimacy. A token that claims to represent a piece of art or a share of real estate is only meaningful if the link between the digital and the physical—the "oracle"—is trusted. Without it, the token becomes a symbol without substance. Much of the confusion around NFTs and digital assets stems from this broken bridge between worlds. The deeper insight, then, is not that we can now trade anything, but that we must learn to design *trust* anew. Technology can encode rules, but only communities can sustain meaning.

This is where the metaphor of ownership as software becomes potent. Just as software can be buggy, insecure, or poorly documented, so too can token systems. The challenge is not to build faster but to build *legible* systems—ones whose assumptions are transparent, whose incentives are balanced, and whose users are protected from their own cognitive limits. A robust token economy must care as much about usability and ethics as it does about code and markets.

If the last two decades of the internet taught us anything, it is that technological revolutions rarely follow our initial hopes. The web promised connection and delivered surveillance; social media promised voice and rewarded outrage. The token economy now carries its own seductive promise: universal access, creator empowerment, financial democracy. It will fulfil none of these unless we address its design flaws early—flaws not in code, but in culture. Tokenisation is not simply a technical shift but a moral and civic one. It forces us to confront what kind of ownership we want to cultivate in a world where value can be infinitely sliced and endlessly traded.

The coming chapters argue that the true measure of a token's worth is not its price on an exchange, but its *function* in a social system. Does it make coordination easier? Does it deepen trust? Does it align incentives without eroding meaning? These are the questions that separate tokenisation as progress from tokenisation as spectacle. By examining real cases—from co-operative infrastructure to creative industries, from decentralised governance to consumer adoption—we can begin to identify the design patterns that make digital ownership both resilient and humane.

The stakes are high. Within a decade, most organisations will hold or issue digital assets in some form. Entire industries—from finance and art to logistics and real estate—are already experimenting with token-based models. But as the frontier expands, so does the risk of overreach. When everything becomes a potential asset, what happens to things that were never meant to be priced? When loyalty points become tradable, when personal data becomes collateral, when cultural memory itself becomes a marketplace—how do we preserve the boundaries of the sacred and the social?

To navigate this future, we need both ambition and restraint: ambition to harness what tokenisation makes possible, and restraint to prevent it from hollowing out the very values it seeks to empower. This balance—between innovation and integrity, between liquidity and meaning—is the thread running through this book. It demands a new literacy: not just technical fluency, but ethical clarity.

The token economy is coming, whether or not we are ready for it. The question is whether it will be built on hype or on understanding. This book aims to ensure it is the latter. What follows is not evangelism, but architecture: a rigorous, human-centred framework for thinking about tokens, ownership, and value. You will find neither utopia nor dystopia here, but a set of tools to discern both. Because when ownership itself becomes programmable, every society becomes, in effect, a software project—and we must learn to code with conscience.

In the chapters ahead, we will explore how to decide *what* deserves tokenisation, *how* to design it responsibly, and *why* it must serve meaning as much as markets. The transformation is already underway. The task now is to make it wise.

Chapter 1
Ownership, Rewritten

In 1535, King Henry VIII dissolved England's monasteries and redistributed their vast lands to new owners. With one stroke of royal will, centuries of spiritual custodianship turned into legal property. The title deeds that followed—inked on parchment and sealed with wax—did more than record possession; they redefined what it *meant* to own. They transformed faith into asset, community into claim, stewardship into trade. Ownership, ever since, has been rewritten not just by power, but by paperwork. Today, the quill has been replaced by code. Instead of parchment and wax, we now have public ledgers and private keys. Yet the question remains the same: what does it *really* mean to own something?

A teenager holding a digital token to a song she co-wrote may not realise she stands in a lineage that stretches back to those royal decrees. She is both heir and innovator—owning not the object itself, but a programmable claim upon it. Her token may grant her rights to revenue, perhaps even to vote on licensing deals or collaborate with others who hold similar shares. This is not ownership as our grandparents knew it. It is modular, fluid, and above all, *recomposable.* Where the industrial age gave us factories that produced goods, the digital age gives us ledgers that produce claims. We are moving from bricks to bundles—from tangible possession to a web of interlinked rights that can be unbundled, exchanged, or automated.

The modern legal scholar Tony Honoré described ownership as "the greatest possible interest in a thing." But even he conceded it was never absolute. To own a house is not to own the air above it or the minerals beneath it; to own a song is not to own every possible use of its melody. Property has always been a mosaic of privileges and prohibitions—a *bundle of rights* rather than a single, solid object. What tokens do is make that mosaic explicit and programmable. They allow us to carve ownership into precise layers: access without possession, income without control, identity without exclusivity. A gallery might sell time-bound passes to view an artwork, while the painting itself remains in public trust. A musician might sell royalties without giving away creative control. In both cases, ownership becomes a system of code—dynamic, divisible, and open to redesign.

This transformation is not merely technical. It asks us to revisit the foundations of trust. Titles, historically, recorded claims sanctioned by institutions: a land registry, a notary, a government. These entities mediated belief—"I trust that you own this because a trusted party says so." But what happens when the ledger itself *is* the trusted party? Tokens shift the axis of verification. They invite us to believe not because a clerk certifies, but because a network attests. The implications are profound. When verification becomes open by default, the architecture of ownership moves from institutional to infrastructural—from authority to protocol. The ledger becomes a living commons, where the act of recording is inseparable from the act of believing.

That shift is easy to romanticise and equally easy to misunderstand. A ledger, however open, cannot eliminate politics. The notion that code alone can replace the messy work of law and governance is a seductive mirage. Yet it is also true that public ledgers have changed the boundaries of trust. In many parts of the world, land rights are opaque, paper records are fragile, and institutional corruption is endemic. A tamper-proof, auditable record—shared and verifiable by all—offers more than efficiency; it offers *legibility*. Ownership ceases to be a private privilege and becomes a public fact. That is not a trivial innovation. It is a reconfiguration of power.

Still, not everything should be eternal or scarce. The internet was born on the principle of infinite copyability—information as a public good, endlessly reproducible. Tokenisation, by contrast, reintroduces scarcity into a digital world that once celebrated abundance. It manufactures exclusivity not through physics, but through consensus. A digital artwork, once freely reproducible, can now be made singular, its uniqueness guaranteed by code. This capacity to *engineer scarcity* is both ingenious and perilous. When used well, it can sustain creative economies, preserve digital heritage, and coordinate shared value. When abused, it breeds speculation, hoarding, and cultural fatigue. The difference lies not in the technology but in the *intent.* A limited-edition game skin that rewards genuine engagement enhances community; a contrived "drop" designed to inflate prices corrodes trust. The token itself is neutral—it is our design of scarcity that determines whether value is created or destroyed.

As this chapter will show, the token economy's most radical promise is not new wealth, but new literacy. To navigate it, we must move beyond slogans like "own your assets" and ask deeper questions. What kind of value does a token embody? Does it provide *use*—a practical function? Does it hold *exchange* value—a price others recognise? Does it confer *identity*—a sense of belonging or recognition? These three dimensions—value-in-use, value-in-exchange, and value-in-identity—form a practical triad, a test for distinguishing meaningful tokenisation from mere novelty. A token that fails all three is little more than a mirage, a shiny placeholder for value that never arrives.

Ownership, then, is being rewritten not through revolution but through recombination. Each technological epoch has redrafted its grammar of possession: feudal oaths became deeds, deeds became shares, shares became database entries. Tokens are the next chapter in that story—a system that lets us *compose ownership* as if we were writing code. Yet this new grammar demands new literacy. To design or adopt tokenised systems responsibly, we must understand not only how they function, but what they signify. Every line of code carries a moral choice about access, power, and permanence. Every token carries within it a philosophy of ownership—whether it invites community or extracts profit, whether it deepens meaning or flattens it into trade.

We stand at a crossroads between two futures of property. One treats tokens as speculative chips in a global casino; the other treats them as building blocks for shared prosperity and transparent governance. The difference is not technological—it is conceptual. To rewrite ownership well, we must recover what it has always meant: a relationship between people, things, and the systems that bind them. The ledger, like the law before it, is only as just as the society that writes upon it.

This chapter will unpack that shift in full: how tokens re-bundle rights, how ledgers alter trust, how scarcity is engineered, and how to discern real value from digital illusion. But for now, hold one thought in mind: ownership has never been static. It is a story humanity keeps rewriting, each time with a new tool in hand. The question before us is not whether we will write it again—but whether we will do so wisely.

Bundles, not bricks

In 1215, on the meadow of Runnymede, King John placed his seal on the Magna Carta, conceding that even a monarch's ownership of land was not absolute. The document did not create private property as we know it, but it planted the seed: that ownership could be divided, limited, and negotiated. What the barons won that day was not the soil itself, but the rights to use, inherit, and protect it under law. Eight centuries later, that same logic—the partitioning of rights into definable claims—is being rewritten in code rather than parchment. A digital token representing a piece of property, artwork, or access permit follows the same principle: ownership is not a monolith, but a *bundle of entitlements*. What changes now is our ability to separate, combine, and automate those entitlements at unprecedented precision.

To describe ownership as a "bundle of rights" is to dismantle the comforting illusion that property is a singular, indivisible thing. When a homeowner in Leeds rents out a spare room through Airbnb, she temporarily transfers *use* rights but retains *title* and *control*. When a band in Bristol sells digital tokens granting holders a share of their future royalties, they are selling *income* rights but keeping *creative* rights intact. The genius of the token lies in its capacity to formalise these distinctions—to write them into logic that executes automatically, without relying on continuous human enforcement. It does not replace the concept of ownership; it *granularises* it. Every permission, restriction, or profit share becomes an instruction that can be programmed, traded, and audited.

This concept has deep roots in property theory. In the early twentieth century, the American jurist Wesley Hohfeld mapped legal relations into eight fundamental "jural correlatives": right, duty, privilege, no-right, power, liability, immunity, and disability. His insight was that ownership is not a relation between a person and a thing, but a web of relations between people about a thing. To own is to have enforceable expectations of others. The brilliance of tokenisation is that it captures this web in executable form. A smart contract can encode that you may enter a digital gallery for one hour, that you receive two per cent of its revenue stream, or that your vote counts only if you hold a certain token balance. Hohfeld's abstraction becomes, quite literally, operational.

Consider the Louvre's digital initiative in 2022, when it explored issuing limited digital passes for after-hours access to the museum's most visited galleries. These passes could, in theory, behave as programmable rights: holders could transfer them, rent them for an evening, or pair them with digital certificates of attendance. The Louvre did not go so far as to issue fully tradable tokens, but the prototype demonstrated how *access* could be decoupled from *ownership* of the institution or its assets. The right to *experience* an object became distinct from the right to *possess* or *profit* from it. This separation is not an abstraction—it is a profound shift in how cultural institutions may fund, govern, and share their value.

Contrast that with the case of the Uffizi Gallery in Florence, which in May 2021 licensed digital reproductions of Botticelli's *The Birth of Venus* as NFTs through a private partner. The sale reportedly generated €140,000, but controversy followed: the museum's leadership later retracted from the programme, citing confusion about what exactly had been sold. The buyers did not own the artwork, of course, but the *representation* of it—and the public struggled to understand the boundary between cultural heritage and commercial token. Here, the bundle of rights was poorly communicated. The token formalised one claim (ownership of a digital file) while leaving others ambiguous (reproduction, resale, cultural context). The incident revealed both the promise and peril of programmable ownership: clarity in code does not guarantee clarity in meaning.

The capacity to separate rights also changes how communities organise around shared assets. In 2019, a cooperative in Berlin known as Spreefeld experimented with digitally recording participatory shares in a collectively owned housing complex. Residents could hold non-tradable tokens representing *use rights* to specific apartments and *voting rights* in governance decisions. Because the tokens were bound by smart contracts, they could prevent speculative resale while allowing limited transfer within the community. Here, ownership ceased to be a static title and became a living constitution. The bundle of rights was not only recorded but *maintained* by consensus.

There is, however, a counterpoint. The more divisible ownership becomes, the easier it is to lose sight of responsibility. In the 2008 financial crisis, mortgage-backed securities demonstrated what happens when property rights are sliced and recombined without accountability. Each bond represented a fraction of a right—income from mortgage payments—but the web of intermediaries became so opaque that no one could trace who truly bore the risk. Tokenisation can replicate that mistake if we mistake programmability for governance. The fact that a right is legible on a ledger does not mean it is ethically or economically sound. Complexity can conceal as much as it reveals.

The implications extend far beyond finance. Think of intellectual property. In 2023, the London-based publisher Faber & Faber explored tokenised rights for limited digital editions of poetry, allowing collectors to hold provable copies while poets received perpetual royalties. The tokens embedded both *access* (the digital file) and *income* (royalties from resale). In effect, ownership was rewritten to recognise ongoing creative participation rather than one-time sale. It was a subtle but radical act: transforming ownership from an endpoint into a relationship. Yet even this elegant experiment faced a tension between exclusivity and openness. When does rewarding creators cross into commodifying art? The bundle of rights, however programmable, still sits within a moral frame that code cannot enforce.

A quiet motif emerges here—the *ledger as lens*. What we choose to record defines what we choose to value. Historically, ledgers—be they royal rolls, shipping manifests, or bank books—captured wealth in tangible form. The digital ledger captures *intention*. It can record not just ownership but participation, reputation, and contribution.

But it can also strip context away. When a museum tokenises entry passes, the richness of cultural experience risks being reduced to a data point. When a neighbourhood tokenises collective ownership, the act of living together risks being mistaken for a series of transactions. The challenge is to make the ledger a *mirror* of meaning, not merely a register of trade.

The same tension appears in the treatment of *governance rights*. Tokens can grant holders a vote in collective decisions—on the distribution of revenue, the curation of content, or the admission of new members. In 2020, Friends with Benefits, a decentralised creative collective, issued membership tokens whose holders could propose and vote on events, partnerships, and funding allocations. It functioned as a club with its constitution encoded in software. Yet as membership value rose sharply, new entrants bought tokens not for participation but speculation, diluting the culture the system was meant to preserve. Governance rights became indistinguishable from market rights. Here, the ledger reflected not democracy, but price. The distinction between *right* and *stake* collapsed.

The question, therefore, is not whether tokens can rebundle ownership—they already do—but how to decide *which* rights to formalise and *how* to balance them. The medieval manor, the modern corporation, and the digital cooperative all perform the same act: distributing access, control, and reward across time and participants. What changes is the medium. A deed on parchment needed a seal; a company share needed a registrar; a token needs a consensus protocol. The historical continuity is striking. Every innovation in property has been, at its core, an attempt to stabilise trust in changing conditions. Tokenisation is no different, but it carries a new possibility: the automation of trust itself.

That possibility tempts us to overreach. Not every right benefits from being explicit or tradable. Informal reciprocity, social norms, and unspoken expectations are forms of ownership too—ones that resist codification. When we tokenise every relationship, we risk eroding the subtle agreements that sustain communities. Consider Wikipedia: millions of contributors maintain it without personal tokens, sustained by reputation rather than property. Would converting that participation into tokenised stakes make it fairer or hollower? The answer depends on whether we believe value is best maintained through markets or meanings. A ledger can distribute profit; it cannot guarantee purpose.

The intellectual clarity of the "bundle of rights" model can, paradoxically, obscure the emotional reality of ownership. To own is to feel attachment, pride, sometimes identity. A token can record rights but not affections. Yet, by making ownership composable, it may also allow more people to share in that feeling. A local resident owning one thousandth of a renewable energy project through a digital token may not physically control the turbines, but she *participates* in their story. She owns a fragment of the future. Perhaps that is what ownership in the twenty-first century will increasingly mean: participation through design, rather than possession through exclusion.

Still, one question must remain unresolved, as it should: at what point does division weaken belonging? Every rebundling of rights creates new freedoms—and new frictions. The art of token design lies in balancing modularity with coherence, ensuring that the sum of parts still feels like a whole. That is the quiet discipline this new age of ownership demands: to build bundles, not bricks, but never forget the hands that hold them.

From titles to ledgers

On 20 April 2017 in Tbilisi, Georgia's National Agency of Public Registry and the Bitfury Group announced that a real-estate registration had been cryptographically anchored to a blockchain, the first step in a system intended to record land titles with public verifiability. The deed itself still lived within Georgian law; the hash of its record, however, now existed on a ledger anyone could audit. A homeowner no longer depended solely on a clerk's stamp or a minister's seal to prove priority. They could point to a public fingerprint of their claim, time-stamped beyond the reach of local politics or office fires. The counter becomes code.

Titles record claims; ledgers coordinate trust. A title says, *you own this.* A ledger shows *how we know and agree that you do.* When the Georgian pilot moved from paper and siloed databases towards a public anchor, it did not abolish the title; it changed the *witness*. The witness was no longer just a registrar in Tbilisi but a network of machines that, taken together, refused to forget. That shift—from a single institutional witness to a distributed one—is what this section examines: what changes when verification is open by default, and how tokens ride on that change.

To see the difference with clarity, start at the counter of a traditional land office. The line is long. You bring passports, forms, sometimes a brown envelope of historical documents. A registrar checks the parcel number, consults a ledger book or a terminal, applies a stamp, perhaps asks for another affidavit. This is institutional trust in practice: a human chain of verification, bolstered by locks, permissions, and reputations. It works, often well. But it relies on the integrity of a single archive and the humans who guard it. Show: a rubber stamp on vellum. Name: the *title* entered into a paper registry. Explain: the claim exists because the institution says so. Implication: if the archive is compromised, the claim is vulnerable, and your recourse is political or judicial rather than technical.

Move to a modern database registry. The counter is quicker; forms are scanned; entries live in a relational schema with role-based access control. The administrator can roll back errors, freeze entries, or correct a typo. Audit logs track who did what and when. Show: a login screen, badges, a ticketing system for updates. Name: the *database* as ledger, owned by an institution. Explain: trust increases via speed, backups, and role separation, yet remains centralised. Implication: resilience improves against fire and misfiling, but the same institution remains the final arbiter of truth, and a single superuser or breach can still rewrite the past.

Now step into a public ledger. There is no counter. There is a protocol. Entries are signed by private keys and propagated across nodes; time is measured in blocks; changes require network consensus. No clerk can quietly "fix" a record. Show: a transaction ID, a block height, an explorer query. Name: the *public ledger*—a database where validation is open, verification amateur-proof, and history append-only. Explain: the system coordinates trust by making falsification expensive and detection trivial. Implication:

power shifts; the authority to attest migrates from an office to a network, and with it the locus of accountability also changes—from discretion to procedure, from private logs to public proofs.

What, then, do tokens add? They package rights with verification. A token is to a ledger what a title is to a registry: an entry that embodies a claim. But when tokens live on public ledgers, their verification becomes *ambient.* Anyone can check ownership, provenance, or transfer without asking permission. In the analogue era, due diligence meant letters, appointments, and photocopies. In the network era, it is a query. The cost of skepticism falls. That alteration—skepticism becoming cheap—is the heart of "open by default".

Sweden's Lantmäteriet provides a careful example of what this shift can promise and what it demands. Between 2016 and 2018 in Stockholm, the land authority ran pilots with ChromaWay, Telia, and others to model property transactions on a distributed ledger, integrating banks, brokers, buyers, and the state into a single workflow. Show: a digitally signed contract that moved through parties without manual re-entry. Name: *Lantmäteriet's blockchain pilot* (Stockholm, 2016–2018). Explain: the system demonstrated that a shared ledger could synchronise steps, reduce reconciliation, and provide a tamper-evident trail across institutions. Implication: the ledger shifts from a single-owner database to a shared coordination layer, promising fewer delays and fewer disputes about "who knew what when".

A different track, equally instructive, comes from Estonia. Since the early 2010s in Tallinn, the state has worked with Guardtime to deploy KSI (Keyless Signature Infrastructure) across government systems, using cryptographic hashes to attest to the integrity of records, including health data. Show: a citizen checks who accessed a medical file and when, backed by hash-linked audit trails. Name: *Estonia's KSI-backed logs* (Tallinn, 2012 onwards). Explain: the ledger here is not a cryptocurrency network but a verifiability layer that makes unauthorised changes detectable. Implication: public verification does not always mean public exposure; a state can keep records private while making integrity proofs widely checkable, blending institutional responsibility with cryptographic accountability.

Yet not all experiments land. In 2015, Honduras announced a partnership with Factom to secure its land registry using blockchain technology. Political turnover, data quality issues, and legal integration challenges meant the project never reached full deployment. Show: a press release, then silence. Name: *Honduras–Factom land registry pilot* (Tegucigalpa, 2015). Explain: an open ledger cannot salvage a closed governance environment; digital integrity means little if the analogue foundation is corrupt or incomplete. Implication: technology cannot conjure trust ex nihilo; ledgers coordinate trust that institutions and communities already sustain.

These examples point to a key distinction between *recording* and *coordinating*. Titles record; ledgers coordinate. The paper registry is a catalogue; the database is a faster catalogue; the public ledger is coordination infrastructure. Coordination shows up as behaviour: fewer reconciliations, fewer duplicate forms, fewer private copies of "the truth". Name the benefit plainly: synchronisation. Explain: when everyone reads and writes to the same auditable substrate, disputes shift from "your system versus mine" to "this entry versus that key". Implication: accountability tightens; excuses thin out.

Open verification also changes incentives. In a paper system, an official can quietly prioritise a friend's file. In a closed database, an administrator can still grant access to a privileged contractor. On a public ledger, favouritism has fewer hiding places; actions leave signatures. Show: a procurement contract posted and time-stamped before bids are opened. Name: an *on-chain procurement registry* run by a city hall as an integrity measure. Explain: officials commit to rules in advance, and the ledger preserves those commitments as public artefacts. Implication: the risk of reputational damage rises for deviation; trust shifts from personalities to proofs.

But openness cuts both ways. Public verification can reveal patterns that endanger privacy or market integrity. A ledger where all transfers are visible can facilitate surveillance or predatory behaviour unless rights are carefully wrapped in privacy-preserving designs. Show: a charity's token-based aid distribution that inadvertently exposes recipients' wallets to analytics firms. Name: a *traceable cash-aid pilot* operated on a transparent chain. Explain: while auditability enables external assurance, it can also create unintended data exhaust about vulnerable people. Implication: "open by default" is not a moral absolute; designers must select what is open and what remains shielded, using techniques like zero-knowledge proofs or off-chain attestations.

For institutions, the move from titles to ledgers also means a move from discretion to *commitment devices*. A registrar used to be able to say, "We will process this within two weeks." A ledger lets the agency *prove* when a transaction was queued, when it was processed, and whether a deadline was met. Show: a service-level timer that starts at submission, visible to all counterparties. Name: a *digital service commitment* encoded into a smart workflow. Explain: metrics replace promises; delays have traces. Implication: performance management shifts from internal dashboards to public accountability, and excuses lose air.

Tokens amplify this because they embody claims that travel. A museum's tokenised pass can be transferred without phoning a clerk. A co-op's governance token can be delegated without convening a meeting. Show: a secondary sale of a time-bound access token that respects blackout dates automatically. Name: a *time-locked access token* enforced by a smart contract. Explain: the ledger is not only recording outcomes but *preventing* rule breaking by design. Implication: compliance becomes behavioural; the system narrows the gap between policy and practice.

There is a catch. Code ossifies. Paper can tolerate ambiguity; a registrar can recognise a widow's affidavit and make a humane exception. A database administrator can issue a one-off fix under supervision. A public ledger resists exceptions. Show: a transfer executed mistakenly and propagated irreversibly. Name: an *irreversible on-chain error*. Explain: the property of finality—which deters fraud—also deters mercy. Implication: societies must reintroduce carefully bounded reversibility—escrow periods, multi-signature releases, or adjudication hooks—if they want the benefits of both integrity and compassion.

The quiet motif returns: the counter. In paper systems, the counter is where discretion lives; in public ledgers, the counter dissolves into protocol. That removal can feel dehumanising unless we replace it with transparent processes for recourse. Show: an appeals mechanism linked to tokens, where a court order can freeze a disputed asset without breaking the ledger's invariants. Name: a *court-controlled freeze function* executed by a designated key under strict oversight. Explain: institutions do not vanish; they change role—from sole authors of truth to authorised editors with traceable pens. Implication: the future is not code *versus* law but code *with* law, the ledger making institutional interventions visible and auditable.

Sweden's pilot and Estonia's KSI share another lesson: success depends on *interfaces*, not just back-ends. A citizen experiences trust at a screen or a counter, not in consensus algorithms. Show: a property buyer who can see, step by step, which party has signed and when funds will release. Name: a *shared settlement dashboard* that unifies banks, brokers, and registry. Explain: the ledger coordinates, but the interface educates; comprehension is the first defence against fraud. Implication: open verification must be consumable; otherwise it remains a specialist toy that the public bypasses with blind faith.

A frequent objection is cost and complexity. Not every registry needs a blockchain; not every token deserves an open rail. The counter-example is plain: when transaction volume is low, parties are stable, and disputes are rare, a well-governed database may be sufficient and cheaper. Show: a small rural land office that processes a handful of transfers each week without incident, maintained by a diligent staff. Name: a *low-volume registry* with excellent audits. Explain: adding a public ledger here could increase overhead without tangible gain. Implication: technology choices should follow risk profiles and coordination needs, not fashion.

How, then, to decide where to anchor titles and where to embrace ledgers? A practical approach starts with failure modes. If your biggest risk is loss of records, robust backups and off-site storage may suffice. If your biggest risk is insider tampering or inter-agency dispute, consider shared ledgers that equalise power between participants. If your persistent problem is the public's mistrust of invisible processes, then open verification earns its keep because it changes the *experience* of trust: anyone can check, not just the privileged few.

This brings us back to the token, a title with legs. Its value rests on how we coordinate belief about it. Paper titles bind us to an office that authorises. Database titles bind us to an organisation that administers. Public-ledger tokens bind us to a network that attests. Each arrangement embodies a philosophy of trust and a set of trade-offs. Show: the three desks—the registrar's, the database admin's, the node operator's. Name: *counter, console, consensus*. Explain: at each desk, verification takes a different shape—stamp, role, signature. Implication: choosing a ledger is not a technical footnote; it is a constitutional decision about where you want truth to live and how you want it to be contested.

There is no universal answer. A city that digitises titles may still prefer a central database if it prizes speed and internal control. A cross-border supply chain, plagued by duplicated paperwork and finger-pointing, might need a shared ledger to keep everyone honest. A cultural institution may anchor provenance to a public chain while keeping donor identities private. Each case is a design of incentives as much as information.

So the counter flickers before us again. Do we keep it, transform it, or let the network take its place? The choice is not binary but a spectrum, and the stakes are plain. When verification becomes open by default, who carries the quill, who holds the key, and who gets to say, *this line here is the truth*?

Scarcity, engineered

In August 2013, Valve Corporation in Bellevue, Washington shipped the Arms Deal Update for *Counter-Strike: Global Offensive*, adding weapon "skins" to a decade-old shooter and tying them to a controlled secondary marketplace. Within months, virtual finishes with no effect on gameplay were trading for hundreds of dollars; by January 2018, a "Souvenir AWP | Dragon Lore" skin reportedly sold for over $61,000 (Polygon, 2018). Nothing physical changed. The rules did. A studio set supply ceilings, encoded provenance, and enforced a marketplace with fees and fraud checks. Scarcity arrived by coordination rather than physics. It worked.

Why did it work? A rifle that shoots the same still feels different when the market can trace its origin, count identical copies, and guarantee that authenticity persists. Skins became signals: of time invested, of event attendance, of luck. The mint was code. The vault was a ledger. Players behaved accordingly. Prices formed, communities policed fakery, and designers tuned drops as if adjusting monetary policy. Five words explain the pivot: *software made scarcity socially credible.*

Engineered scarcity is not new. Limited editions have long supported art and fashion. But tokens and ledgers let us do something those markets could only approximate: publish the rulebook for supply, bind it to transfers, and make the history of each unit inspectable by anyone. Show a cap. Name the cap. Explain how it's enforced. Then let strangers coordinate around that knowledge. The implications are profound—sometimes healthy, sometimes hazardous. The question is when constraint sharpens value, and when it curdles into speculation.

Start with the behaviour we can see. In *CS:GO*, the Arms Deal Update (August 2013) did three things that matter: it created item classes with fixed minting ranges; it attached visible provenance (tournament "Souvenir" drops, team stickers); and it hosted exchange on an official market tied to Steam accounts. The show is a trading page with a unique item ID and price history. The name is a *programme of scarcity* authored by Valve. The explanation is coordination: players agree a red-tier skin is rarer because the drop tables and supply ceilings say so, and the platform prevents counterfeits and double-spends. The implication is enforceable meaning: if you own a celebrated skin, others can verify it without trusting you or a third-party forum. A token is a promise with receipts.

Now consider a second example beyond games. In October 2020, Dapper Labs in Vancouver opened *NBA Top Shot* to the public, selling officially licensed basketball "moments" as NFTs with stated mint counts and clear serial numbers. Sales surged in early 2021; at the peak, individual packs sold out in minutes and secondary transactions cleared at premium prices. Show: a numbered LeBron James dunk with a stated "Limited Edition" of 79. Name: *NBA Top Shot* (Vancouver, 2020–2021). Explain: scarcity was engineered by capping mints per moment, publishing serials, and guaranteeing provenance under the NBA's licence. Implication: mainstream consumers responded not to cryptography in the abstract but to *transparent limits* attached to a cultural narrative they recognised.

The mechanism here is not alchemy. It is disclosure plus enforcement. Tokens publish conditions ex ante (supply limits, unlock schedules, access constraints), then keep those conditions visible and hard to subvert. This pushes two behaviours. First, participants monitor supply more than they monitor rhetoric; the mint schedule becomes the news. Secondly, designers are tempted to *play the mint*: raise prices, game scarcity with micro-variants, or pace releases to drive fear of missing out. The mint becomes a metronome that can either guide a healthy rhythm or produce manic swings.

We should name the risk. Engineered scarcity can amplify speculation, especially when the token's *use* is thin. When *CS:GO* skins became chips for unregulated gambling in 2016, Valve intervened and issued cease-and-desist letters to major betting sites, citing terms-of-service violations and prompting shutdowns and lawsuits (2016). Show: teenagers in Twitch chats wagering skins on match outcomes. Name: *skin gambling crackdowns* (2016). Explain: the same properties that made skins verifiable and tradable also made them liquid enough for betting markets outside the game's design intent. Implication: scarcity without boundaries invites external uses that can damage trust and draw regulators' attention.

A contrasting limitation appears in markets where artificial caps are abundant but *meaning* is not. Ubisoft announced Quartz, an NFT experiment for *Tom Clancy's Ghost Recon Breakpoint*, in December 2021. The items were branded "Digits", individually numbered and tied to playtime requirements. Uptake was muted; after a few additions, updates paused and the game itself ended active development (2022). Show: a marketplace listing languishing with no bids. Name: *Ubisoft Quartz* (Paris, December 2021). Explain:

engineered scarcity could not compensate for weak cultural attachment to the items, unclear benefits, and a wary audience. Implication: caps without narrative and utility are caps without buyers; the ledger can certify authenticity, not desire.

What separates constructive constraint from empty hype is alignment. A rule that curbs free riding or rewards contribution produces durable incentives; a rule that merely rations access produces queues and resentment. Consider *Dota 2*'s International Compendiums (Seattle, 2013–2019), which offered time-bound digital items and in-game features while allocating a portion of sales to the tournament prize pool. Show: an evolving digital book with stretch goals and limited cosmetics. Name: *The International Compendium* (Seattle, first launched 2013). Explain: engineered scarcity—seasonal cosmetics that would not return—was tied to a collective outcome: funding competition and unlocking features as thresholds were met. Implication: participants bought because scarcity was *socially productive*; they could measure impact in prize-pool growth, not just in resale prices.

Tokens let us tether scarcity to performance conditions more tightly still. A museum can mint 10,000 year-passes but enforce that only passes recorded as "used" three times unlock a curator talk. A game studio can release a skin that levels up its visual effects only if a player completes a set of community challenges. Show: a contract that increases an NFT's metadata tier after verifiable milestones. Name: *progressive scarcity*. Explain: supply is still capped, but *quality* within the cap evolves according to effort and collaboration, not merely luck at mint. Implication: speculation becomes harder when value depends on visible, non-trivial behaviours; engineered scarcity now rewards what designers deem healthy for the community.

However, we must not romanticise the instrument. Scarcity works because people believe rules will hold. That belief can fade. *NBA Top Shot* faced complaints in mid-2021 as Dapper introduced more "Circulating Count" moments, blurring the line between limited and open editions. Show: a collector checking a serial number, then seeing supply later expand in a different tier. Name: *edition creep* (2021). Explain: even with explanations, changing categories can feel like retroactive debasement; the social contract around scarcity weakens when boundaries slip. Implication: coordination needs credible commitment; if the mint is a metronome, do not change its tempo mid-song without consent.

There is also the physics of attention. Even perfect scarcity can meet a cold market when narratives tire or alternatives bloom. This is where the motif of the mint returns. A mint is loud at birth, then quiet. It cannot be a constant siren without exhausting its audience. Designers who overuse limited drops—weekly "grails", incessant micro-caps—teach participants to hold cash and wait for "the next". Liquidity fragments. Price discovery skews. Show: a chart of daily active traders falling after a glut of releases. Name: *drop fatigue*. Explain: when every week is special, no week is special; engineered scarcity becomes white noise. Implication: cadence should follow context—moments of real significance, not calendar compulsion.

To judge whether engineered scarcity aligns incentives, we can ask three grounded questions. What behaviour does scarcity reward tomorrow that the system actually needs? Who bears the downside risk if demand falls—creators, platforms, or late buyers? How visible and unchangeable are the rules that govern supply? Pair each with an observable indicator. For behaviour, track retention among purchasers versus non-purchasers one month after a drop. For risk, examine buy-back policies or floor-price support mechanisms; measure how often they trigger. For rules, audit contract metadata and versioning; verify whether keys that can change supply are time-locked or multi-sig controlled. These are mundane checks. They prevent magical thinking.

The game-skin economy offers a concrete lesson here. In *CS:GO*, Valve rarely reissues identical rare skins; when it does introduce variants, they carry distinct names, wear values, or capsule origins, preserving old lines' identity. Show: a veteran "2014 Katowice" sticker that remains prized even as newer designs flood in. Name: *provenance segmentation*. Explain: supply expands, but it expands along new branches rather than through dilution of old ones. Implication: scarcity maintains narrative integrity; early commitments retain meaning because history is legible and cannot be overwritten by a quiet patch.

Contrast that with *Diablo III*'s Real Money Auction House (2012), which let players trade gear for cash. Blizzard removed it in March 2014, explaining that it undermined the core game loop by making the most efficient path to power a financial transaction rather than play. Show: a developer blog announcing the closure and a patch that increased in-game drop rates. Name: *Real Money Auction House shutdown* (Irvine, March 2014). Explain: the market was efficient at pricing items but misaligned with the experience; scarcity of powerful gear had become a paywall, not a challenge. Implication: when engineered scarcity diverts effort from the activity to the marketplace, trust in the system's purpose erodes, and even a functioning market must be dismantled.

One might object that these are entertainment examples, not weighty public goods. Yet the same mechanics now shape culture, tickets, and membership. When Live Nation experimented with token-gated pre-sales in 2022, fans saw earlier access attached to provable fandom rather than opaque queues. Show: a wallet verifier at checkout that checks event NFTs or prior purchase badges. Name: *token-gated ticketing pilots* (2022). Explain: scarcity—the pre-sale window—is assigned by participation signals captured on a ledger, not by arbitrary codes distributed to mailing lists. Implication: allocation can feel fairer because criteria are visible and consistent, though it can also create new exclusion lines that must be justified.

So, how to engineer scarcity without engineering regret? Treat the mint like a covenant. Publish supply ranges and keys. Bind changes to procedures that require time and consensus. Tie caps to contributions people respect—attendance, craft, service—so that price signals roughly reflect participation, not merely timing. When the value is cultural, invest in provenance storytelling: dates, places, collaborators. When the value is utility, invest in service reliability: uptime, redemption UX, anti-fraud. The ledger can only carry meaning that institutions and designers put into it.

We return to the mint one last time. It is a small square of metal in the imagination, stamping a serial onto a coin. In tokens, the stamp is a block height and a signature. In both cases, it says: this is counted; this is bounded; this belongs to a set we can all see. Counting and bounding are not oppressive by nature; they are the scaffolds of cooperation. The danger arrives when the scaffold becomes the spectacle, when the stamp is prized more than the coin's use.

A studio can cap a skin at 500 copies. A museum can mint 1,000 passes. A collective can issue 10,000 governance badges. The act is easy. The consequence is not. What will you make scarce: admission, attention, or achievement? Who enforces the cap, and how visible is that power? If demand cools, what breaks first—the promise, the price, or the trust?

The three tests

In March 2021, Jack Dorsey, then chief executive of Twitter, sold an NFT of his first tweet—"just setting up my twttr"—for $2.9 million through the platform Valuables by Cent. The buyer, Sina Estavi, called it "a piece of digital history". A year later, when Estavi tried to resell it, bids barely reached a few hundred dollars. The code was intact; the certificate still pointed to the tweet; yet the market had vanished. The episode distilled a hard truth: not everything that can be tokenised has value that endures. The ledger had preserved the record perfectly, but it could not preserve *meaning*. That gap—between what can be recorded and what should be—is what the following triad helps to close.

Tokens sit at the intersection of three forms of value: use, exchange, and identity. A project that fails all three is a collectible mirage; one that satisfies only one dimension may function but rarely flourish. The tests are simple to describe and difficult to pass. Each exposes a different weakness in the "just tokenise it" reflex that has dominated the last decade. *Value-in-use* asks whether the token does something worth repeating. *Value-in-exchange* asks whether others recognise and can trade that utility fairly. *Value-in-identity* asks whether owning or using the token says something that people wish to keep saying. Together, they form a diagnostic lens through which to separate durable economies from disposable experiments.

Begin with value-in-use. Show: a verifiable service or function that a token performs repeatedly and reliably. Name: *Helium Network* (San

Francisco, launched 2019). Explain: Helium rewards users for providing wireless coverage to connected devices; tokens circulate as payment for data transmission and as incentives for network maintenance. The token is not a speculative chip detached from activity—it *pays for bandwidth*. Implication: when use precedes hype, markets price performance rather than promise. The daily metric is measurable—number of packets transmitted—and the price adjusts accordingly. The system may face competition, but its economic gravity lies in action, not attitude.

Contrast this with the NFT avatar boom of 2021. Projects such as *Bored Ape Yacht Club* (Yuga Labs, Miami, April 2021) offered holders cartoon primates with commercial rights and social cachet. Value-in-use was minimal—display rights, community access—but value-in-identity was immense. Owners signalled wealth, taste, or early adopter status. Secondary markets exploded, with some sales surpassing $1 million. When the speculative tide receded, use-value did not backstop prices; those who still held their apes did so for affiliation rather than function. The lesson: use anchors, identity floats. Without a tether between them, volatility becomes destiny.

Value-in-exchange is more delicate. It asks whether a token can be *priced* without being trivialised. Traditional securities achieve this through standardised disclosure; currencies do it through deep liquidity and consistent demand. Tokens exist between these worlds, often too idiosyncratic for transparent markets and too open-ended for strict regulation. Show: *Ethereum gas fees*—micro-payments that power computation. Name: *Ether (ETH)*, live since July 2015. Explain: its exchange value emerges from a clear service constraint: every smart contract consumes gas, and gas requires Ether. The market price of ETH thus tracks both speculation and computational demand. Implication: exchange value stabilises when it corresponds to a measurable constraint, not merely narrative momentum.

A credible counter-example helps. During the ICO surge of 2017, dozens of projects issued tokens with grand promises—"decentralised storage," "AI marketplaces," "blockchain for healthcare"—but no binding use case. Many traded heavily at launch, then withered as activity failed to materialise. Their exchange value proved unmoored because their use value was fictional. Tokens like *Filecoin* (protocol launched October 2020) eventually recovered by delivering real infrastructure, but hundreds vanished into regulatory archives. The reconciliation is straightforward: liquidity amplifies reality, not fantasy, over time. Tokens that cannot measure their own circulation decay into trivia.

The third test, value-in-identity, may be the most subtle. Ownership is a social signal; the token is a badge that carries context. A university degree, a season ticket, or a veterans' medal all encode belonging and history. Tokens can formalise such identity links, but they also risk flattening them into tradeable trinkets. Show: *Proof of Attendance Protocol* (POAP, Buenos Aires, 2019), which issues non-transferable badges to attendees of events. Name: *POAP tokens.* Explain: each badge functions as verifiable memory—evidence of participation rather than property for sale. Because they cannot be resold, their value-in-identity grows with personal significance and social recognition. Implication: scarcity here reinforces authenticity, not speculation; the holder's story matters more than market price.

Identity value can also decay when transferability exceeds meaning. In 2022, fashion house *Dolce & Gabbana* released digital wearables and NFTs with exclusive access to events. While initial auctions raised millions, subsequent trading volumes plunged as buyers realised that resale stripped away the experiential privileges—the dinners, fittings, and backstage access—that made ownership desirable. The market priced what remained: pixels detached from privilege. Tokens, when dislocated from identity context, reveal how fragile symbolic value can be once treated as liquid capital.

The triad functions best when its dimensions reinforce each other. A museum token that grants entry (use), trades on secondary markets (exchange), and signals patronage (identity) satisfies all three. The Tate Modern's hypothetical *Digital Patron Pass*—if it were to exist—could illustrate this structure. The pass might entitle holders to free visits and priority exhibitions (use), be exchangeable among art enthusiasts (exchange), and convey ongoing recognition in donor walls or digital galleries (identity). The coordination of these layers is what gives the design dignity. A token with only exchange value risks becoming a lottery ticket; with only identity value, a badge of vanity; with only use value, a coupon. Tokens that pass the three tests inhabit all three states at once.

The motif threading these dimensions is *continuity*. Use value keeps activity continuous; exchange value keeps recognition continuous across participants; identity value keeps meaning continuous across time. When one layer breaks, continuity collapses. The Dorsey tweet failed on all three counts: no functional use, collapsing exchange, and fading identity once the cultural moment passed. Its failure is instructive because it followed all technical rules correctly—the minting was verifiable, the ledger indelible—but none of the social ones that give permanence.

The triad also resists the seduction of "universal valuation". In late 2022, digital artist Beeple opened his physical studio in Charleston, South Carolina, turning his NFT fame into a hybrid practice that combined on-chain provenance with in-person installations. The artwork's use value (as visual experience) regained primacy, while its exchange and identity values intertwined through exhibitions and verified owners' communities. Here, tokenisation served craft rather than replacing it. Scarcity supported art; art did not depend on scarcity. This is how engineered scarcity and the three tests cohere: each token must justify its existence through some combination of function, tradability, and meaning that outlives its hype cycle.

A critic might ask whether these distinctions overcomplicate what is, at root, speculation. Yet even in speculation, these forces are measurable. Metrics exist: active use addresses for use value; liquidity and turnover ratios for exchange value; community retention or engagement for identity value. Projects that publish these metrics visibly—on dashboards, not slogans—tend to mature beyond the "crypto toy" stage. They invite empirical scrutiny, which itself strengthens trust. When use can be graphed, exchange priced, and identity tracked through credible participation, the triad ceases to be theoretical. It becomes a governance tool.

Still, passing all three tests does not guarantee virtue. A well-designed pyramid can also align use, exchange, and identity: the use is recruitment, the exchange is inflow, the identity is belonging. Coordination alone cannot redeem intent. This is the enduring tension in token economies—they make collective belief efficient, which magnifies both wisdom and folly. The triad can diagnose value; it cannot dictate ethics.

The task for designers and regulators alike is to treat the three tests as a compass, not a certificate. Before minting a token, they might ask: what daily action makes this token useful enough to keep? Who could buy it without losing its essence? What shared story would holders be proud to continue? Each question is empirical, not ideological. Tokens that cannot answer them are destined for quiet oblivion once novelty fades.

We return, finally, to the image of the ledger. A ledger can record any claim, but not every claim deserves recording. The three tests are a way of asking what should leave a trace. Value-in-use binds the ledger to behaviour, value-in-exchange to community, value-in-identity to culture. Together they measure whether a token connects economy, society, and self. The triad does not end debate; it begins it. The open question is whether, as we continue to mint our futures, we will remember to ask not only *what* we can tokenise, but *why* anyone would care to keep it.

Chapter 2
Tokenisation Explained (Without Mystique)

On 11 March 2021, a digital collage by the artist Beeple sold at Christie's for $69.3 million. The work, titled *Everydays: The First 5000 Days*, existed entirely as pixels—a vast composite of images uploaded online over thirteen years. Yet what changed hands in the auction was not a file, but a token: a cryptographic certificate on the Ethereum blockchain, recording who owned what. The buyer could download the artwork like anyone else, but only they could *prove* possession of that particular digital inscription. It was a transaction that captivated headlines and confused logic. How could something infinitely copyable become scarce? How could a string of data confer ownership of an idea? Beneath the spectacle, the sale exposed a deeper shift: value itself was being rewritten in code.

The Beeple auction crystallised the paradox of tokenisation. The file remained public; the claim to it became private. The artwork was as accessible as before, but now *anchored*—or perhaps *trapped*—in a new frame of verifiability. For some, this was liberation: a long-awaited way to recognise digital labour and creativity. For others, it was a hall of mirrors, a marketplace built on signatures detached from substance. Both views contain truth, but neither captures the whole. The phenomenon cannot be dismissed as hype, nor worshipped as revolution. It demands dissection, not devotion. Tokens, stripped of their marketing aura, are coordination tools. They do not conjure new realities; they make pre-existing claims machine-readable.

At its core, a token is not the right itself, but a *pointer* to rights. It gestures towards something—an asset, a privilege, a relationship—that must exist beyond the code. The blockchain records the gesture impeccably but knows nothing of its referent. The bridge between the on-chain and the off-chain world is where truth must be maintained, and where failure often begins. Consider the thousands of NFTs whose image files vanished when hosting servers expired. The tokens remained intact, yet pointed to nothing. Proof of ownership without proof of existence is a void in disguise. The lesson is straightforward and sobering: the technology guarantees that something happened, not that it mattered.

That distinction—between representation and reality—is the key to understanding tokenisation without mystique. It is the difference between a passport and a journey, a map and a territory. The passport can be forged or lost; the journey, once lived, cannot. Tokens allow us to formalise, exchange, and trace claims at extraordinary scale, but they cannot conjure legitimacy from code alone. Every token, however cryptographically pure, ultimately depends on a social substrate: legal contracts, cultural norms, or institutional enforcement. Without these anchors, the digital promise drifts into abstraction.

Yet abstraction can be powerful when structured properly. Standards—those technical conventions often dismissed as dull—are where social order meets code. The Ethereum ERC-721 standard, introduced in 2018, defines how non-fungible tokens (NFTs) are created, transferred, and recognised across platforms. It was not merely a software update but a social contract: a shared grammar for ownership in the digital commons. Because developers could rely on predictable behaviour, marketplaces, wallets, and analytics tools could interoperate, forming an ecosystem where each new token amplified the value of the others. The standard's real achievement was not technical interoperability, but *cultural predictability*. It made digital ownership legible to machines and, by extension, to markets.

Every standard encodes choices about power and protection. The decision to make tokens transferable, for instance, assumes liquidity is good and permanence is optional. The decision to allow metadata changes assumes evolution outweighs immutability. These are not neutral design decisions—they are philosophies of value, written in syntax. When we call standards "open," we often mean "shared under particular assumptions." To understand tokenisation fully, one must read not only the white papers but the social contracts embedded between the lines.

Nowhere is that social layer more fragile than in custody. "Not your keys, not your coins" became a mantra of early crypto enthusiasts—

a warning that control lies with whoever holds the private cryptographic keys. Yet that purity of self-custody has proved brittle against human behaviour. People forget passwords, lose devices, die without recovery plans. In 2019, the Canadian exchange QuadrigaCX collapsed after its founder, Gerald Cotten, died allegedly holding sole access to customer wallets; roughly $190 million in assets were trapped irretrievably. The event underscored a paradox: the technology that promised independence also magnified isolation. The more perfectly decentralised the system, the less forgiving it became of human error.

Since then, alternative custody models have emerged: managed accounts, multi-signature safes, and social recovery mechanisms where trusted parties can restore lost access through collective verification. Each trades autonomy for assurance. For institutions—banks, museums, public archives—such trade-offs are not weaknesses but necessities. Risk management requires thresholds, audits, and fallback paths. The old logic of custody reasserts itself: control is never absolute; it is distributed between systems, procedures, and people. What tokenisation forces us to confront is that *trust does not disappear—it migrates.* From vaults to keys, from clerks to code, from institutions to interfaces. The challenge is not to eliminate intermediaries, but to design better ones.

This interplay of control and coordination extends to the problem of interoperability. A token that can move freely between platforms seems like an obvious good—why trap value when it can circulate? Yet freedom without friction invites contagion. The same standards that enable composability—letting tokens interact across decentralised apps—also create pathways for bugs, exploits, and scams. The 2022 Nomad bridge hack, in which a vulnerability in a cross-chain protocol allowed attackers to drain roughly $190 million, illustrated the cost of openness untempered by caution. When every ledger talks to every other, an error in one can echo through all.

To navigate this tension, designers are experimenting with "safety rails": automated circuit breakers, permission layers, and auditing frameworks that preserve openness while containing damage. These mechanisms are less glamorous than token drops or speculative art, but they are what make digital economies survivable. A bridge that never closes is not a marvel; it is a hazard. The same holds for markets. Portability must coexist with prudence, or else the infrastructure of trust collapses under its own connectivity.

The quiet motif running through these debates is *translation*. Tokens translate human agreements into machine-executable form. Standards translate expectations into code. Custody translates control into practice. Interoperability translates innovation into shared space. Each translation preserves intent but risks distortion. The art of token design lies in knowing which meanings can survive translation and which must remain human. We cannot legislate empathy in a smart contract, nor can we automate forgiveness after a mis-sent transaction. But we can design systems that make such qualities easier to practise, not harder.

To explain tokenisation without mystique is to strip away its aura of inevitability. Tokens are not the destiny of ownership, merely its latest instrument. They succeed when they clarify relationships, not when they obscure them. They thrive when anchored in law, language, and lived use, not when floating in speculation. What gives tokenisation moral weight is not its mathematics but its capacity to encode commitments transparently: who owes what to whom, under what conditions, and with what safeguards. That transparency, properly governed, can widen participation and sharpen accountability. Poorly governed, it can turn economic life into a brittle ledger of irreversible mistakes.

The chapters that follow trace this delicate architecture: how tokens point to rights, how standards stabilise trust, how custody defines control, and how interoperability can both enable and endanger. Each is a layer of the same structure—a bridge between human institutions and the software that now mediates them. The promise is clarity, the peril is illusion. To grasp tokenisation in full, we must learn to see through the spectacle of price and the glamour of code, down to the simple question every ledger must answer: what, exactly, does this record *mean*?

What a token is (and is not)

On 11 March 2021, at Christie's in London, a JPEG file changed hands for $69.3 million. The artist was Mike Winkelmann—better known as Beeple—and the artwork, *Everydays: The First 5000 Days*, was not sold as an image but as a token. The file itself was freely viewable online; the token, minted on the Ethereum blockchain, was a record declaring who owned it. The buyer, Singapore-based entrepreneur Vignesh Sundaresan, did not receive a hard drive, canvas, or certificate. He received a cryptographic signature in a distributed ledger. The sale shocked traditionalists not for its price but for what it implied: that ownership could now be claimed in code, detached from any physical object. Yet what exactly had been purchased? A digital asset, a concept, or merely an entry in a database? The question remains unsettled.

A token, in its most elemental form, is a pointer—a programmable marker that refers to something else. It says, "this address holds a claim to that thing." Sometimes the thing is a file; sometimes it is a financial right; sometimes it is nothing more than a social acknowledgement. The token itself is not the object or the right; it is the *record* of association. This distinction sounds pedantic until it fails. When the underlying reference disappears—when the artwork's URL dies, or the platform hosting it collapses—the token still points faithfully, but to emptiness. It is like a street sign in a demolished town.

The Beeple case embodies that risk. The token contains a link, not the artwork. If the server storing that file ever ceases to exist, the blockchain entry will still affirm ownership, but of what? A void made permanent. This is not a flaw in the blockchain; it is a misunderstanding of what the blockchain records. The ledger preserves signatures, not substance. Code can immortalise a claim, but it cannot keep the claimed object alive. The lesson, unglamorous but crucial, is that verification of *what* is owned remains a social and legal task, not a computational one.

A token can therefore be thought of as an interface between two realities: the cryptographic and the contractual. On-chain, it exists as a unique identifier governed by code—immutable, traceable, and transferrable. Off-chain, it derives its meaning from context: a promise, a law, or a shared belief that gives the record weight. This duality makes tokenisation powerful but precarious. A share certificate printed on paper derives legitimacy from company law; an NFT of a song derives legitimacy only if a court, a contract, or the artist's community agrees that the token indeed represents that work. The blockchain ensures integrity of data, not integrity of meaning.

This is why the metaphor of "owning" a tokenised asset is often misleading. One does not own the castle by holding its illustration. The token might grant access to income or governance, but without a binding link to the physical or legal layer, it is merely expressive. The British courts began to acknowledge this nuance in 2022, when the High Court ruled that NFTs could constitute property under certain conditions, extending protections against theft or misuse. The ruling did not make every token an enforceable right; it recognised that enforceability depends on identifiable parties and objects. Law met code halfway.

The misalignment between representation and reality can be traced across industries. In 2018, the start-up *Monegraph*, once hailed as a pioneer of digital art certificates, quietly wound down operations when artists discovered their tokens referenced files hosted on servers that expired. The ownership claim survived cryptographically, but the artefacts did not. Similarly, in 2020, the NFT marketplace *Mintable* faced user backlash after a database misconfiguration broke links between tokens and the files they represented. The assets were not "lost" on-chain; they were lost in translation between technical and legal truth.

Contrast this fragility with examples where the bridge holds. The city of Zug in Switzerland, dubbed "Crypto Valley," has issued blockchain-based digital identities since 2017, linking each token to a citizen's verified municipal record. The token does not exist in a vacuum; it is anchored in an official registry backed by the Swiss government. Here, the pointer is backed by process. The system demonstrates how on-chain data can meaningfully map to off-chain legitimacy when institutional frameworks align. The ledger does not replace the state; it extends it.

The motif of the *pointer* helps clarify the boundary between token and asset. A pointer directs attention, but the value lies in what it points to. A cinema ticket is valuable because it grants entry, not because the paper itself is rare. When digital scarcity first became programmable, the industry mistook the pointer for the prize. That confusion fuelled speculative bubbles, yet it also accelerated experimentation. The enduring projects—the ones building infrastructure rather than spectacle—understand the pointer as a relational tool.

Take the case of *Harberger taxes*, a concept revived by economist Glen Weyl and implemented experimentally in several blockchain property projects after 2018. Under this model, property owners must continuously declare a self-assessed value for their asset and pay a tax on it, with anyone free to purchase the asset at that declared price. Here, the token does not merely denote ownership but enforces a rule of circulation. It represents an active claim—maintained by behaviour, not merely held. The design demonstrates that a token's power lies not in static representation but in dynamic coordination: making rights executable.

This functional view also illuminates why "proof of ownership" often misleads the public. A blockchain entry can prove that someone signed a transaction; it cannot prove that they had the authority to sell what the transaction described. In 2021, several artists found their work minted without consent on popular NFT marketplaces. The blockchain dutifully recorded these mints, but law recognised them as forgeries. Verification was perfect; legitimacy was absent. The network was right about the data and wrong about the world.

Failure modes like these arise when we confuse computational truth with social truth. The blockchain can confirm *what happened*—that a signature was made at a certain time by a certain key. It cannot confirm *why* it happened, or whether it should have. That distinction may sound academic, but it shapes everything from art sales to land registries. A token-based property deed is only as reliable as the system that recognises it. If the land office burns, the blockchain record still exists—but it exists alone, like a passport to a vanished country.

To bridge this divide, token systems increasingly rely on oracles—mechanisms that feed verified off-chain data into smart contracts. Oracles can connect a shipping token to real-time freight logs, or an insurance policy to weather feeds. Yet oracles reintroduce trust: someone must maintain them, verify their sources, and update their protocols. Each oracle becomes a miniature institution, complete with governance and liability. The dream of trustless automation returns to the human world by another door. The pointer still depends on its witness.

This interplay between autonomy and dependence defines the philosophy of tokenisation. The blockchain eliminates one class of intermediaries—clerks, brokers, registrars—while creating another: coders, maintainers, auditors. It does not abolish trust; it redistributes it. The mature question is not "can we remove trust?" but "where shall we locate it, and how transparent shall we make it?" Tokens, when designed honestly, make these locations visible. They show who is responsible for what, and where the boundaries of automation end.

The counterpoint comes from projects that pursued purity over practicality. The decentralised marketplace *OpenBazaar*, launched in 2016 as a peer-to-peer alternative to eBay, prided itself on having no intermediaries. Transactions occurred directly between users through smart contracts, with payment in Bitcoin. Despite its elegant architecture, the platform closed in 2021 after struggling with disputes, spam, and user support. Without any trusted anchor—no customer service, no guarantees—most participants drifted back to platforms that offered safety nets. The pointer worked perfectly; the relationship it described did not.

In contrast, the *UK Land Registry*'s 2019 pilot for blockchain-backed property transactions in South Wales demonstrates a more grounded approach. Rather than replacing legal infrastructure, it used tokens to mirror and verify official records, reducing reconciliation times from weeks to hours. The pilot showed that when legal authority and cryptographic integrity are synchronised, the ledger becomes not a replacement for institutions but their ally. The pointer and the object move together.

Throughout this evolution, one principle endures: a token without anchorage is a gesture without consequence. To treat tokens as assets in themselves is to mistake record for reality. The true innovation lies in programmability—the ability to define conditional relationships between rights, actions, and verification. A token can say, "transfer this share if payment clears," or "grant access if membership remains valid." It can coordinate without intermediaries. But to assert ownership in a world still governed by law, it must ultimately plug into frameworks of recognition—contract, identity, and enforcement.

The tension between autonomy and anchorage will not disappear. Every advance in tokenisation sharpens the same question: when does a claim in code become a claim in fact? The answer depends on what we anchor and how rigorously we maintain those anchors. A broken link is not merely a technical failure; it is a fracture in meaning. The blockchain records that the bridge once existed, but it cannot rebuild it.

So before declaring that something has been "tokenised," one must ask: tokenised *how*, tokenised *to what*, and tokenised *for whom*? The token may be immutable, but its referent is not. The signpost stands only as long as the road remains.

Standards as social contracts

In November 2017, Axiom Zen in Vancouver released CryptoKitties, a web game where players bred and traded cartoon cats on Ethereum. Within days, the cats clogged the network and spread beyond the developer's website to third-party wallets and marketplaces. The reason was prosaic and powerful: the cats' data followed a public format that other tools could read. A standard took shape at speed. In January 2018, the ERC-721 specification crystallised that format, defining how non-fungible tokens should behave across contracts and interfaces. The result was immediate. Wallets could display cats without bespoke code. Marketplaces could list them without private deals. The cats spread everywhere fast. A toy hardened into precedent: when we standardise token behaviour, we standardise the expectations that bind economic life.

To watch an ecosystem fall into step with a new standard is to witness a social contract enter code. Show: hundreds of wallets rendering the same asset correctly without coordination. Name: ERC-721, a public, reviewed template for non-fungible tokens on Ethereum (2018). Explain: by agreeing on functions such as ownerOf, transferFrom, and tokenURI, developers created a common grammar for digital items. Implication: once that grammar existed, every new token authored in it inherited distribution, tooling, and market access as if by default. Interoperability is not magic; it is consensus about verbs.

Standards embed choices. They are constitutions with syntax. ERC-721 assumes that tokens are individually distinct, that they can be transferred freely, and that their descriptive metadata lives at a retrievable address. Those are not neutral assumptions. They privilege liquidity and visibility over secrecy and restraint. They make some values cheap (resale, display) and others costly (privacy, non-transferability). A standard is not merely a wire format; it is a policy. Once adopted widely, it becomes a promise that strangers rely on without a handshake.

Consider what that promise does to coordination costs. Before ERC-721, every project taught wallets, analytics, and markets a new dialect. After ERC-721, a wallet author in Berlin could render an artist's work minted in Buenos Aires without prior contact. Show: OpenSea and Rarible indexing a new collection within minutes because methods and events match a predictable ABI. Name: *indexability by design*. Explain: when events like Transfer emit in known shapes, indexing software can catch them blindly, then present holdings in user interfaces without one-off integration. Implication: the marginal cost of reaching one more venue approaches zero; network effects take the wheel.

Network effects here are specific, not mystical. Each conformant token increases the value of the standard to users (more items visible in their wallet), to markets (more listings without custom code), and to developers (more libraries and documentation). The flywheel is measurable: time-to-integration shrinks; number of venues grows; liquidity tightens spreads. That is how a format becomes an economy. The social contract becomes a habit.

But there is a shadow to such clarity. When a template becomes ubiquitous, its omissions calcify. ERC-721 famously did not encode royalties. Designers assumed marketplaces would enforce creator payments off-chain. In late 2022 and 2023, several major platforms changed their enforcement posture, and resale royalties—long treated as implied—fell into dispute. Show: a creator watching secondary fees drop as a marketplace toggles settings. Name: *implicit royalties broken by policy drift.* Explain: the standard left a gap, and platforms filled it unevenly; when priorities shifted, the gap widened. Implication: what is not in the template is at risk; social contracts need explicit clauses, not vibes.

The ecosystem reacted by proposing ERC-2981 (2021), a royalty information standard that allows a contract to state a recommended fee recipient and percentage. It did not compel payment, but it restored a focal point. Show: a marketplace reading royaltyInfo at sale time and presenting the suggested split. Name: *soft enforcement through published intent.* Explain: by publishing a convention, projects reduce confusion and pressure compliant venues to play fair, even where law is silent. Implication: standards do not require force to shape behaviour; clarity alone can move markets.

Not all clarity is worth the lock-in. This is the counter-example worth reckoning with. Rigid standards can slow evolution. ERC-721's one-ID-one-item model made batch transfers inefficient and led to gas waste in gaming projects with thousands of semi-fungible items. The answer was ERC-1155 (proposed 2018), which treats items as IDs within a single contract and allows batched operations. Show: a game sending 50 swords in one transaction instead of 50 transactions. Name: *ERC-1155's multi-token design.* Explain: a new template addressed a pain point that the older one created; projects migrated where it fit. Implication: standards must compete and specialise; longevity comes from fitness, not early dominance.

This tension—stability versus flexibility—is perennial. History offers a useful analogy: the ISO shipping container (1968) transformed trade because its dimensions were fixed across ports and cranes. But the standard did not specify cargo; it specified the box. In tokens, the analogue is to stabilise behaviours (transfer, metadata, permissions) while leaving content and governance malleable. The better a standard separates mechanism from meaning, the longer it will serve. When standards overreach into business logic, they bake in a business model that may not age well.

Standards also stage power. Who writes them? Who ratifies them? Who can amend them? In Ethereum, improvement proposals (EIPs) travel through public discussion, reference implementations, and editorial review. That process is open but not democratic in a majoritarian sense; influence accrues to those who write code, run infrastructure, or convince others. Show: a GitHub discussion where a contentious field name is debated for weeks. Name: *rough consensus and running code.* Explain: the social contract here values technical argument and operational proof over votes. Implication: legitimacy is earned in public, but minority voices can be drowned unless process stewards actively surface edge cases.

Edge cases matter because standards become rails for capital. A mis-specified field can cost real money. Recall the early days of token metadata where many projects pointed tokenURI to fragile HTTP addresses. When hosting expired, images vanished. The standard permitted it; the market assumed permanence; reality intruded. The community adapted by using IPFS or Arweave for content addressing, then publishing best-practice guides and linting tools. Show: a deploy script that rejects non-content-addressed URIs. Name: *norms layered atop standards.* Explain: a standard can set the floor, while norms, libraries, and audits raise the ceiling. Implication: safety is a stack; templates are necessary but insufficient.

The quieter gift of standards is expectation management. They tell participants what will not happen as much as what will. ERC-721 tells you that token IDs will not collide across a contract, that transfers will emit events in a predictable shape, and that ownership queries will not arbitrarily fail. This predictability allows downstream contracts to compose safely. Show: a lending protocol accepting any ERC-721 as collateral because it trusts the interface. Name: *composability by contract.* Explain: when two strangers share the same verbs, they can co-operate without meetings. Implication: innovation speeds up because coordination costs drop, not because genius increases.

Yet safety can evaporate when composability outruns caution. In 2022, a bug in a widely used NFT marketplace's listing flow allowed attackers to buy items at stale prices after owners believed they had delisted them. The standard behaved as written; the off-chain listing system did not. Show: a victim's wallet showing a sudden, unexpected sale at a deep discount. Name: *interface-protocol mismatch*. Explain: the social contract was honoured at the smart-contract layer but broken in UX; users expected an action to mean "cancel" when it meant "replace". Implication: standards need parapets—reference UIs, explicit state diagrams, and warnings—so that human expectations converge with machine behaviour.

This is where "standards as social contracts" reveals its full sense. A social contract is not just a law; it is a repeated pattern of behaviour under shared rules. Technical templates only become social contracts when the broader system—wallets, markets, auditors, educators—teaches and enforces the rule as a habit. Show: a wallet refusing to sign a transaction that would transfer a non-transferable token, because the metadata says soulbound: true. Name: *normative enforcement at the edge*. Explain: the template signals intent; the interface enacts it; the ecosystem aligns. Implication: standards are living; they need guardians in code and culture.

Two more examples clarify how standards carry values. First, consider *EIP-2612* (2020), which introduced "permit" for ERC-20 tokens, enabling approvals via signatures rather than on-chain transactions. Show: a user authorising spending with one signed message instead of two transactions. Name: *gasless approval for tokens*. Explain: the standard placed user convenience over purity, reducing friction and thereby inviting wider adoption. Implication: humane design choices in standards expand the circle of participants; small syntactic changes can have social effects.

Second, look at *EIP-1271* (2019), which specifies how contracts can validate signatures, enabling smart-contract wallets to act like people. Show: a DAO signing a message via a multi-signature safe to authenticate on an app. Name: *contract-level signature validation*. Explain: the standard recognises that "an account" can be a group; it writes pluralism into authentication. Implication: standards can recognise different kinds of persons; they can widen who gets to act, not just what actions are allowed.

A limitation is equally instructive: standards are slow. They stabilise after painful lessons, not before. That frustrates builders facing immediate threats. The reconciliation is strategic: design locally, then standardise globally. A project can pioneer a pattern—say, enforced on-chain royalties with OperatorFilter logic or time-locked metadata updates—prove it in production, and only then seek inclusion in a broader template. Show: a draft EIP citing two independent implementations and audits. Name: *evidence before elevation*. Explain: the social contract hardens once the behaviour is observed to work across contexts. Implication: standards should be fossils of success, not bets on taste.

The quiet motif through all of this is *language*. Standards give a shared language to strangers who may never meet. That language is not neutral; it encodes what we care about. Do we care more about permanence or mutability? About privacy or portability? About creator power or buyer freedom? Each field and function is a sentence in that debate. When we adopt a standard, we assent to the story it tells about ownership and exchange.

So the forward test is direct and demanding. If you are proposing or adopting a token standard, what social commitments does it smuggle in? Which risks does it conceal by omission? Where does it place the burden of care—on the creator, the marketplace, or the holder? And when the next CryptoKitties arrives—surprising, messy, generative—will the grammar you have chosen flex to include it, or force the world back into last year's shape?

Custody, keys, and risk

In February 2019, the Supreme Court of Nova Scotia placed QuadrigaCX, Canada's largest cryptocurrency exchange, into creditor protection. Its founder, Gerald Cotten, had died two months earlier in Jaipur, India, reportedly holding sole access to digital wallets containing over 100 million Canadian dollars in customer assets. When auditors later examined the wallets, most were empty. The platform's users were locked out of their own funds—technically "their" assets, but in practice held by a single man's laptop. The tragedy exposed an awkward truth: decentralised technology cannot save us from human centralisation. Control follows keys; people forget, lose, or die.

That case is not an anomaly—it is a pattern written across the short history of digital custody. In 2014, Tokyo-based exchange Mt. Gox collapsed after losing hundreds of thousands of bitcoins, much of it due to inadequate private key management. The supposed "trustless" system failed not because of code, but because of concentration. Both Quadriga and Mt. Gox demonstrate how digital assets revert to the oldest problem in finance: who holds the keys, and who can be trusted to act when something goes wrong.

Custody, in any form, is the quiet architecture of power. In traditional finance, the term refers to institutions that safeguard clients' securities, ensuring they are neither stolen nor misused. In token economies, custody takes on a new dimension: whoever controls the private key controls the asset absolutely. That simplicity is both its elegance and its flaw. No forgotten password can be reset by customer support. No court order can unlock a wallet without the key. The blockchain is not cruel; it is indifferent.

Self-custody emerged as the ideological core of cryptocurrency—a declaration of autonomy. To hold one's keys is to hold one's sovereignty. The early mantra "not your keys, not your coins" embodied a revolutionary ethic: reject intermediaries, assume full responsibility. Show: an individual generating a hardware wallet, writing down a seed phrase, locking it in a drawer. Name: *self-custody in practice*. Explain: the private key acts as a digital signature proving control over assets; losing it severs access permanently. Implication: autonomy here is binary, not partial. It is freedom sharpened into risk.

The scale of that risk is measurable. In 2022, blockchain analytics firm Chainalysis estimated that about 20 percent of all Bitcoin in circulation—worth tens of billions of dollars—was trapped in inaccessible wallets. Each case is a personal disaster, often unfixable. Human memory, not cryptography, becomes the weakest link. When the burden of custody falls solely on the individual, the system inherits the fragility of human behaviour: distraction, loss, death.

The industry's response has been to reintroduce delegation—ironically, the very practice early crypto sought to escape. Managed custodians such as Coinbase Custody, Anchorage Digital, and BitGo now hold billions in institutional assets. These firms combine cryptographic key management with insurance, compliance, and disaster recovery. Show: an institutional custodian splitting keys across multiple secure vaults and requiring multi-signature authorisation for transactions. Name: *managed custody architecture*. Explain: by distributing key fragments and enforcing procedural controls, managed custody restores redundancy. Implication: autonomy gives way to accountability; users regain safety at the cost of dependence.

For institutions, this trade-off is acceptable, even desirable. Regulatory frameworks such as the UK's Financial Conduct Authority (FCA) rules or the EU's Markets in Crypto-Assets Regulation (MiCA, 2023) mandate specific custody protections. Investors prefer recoverability over purity. They want recourse, not heroism. For retail users, however, the tension remains unresolved. Should one entrust keys to an exchange that might fail, or hold them personally and risk irretrievable loss? The question has no universal answer—only a spectrum of comfort with responsibility.

Between these poles lies a third frontier: social recovery. This model, popularised by Ethereum co-founder Vitalik Buterin in 2021, distributes the power of restoration across trusted peers or institutions. Show: a user designating five "guardians"—friends or entities—who can collectively authorise a new key if the original is lost. Name: *social recovery wallets*. Explain: control remains individual in daily use, but emergency recovery requires collective consent. Implication: the model blends cryptography with community, reintroducing social trust as a programmable feature rather than a vulnerability.

Social recovery attempts to re-humanise custody without reverting to full centralisation. Yet it raises delicate questions: whom do you trust enough to rescue you, and what happens if they collude or disappear? The model assumes the same social integrity that traditional systems once outsourced to banks. It reimagines fiduciary responsibility as a network of relationships rather than a corporate service. The trade-off is subtle: resilience through friendship, not regulation.

A limitation becomes clear when scale enters the equation. Social recovery works for individuals, but less so for funds or organisations managing large sums. When thousands of stakeholders must agree on recovery rules, coordination becomes a governance problem. This is where *multi-signature custody*—requiring multiple keys to execute transactions—bridges the gap. Show: a corporate treasury requiring three of five executives to co-sign any movement of assets. Name: *multi-sig governance*. Explain: by distributing authorisation, the system reduces single points of failure without sacrificing control. Implication: the pattern mirrors checks and balances in corporate law; technology echoes old prudence.

These different custody forms—self, managed, social—map a triangle of trade-offs. Self-custody maximises autonomy but amplifies personal risk. Managed custody provides safety through intermediaries but revives central dependence. Social recovery and multi-signature models distribute trust, offering middle paths. The triangle cannot be collapsed without losing a vertex; every design is a negotiation between freedom, safety, and scalability.

History shows that societies oscillate between extremes of trust and control. In 1999, the UK experienced a surge in online banking fraud after early systems placed full responsibility on users. Banks eventually shifted to multi-factor authentication and consumer protections, acknowledging that pure user control was untenable. The same lesson now re-emerges in token economies: systems mature when they absorb, rather than reject, human imperfection. Custody design is, at heart, an exercise in anthropology.

One visible behaviour that crystallises this evolution is delegation. Despite rhetoric about independence, most users prefer custodial solutions that mimic familiar patterns—password resets, customer service, and recovery options. Exchanges like Binance and Kraken operate as hybrid models: they manage keys internally but allow users to withdraw at will. This hybridisation reflects a pragmatic truth—people crave convenience as much as sovereignty. Control, when too absolute, feels more like burden than freedom.

Yet trust outsourced blindly can rot. The collapse of FTX in November 2022 proved that even sophisticated investors failed to audit who actually held their assets. FTX was a custodian masquerading as a marketplace; billions were misused behind a façade of credibility. The lesson, echoed across financial history, is that transparency must accompany trust. Managed custody without verifiable proof is a liability dressed as comfort. Emerging models like *proof of reserves* audits attempt to bridge that gap, allowing exchanges to cryptographically verify holdings against liabilities without revealing private data. The mechanism shows that even institutional custody can evolve towards measurable integrity.

Still, no system can remove risk; it only relocates it. The quiet motif throughout custody is *control as concentration*. Whether in a cold wallet, a server farm, or a social network of guardians, the question remains: who can act unilaterally, and under what conditions? In 2021, a dispute between users of the decentralised finance protocol Compound demonstrated this tension. A bug in a governance upgrade distributed millions in unintended rewards, and the protocol lacked an override to reclaim them. Total self-custody for code left the community powerless. Immutability became impotence.

This is the paradox of decentralised control: when everything depends on private keys, systems become simultaneously sovereign and brittle. Legal scholars have compared this to a "digital bearer asset" regime—possess the key, own the right. But bearer instruments went out of fashion in the twentieth century precisely because they were untraceable and irrecoverable. Modern law prefers systems of registered ownership, where loss does not equate to disappearance. The challenge for token economies is to reconcile these philosophies: digital bearer freedom with institutional recoverability.

Experiments continue. Wallet providers such as Argent and Safe (formerly Gnosis Safe) now blend smart contracts with usability features—daily transfer limits, recovery delays, and approval hierarchies. Show: a user accidentally authorising a large transfer but able to cancel it during a 24-hour buffer. Name: *programmable safety margins*. Explain: these features translate human hesitation into machine logic, reducing irreversible mistakes. Implication: safety re-enters through code, not bureaucracy.

But code cannot anticipate every human tragedy. The question of inheritance—what happens to assets when an owner dies—remains largely unsolved. A seed phrase in a safe is useless if no one knows it exists. Some projects propose *dead man's switches* that transfer assets after inactivity; others integrate legal executors as co-signers. Each approach tries to align cryptographic certainty with human continuity. The results are uneven, but the direction is clear: custody must evolve from possession to stewardship.

Control follows keys; people forget. That five-word sentence is the truth at the core of digital ownership. The future of token economies depends on designing systems that respect autonomy without demanding perfection. Custody is not a single decision but a continuum of trust relationships—some human, some institutional, some algorithmic. The right choice depends less on technology than on temperament: how much risk one can bear, and how much trust one can extend.

So the open question remains. If ownership is now a function of keys, who—or what—should hold them when the human mind, with all its fallibility, remains the final custodian? The answer will define whether digital property becomes an instrument of empowerment or another chapter in the long history of misplaced trust.

Interoperability vs safety

On 14 February 2022, hackers exploited a vulnerability in the Wormhole bridge, a protocol linking Ethereum and Solana, to steal cryptocurrency then valued at more than 320 million US dollars. The attack did not breach either blockchain's core consensus; it exploited the connection between them. A single unchecked function in the bridge's smart contract allowed the attacker to mint wrapped tokens without depositing collateral. One missing verification turned interoperability—the ability to move value freely across networks—into an instrument of loss. The same quality that makes token systems fluid also makes them fragile.

Portability fuels innovation. It lets a token minted in one environment circulate through many others without friction. That feature distinguishes blockchain economies from walled-garden platforms. Yet each open door invites more than opportunity; it invites contagion. Show: the Wormhole incident cascading into temporary price shocks across ecosystems. Name: *cross-chain exposure*. Explain: as assets moved between incompatible rule sets, a single point of weakness replicated across systems. Implication: interoperability is not a neutral design choice; it is a decision about how much shared risk a network is willing to bear.

The metaphor that fits is plumbing. Interoperability connects blockchains as pipes connect reservoirs. When water flows, prosperity follows; when one pipe bursts, contamination spreads. The challenge is to design valves—safety rails—that preserve flow while containing damage.

Three years before Wormhole, in September 2019, another bridge project, Loopring, introduced circuit-level proofs to verify transfers without trusting intermediaries. Show: zero-knowledge proofs confirming that assets had been locked before minting their representations elsewhere. Name: *cryptographic containment*. Explain: rather than assuming honesty, the system required mathematical evidence before value could cross domains. Implication: safety rails work best when they minimise faith and maximise verifiability.

Interoperability first gained moral weight during the rise of decentralised finance (DeFi) in 2020. Tokens became composable building blocks: a liquidity pool fed a lending protocol, which fed a derivatives engine. Each connection expanded utility—and multiplied failure paths. When Compound or Aave adjusted interest-rate models, hundreds of dependent projects rippled in response. Show: a developer's decision to alter one parameter leading to liquidation cascades across integrated contracts. Name: *composability risk*. Explain: the very property that makes DeFi efficient—

automatic interoperability—also amplifies unintended interactions. Implication: systems built for permissionless innovation must plan for permissionless failure.

Safety rails take many forms. Some are procedural, others architectural. Formal verification—mathematically proving that code behaves as intended—offers one defence. The MakerDAO community, for instance, requires independent audits and simulation tests before major upgrades to its core contracts. Show: pre-launch "shadow networks" replicating real-world conditions to stress-test behaviour. Name: *sandbox validation*. Explain: by quarantining experiments, developers prevent unproven logic from reaching user funds. Implication: openness need not mean recklessness; it can be bounded by deliberate staging.

Yet not all safety can be engineered. Human vigilance remains the final circuit breaker. In March 2023, when a compromised wallet drained millions from the Euler Finance protocol, rapid coordination between teams across multiple networks froze stolen assets before they could be laundered. Show: rival DeFi platforms collaborating in real time to flag tainted funds. Name: *crisis coordination*. Explain: decentralised systems often lack central emergency powers, but community response can substitute institutional intervention. Implication: social trust, though informal, becomes a last line of defence when automation fails.

The counter-example comes from Terra's collapse in May 2022. Its stablecoin, UST, maintained parity with the US dollar through an algorithmic swap with its sister token, LUNA. Interoperability between exchanges and protocols meant that when confidence cracked, automated arbitrage drained liquidity everywhere at once. Show: a spiral of redemptions that erased over 40 billion US dollars in value within days. Name: *reflexive meltdown*. Explain: open connectivity accelerated panic; safeguards that might have paused redemptions were absent. Implication: safety rails are not censorship—they are shock absorbers that buy time for reason.

The motif through all of this is flow. Tokens, like water, seek the path of least resistance. Engineers must decide where resistance belongs. Every bridge, adapter, or marketplace API represents a balance between convenience and control. If safety rails are too tight, innovation stagnates; if too loose, contagion spreads. The right question is not "should we be open?" but "how open can we be without erasing accountability?"

One design pattern that advances this balance is *modular permissioning.* Instead of binary states—open or closed—protocols can tier their integrations by trust level. A lending platform might allow instant composability for audited partners while sandboxing unaudited ones until review. Show: Curve Finance maintaining a whitelist of verified pools alongside an experimental section flagged as risky. Name: *tiered interoperability.* Explain: this approach mirrors airport security—fast lanes for trusted travellers, checks for unknowns. Implication: openness remains, but exposure becomes a managed spectrum, not an unbounded field.

Another approach is *circuit breaking*—a mechanical pause under abnormal conditions. Decentralised exchanges such as dYdX introduced automated halts that trigger when price feeds diverge beyond set thresholds. Show: an oracle mismatch prompting a brief suspension of trading to prevent cascade liquidations. Name: *automated containment.* Explain: temporary pauses violate no decentralisation principle if defined transparently in code. Implication: restraint can be programmed; freedom can include brakes.

Critics argue that such controls reintroduce centralisation by stealth. Who decides the thresholds? Who restarts the flow? These are legitimate worries. Safety rails that depend on human intervention risk repeating the governance pitfalls of traditional finance. The reconciliation lies in *transparent governance*: decision logic visible on-chain, with accountability encoded. MakerDAO, again, exemplifies this by recording every executive vote and delay period in the public ledger. Show: a "time-lock" smart contract enforcing a 24-hour delay between approval and activation. Name: *delayed enactment.* Explain: even when humans decide, machines guarantee time for review. Implication: transparency transforms discretion into process.

Beyond code, education functions as infrastructure. Wallets like MetaMask and Phantom now display transaction warnings that interpret contract data in plain language. Show: a user attempting to approve unlimited token spending receiving a prompt detailing potential consequences. Name: *informed consent through interface design.* Explain: most exploits depend on ignorance, not ingenuity; reducing opacity is itself a safety rail. Implication: UX design is a form of consumer protection, not mere polish.

The drive for interoperability also intersects with regulation. As jurisdictions impose compliance demands—anti-money laundering, consumer safeguards, and data privacy—protocols must reconcile open architecture with legal accountability. The European Union's MiCA framework (2023) and the UK's forthcoming digital asset regulation both highlight traceability as a baseline requirement. Show: cross-chain analytics firms such as Chainalysis or Elliptic mapping token flows to comply with sanctions regimes. Name: *regulated transparency.* Explain: law now enters the design space; interoperability must coexist with auditability. Implication: technical freedom cannot outpace civic responsibility forever.

There is, however, a cultural danger in overreacting. Each safety mechanism can morph into a gate. History offers caution: the early Internet's end-to-end principle allowed email and the Web to flourish because the network core imposed minimal rules. Over-regulation of interoperability risks repeating the mistakes of closed app stores—stifling the very diversity that yields resilience. The strongest networks do not eliminate risk; they distribute it.

So the trade-off persists. To build open systems that billions can trust, designers must think like both plumbers and public-health officials—keeping the pipes wide but clean. Every cross-chain bridge, every composable API, every interoperable token format carries an implicit oath: to extend access without magnifying harm.

The forward test is deceptively simple. When proposing a new link between systems, ask: if this connection fails, who gets hurt, how quickly, and how far will the damage travel? If the answer is "everyone, instantly," the bridge needs more valves. Innovation flows fastest when its channels are strong enough to hold the pressure.

Chapter 3
Real-World Assets, Carefully

In April 2021, the Swiss city of Zug—already nicknamed "Crypto Valley"—quietly issued a pilot digital bond on a public blockchain. The bond, valued at 100 million Swiss francs, was not a tokenised meme or a speculative experiment in decentralisation; it was a government-backed security, underwritten by a consortium of regulated banks, governed by Swiss law. The ledger did not replace the law—it extended it. The issuance took mere hours instead of weeks, and the settlement cost was negligible. Yet what fascinated observers was not the speed but the shift in trust: a real-world asset, born of paper and signatures, was now verifiable by code. Something foundational had changed. Ownership of tangible value—property, debt, machinery, even art—was beginning to migrate from notarised paper to programmable tokens.

That migration is often celebrated as a triumph of innovation, a frictionless merging of atoms and bits. But behind the enthusiasm lies a quiet and complicated truth: tokenising real-world assets (RWAs) is less about technology and more about translation. It requires mapping the messy, contingent world of legal rights, physical assets, and human error into the exacting precision of code. Where digital-native tokens can live wholly on-chain, RWAs straddle two realities—one governed by mathematics, the other by law. The bridge between them is not built of blockchain protocols alone; it is built of trust, compliance, and process discipline.

The promise is seductive. Imagine property deeds that transfer instantly, invoice loans settled automatically, machinery that pays rent to its owner as it operates. Tokenisation invites us to see the material world as liquid capital. Every asset, once illiquid or trapped in bureaucracy, can be made tradable, divisible, and programmable. A warehouse can be fractionally owned by thousands. A song's royalties can be distributed by smart contract. Capital that once stagnated in paper form begins to circulate. The rhetoric is bold—some say inevitable. But the question worth asking is quieter and more difficult: should everything be made liquid, and at what cost?

The central theme of this chapter is caution—not technophobia, but design realism. When we move from bits to atoms, we import physics, politics, and human fallibility. Unlike digital art or native tokens, real-world assets do not exist purely as entries on a ledger; they must be linked to physical or legal anchors through mechanisms known as oracles and wrappers. These are the interfaces that assert, with auditable evidence, that a token's claim in code matches something verifiable in the real world. If that link fails, no amount of cryptographic integrity can compensate for missing substance. A beautifully engineered bridge collapses if it lands on a swamp.

The "last metre problem"—that stubborn distance between code and context—is what separates robust tokenisation from illusion. It is where the work of engineers meets that of lawyers, auditors, and regulators. This boundary is not glamorous; it involves paperwork, inspection reports, and legal opinions. Yet this is where legitimacy is earned. A tokenised bond is not trustworthy because it is on a blockchain; it is trustworthy because an enforceable legal contract confirms that its holders have recourse in the event of dispute. Technology may verify possession, but law defines ownership.

Liquidity, often invoked as virtue, must also be interrogated. It lowers transaction costs, improves price discovery, and releases dormant capital—but it also invites churn, speculation, and misalignment. The history of finance is full of markets that became too liquid for their own good: housing derivatives in 2008, or short-term credit instruments that eroded long-term investment discipline. The same dynamic threatens tokenised assets if liquidity becomes an end in itself. The aim should be purposeful liquidity—markets that improve efficiency without corroding stewardship. A tokenised invoice that helps a small business access working capital faster is productive. A tokenised claim flipped hundreds of times before payment becomes noise.

There is also a governance trap in excessive fractionalisation. The idea that "everyone can own a piece" carries democratic appeal, but ownership dispersed too thinly can paralyse decision-making. A rental property co-owned by a thousand wallet addresses risks falling into disrepair because no one is accountable for repairs. Voting mechanisms may exist in theory, but collective action in small sums is a fantasy few systems have solved. The logic of financial democracy collides with the psychology of responsibility. Without careful design—delegation, quorum thresholds, custodial trusts—fractional ownership risks hollowing the very notion of ownership it claims to expand.

To proceed *carefully* is to recognise that operational discipline matters more than grand narratives. Tokenisation succeeds when it satisfies the tests that any good auditor would apply: proof of existence, proof of control, cash-flow mapping, and clear dispute resolution. These are not glamorous concepts, but they are what turn digital experiments into functioning markets. The difference between a toy token and an asset-backed instrument is traceability—who verifies the asset, how it is managed, and what happens if something goes wrong. This chapter will argue that process maturity, not innovation theatre, is what earns institutional trust.

This theme connects directly to the broader thesis of *The Token Economy*: that the token is not magic, but mechanism. The chapters before explored the grammar of ownership and the abstraction of tokens as programmable rights. Here, we return to the material—the world that resists perfect digitisation. Tokenising real-world assets is not about conquering that resistance but respecting it. The work lies not in erasing friction but in making friction transparent.

Consider the emerging field of RWA platforms that tokenise government bonds, carbon credits, or real estate. Projects like MakerDAO's integration of real-world collateral (2022) show that institutional-grade tokenisation can work—but only when every component, from legal wrapper to reporting oracle, is auditable. It is no accident that the most trusted RWA projects are often the least flashy. Their code is boring, their documentation exhaustive, their lawyers busy. They succeed because they blend two disciplines often held apart: engineering precision and legal prudence.

Yet the lure of spectacle endures. For every compliant RWA initiative, there are dozens of shallow imitations—tokens claiming to represent assets that cannot be verified, whose issuers vanish when markets turn. These failures are not marginal; they are symptomatic. They reveal how easily a market obsessed with novelty neglects due process. The "carefully" in this chapter's title is not decorative—it is directive.

The recurring motif here is the bridge: between atoms and code, between finance and law, between speed and scrutiny. A bridge, if built properly, can bear extraordinary weight. Built hastily, it becomes a hazard. The test of tokenisation will be whether it produces more functioning bridges than collapsed ones. Each design choice—how to verify assets, structure liquidity, manage governance, or enforce compliance—determines which side of that ledger the project lands on.

The chapters ahead will traverse these questions methodically: how to connect code to physical and legal proof without delusion; how to build liquidity that serves use rather than speculation; how to structure ownership so that collective action remains possible; and how to embed compliance as practice rather than slogan. The reward for those who learn to build *carefully* is immense: systems that make capital more accessible, more transparent, and ultimately more human.

So we return to that Swiss bond, circulating quietly on its blockchain, performing the same economic function as before but with radically different plumbing. Its lesson is deceptively simple. Technology does not abolish the old disciplines—it demands we honour them more rigorously than ever. The bridge between atoms and code will hold only if those who build it remember that integrity is not a protocol; it is a practice. The next sections will show what that practice looks like when design meets the real world.

Bridging atoms to code

In April 2023, the Monetary Authority of Singapore and HSBC executed the tokenisation of a bond representing a parcel of trade invoices from a logistics company operating in the Port of Singapore. The pilot, conducted under *Project Guardian*, aimed to prove that financial instruments grounded in physical commerce could move with the same efficiency as digital-native assets. The bond itself was not stored in a vault or a server; it referenced real invoices, issued by a company moving actual containers through customs. The transaction settled on a public blockchain within minutes. Yet behind the apparent simplicity lay months of legal drafting, audit protocols, and system integrations to ensure that what the code claimed—the existence and value of the invoices—was verifiably true. The code worked. The paperwork mattered more.

Tokenising real-world assets promises to merge the physical and digital economies. But between atoms and code lies a treacherous gap—the *last metre problem*. This is the distance between what a smart contract believes and what actually exists. A token can represent a building, a shipment, or an engine, but only if an external system—an *oracle*—feeds trustworthy information about that building, shipment, or engine into the blockchain. It is in this translation, not the token minting itself, that most failures occur. The most elegant code cannot compensate for a fraudulent input or a broken legal wrapper.

Show: a machine-readable statement that "Asset X exists and is owned by Y." Name: *tokenisation premise*. Explain: the blockchain records a proof of ownership, but it relies on external confirmation that Asset X exists and that Y indeed controls it. Implication: the token is a mirror, not a container; when the reflection diverges from reality, value vanishes.

The first generation of tokenisation experiments—2017 to 2020—revealed this gap brutally. In 2019, the German firm Bitbond attempted to tokenise small-business loans under a licensed prospectus. The project raised several million euros, but when borrowers defaulted, token holders discovered that the legal connection between the blockchain record and enforceable debt was tenuous. The tokens pointed to receivables that no longer existed. The failure was not technical; it was procedural. The oracle layer—the mechanism verifying repayment—depended on manual reporting. When human discipline faltered, automation amplified the error.

Contrast this with the later model of Centrifuge, a Berlin-based protocol that launched in 2021 and continues to issue tokenised invoices for institutional credit pools. Each invoice token passes through layers of off-chain verification—audited cash-flow data, verified identities, signed legal assignments—before being mirrored on-chain. The code here serves as a ledger of entitlement, but the truth comes from certified off-chain records. Show: an oracle feed delivering signed proofs from a regulated custodian. Name: *verifiable attestation.* Explain: trust is not assumed; it is constructed through documentation. Implication: the credibility of tokenised assets grows in proportion to the auditability of their inputs.

This principle—auditable processes over flashy code—recurs across sectors. In 2022, the Swiss bank Sygnum tokenised an ownership stake in Picasso's *Fillette au béret.* The artwork never left the museum, yet fractional ownership could be traded digitally under Swiss law. What made this possible was not just blockchain infrastructure but a precise legal wrapper: a special-purpose vehicle (SPV) governed by enforceable rights. The digital token represented shares in that SPV, not the painting itself. If a holder wished to assert ownership, they would do so through corporate law, not cryptography. The art remained physical, but its economic representation became liquid. The success of the scheme lay in legal engineering, not technical novelty.

This illustrates a broader truth: tokenisation without enforceability is theatre. For a token to have durable value, its claim must be recognised by institutions that arbitrate reality—courts, regulators, and auditors. Code alone cannot compel a landlord to transfer property or a debtor to repay a loan. The legal wrapper performs that conversion. It translates digital statements into obligations that the world will honour. This is the real bridge between atoms and code.

Yet the desire to bypass this bridge remains strong. Some projects attempt to tokenise property deeds directly, arguing that blockchain's immutability could replace registries. In 2018, the Republic of Georgia's National Agency of Public Registry launched a pilot with Bitfury to anchor property titles on a blockchain. The system worked technically, but the government retained ultimate authority over what counted as the official record. The blockchain provided transparency, not sovereignty. That outcome was instructive: technology can enhance institutional trust, but it cannot substitute for it.

There are counter-examples worth examining. Projects such as Chainlink (founded 2017) have developed decentralised oracle networks that aggregate data from multiple independent sources, reducing single points of failure. This improves integrity but does not solve the *semantic gap*: an oracle can confirm a sensor's reading or a database entry, but it cannot confirm that a warehouse actually exists or that a debtor intends to pay. Physical verification still depends on humans, inspectors, and contracts. The oracle can attest to data, not to reality itself.

The motif running through all these cases is verification as choreography—a sequence of human and machine actions that must align precisely for the system to hold. When it works, the bridge between atoms and code functions invisibly; when it fails, it fails dramatically. A warehouse token without a warehouse becomes a fiction instantly discoverable yet legally unfixable. The blockchain records the absence perfectly.

The "last metre" also exposes the fragility of assumptions about automation. Engineers often imagine that adding sensors or IoT devices will solve verification. A temperature sensor on a refrigerated truck can indeed feed real-time data into a smart contract, triggering payments automatically. But what if the sensor malfunctions, or the truck operator tampers with it? The data remains valid to the blockchain even when false to the world. Auditable processes—routine calibration, custody logs, and tamper-evident seals—turn automation from convenience into reliability. The chain of evidence matters as much as the chain of blocks.

Financial institutions are learning this pragmatically. When JPMorgan's Onyx platform launched tokenised deposits in late 2020, it did not promise disruption but reconciliation. Each token corresponded precisely to fiat held in reserve, verified through existing audit procedures. The innovation was not the token but the proof mechanism linking digital and traditional ledgers. Show: an internal reconciliation report tying every token to a balance sheet entry. Name: *dual-ledger assurance*. Explain: the value of tokenisation scales only when it integrates with existing financial infrastructure. Implication: the path forward is hybrid, not utopian.

The same logic applies to physical assets. Tokenising equipment or commodities requires control verification—proof that the custodian cannot secretly substitute, sell, or destroy the asset without detection. Warehouse receipts, inspection certificates, and GPS-tracked seals are not bureaucratic relics; they are the sensory organs of the system. Without them, digital ownership becomes metaphysical. Each token must point to an asset that can be located, inspected, and legally claimed. Anything less invites the same illusion that doomed early asset-backed stablecoins, where "audits" consisted of screenshots.

The limitation of this model is cost. Full auditability requires intermediaries—lawyers, accountants, inspectors—whose fees can erode the efficiency that tokenisation promises. Critics argue that such overheads defeat the point. But the reconciliation lies in scale and automation: once processes are standardised, verification can become a service layer shared across assets. Standardised legal templates, automated reporting, and common attestations can reduce friction without abandoning scrutiny. The industry is already moving towards this: the International Swaps and Derivatives Association (ISDA) in 2023 released a digital asset derivatives framework designed to harmonise legal terms across tokenised instruments. The result is dull but transformative—a grammar of trust encoded into paperwork.

So, what does the "bridge" truly consist of? Not marble code or grand declarations of decentralisation, but a set of disciplined, repeatable practices: every asset verified, every claim traceable, every exception logged. The glamour lies in the precision. A trustworthy oracle is not one that dazzles with decentralised complexity but one that can be audited, tested, and held accountable. A sound legal wrapper is not one that promises revolution but one that holds up in court.

This subchapter's quiet motif—the bridge—returns as both metaphor and method. To bridge atoms and code is to translate responsibility, not merely information. Each party along the bridge—the engineer, the auditor, the regulator—must see the same facts and agree on their meaning. That alignment, not the blockchain itself, is what creates digital trust.

The unresolved tension is the same that has haunted finance for centuries: how to verify claims about the physical world in ways that scale faster than deceit. Tokenisation does not abolish that challenge; it rephrases it. The test for every new project is simple, almost disarmingly so: if the server disappears, if the oracle fails, if the custodian absconds—does the token still correspond to something recoverable, enforceable, and real?

Until that answer is consistently "yes," the bridge between atoms and code remains under construction.

Liquidity where it helps

In March 2021, Greensill Capital, headquartered in London, collapsed after credit insurers withdrew cover and key funders halted purchases of its short-term notes. Supply chain finance—sold as a lubricant for commerce—had become a funnel for concentrated risk. In theory, the market's liquidity should have reduced waste: pay suppliers faster, price invoices transparently, cut financing costs. In practice, opacity met speed. When confidence cracked, liquidity sluiced away, leaving manufacturers and investors exposed. The lesson was harsh and specific. Liquidity is not a virtue in itself.

Set beside that failure, consider a quieter success. In 2011, MarketInvoice—now MarketFinance—in London began auctioning individual invoices from British SMEs to a network of investors. The mechanics were plain: verified receivables, clear eligibility criteria, visible discount rates, and legal assignments that could be enforced if a debtor defaulted. The platform priced time. Suppliers chose whether to sell a £50,000 invoice due in 60 days at a given discount; buyers competed on yield. The market did not need spectacle. It needed a fair clock and a reliable contract. One result was measurable: faster cash conversion for firms that would otherwise wait months for payment. Less waiting. Fewer write-offs. More working capital where it counts.

What distinguishes the two cases is not technology but *discipline about where liquidity sits*. Show: invoices with verified purchase orders placed into a marketplace with knowable settlement procedures. Name: *purposeful secondary markets*. Explain: when the claim and its risk are legible, a secondary buyer can price a receivable as a dated cash flow rather than a mystery. Implication: liquidity reduces waste when it shortens dead time between value created and value paid, not when it merely reshuffles exposure at speed.

Tokenisation promises to extend this logic. A token representing a verified invoice, a rental stream, or a piece of equipment turns a future cash flow into a present instrument that many can evaluate. If the instrument moves through an open, auditable ledger, more buyers can compete, spreads may tighten, and capital costs for the originator can fall. That is the virtuous story. But tokens also make speed cheap. A claim that changes hands ten times before maturity invites a different dynamic: attention drifts from the underlying performance to the next flip. The clock remains, but the gaze moves from the dial to the ticker. Markets stop asking, *Will this cash flow arrive?* and start asking, *Can I pass the parcel before the music stops?*

To use liquidity well, we must anchor it to *verifiable cash flows* and *bounded risk*. Show: a logistics firm in Rotterdam sells a batch of invoices to a token market that requires debtor confirmation and bank-feed proofs of payment on settlement. Name: *attested receivables*. Explain: oracles deliver signed evidence that the invoice exists, the goods shipped, and the debtor acknowledged liability. Implication: secondary buyers price a narrow uncertainty—timing and credit—not a fog of unknowns. That makes the discount a signal, not a guess.

The motif that helps here is the *tap*. A good market is a tap you can open to fill a precise need—bridging a gap between delivery and payment—then close. It is not a firehose you leave running because speed feels like progress. The question is always: how wide should the tap be, and who controls it?

Liquidity lowers costs when it reduces *idle inventory of claims*. Show: a manufacturer in Birmingham with £2 million locked in receivables finds buyers within hours on a tokenised exchange that enforces standard contracts. Name: *time compression*. Explain: the firm's days sales outstanding fall; the opportunity cost of stuck capital shrinks. Implication: liquidity here is a productivity tool—less waste in the system, not more speculation around it.

A second named example clarifies the boundary. In May 2019, Santander in Madrid issued a blockchain-settled bond and managed coupon payments on-chain. The novelty was not yield but plumbing: issuance, settlement, and payment reconciled in near real time, with fewer intermediaries rekeying data. The bond was ordinary. The ledger made its motion efficient. Show: a coupon payment posting across holders' wallets without reconciliation delays. Name: *operational liquidity*. Explain: administrative friction dropped, reducing cost without changing the risk profile of the bond. Implication: not all liquidity is about resale; some of it is about removing clerical dead zones that waste time and money.

Greensill's collapse serves as a counter-example. Its promise—pay suppliers early, finance buyers cheaply—was not inherently flawed. The flaw was concentration and opacity: exposure to a small set of borrowers, soft definitions of "future receivables," and a dependence on external funds with their own redemption cycles. Show: funds forced to sell notes to meet withdrawals, pushing yields up and confidence down. Name: *churn risk*. Explain: when secondary demand is the only thing keeping primary issuance afloat, the market becomes reflexive; short-term flows dictate long-term viability. Implication: liquidity can migrate from service to spectacle, and then it feeds on itself.

Reconcile the cases by specifying a test: *Does secondary trading improve primary discipline?* In the best invoice markets, yes. Stricter onboarding, cleaner data, and standard contracts emerge because sellers want access to cheaper capital. In showy markets, no. Sellers chase form over substance; buyers chase momentum over diligence. The fix is design, not rhetoric.

Design choices turn a market into a tap rather than a firehose. First, insist that liquidity points at *settlement events*. Show: automated triggers that close a token's lifecycle when a debtor pays, with proceeds swept on-chain to holders pro rata. Name: *hard maturities*. Explain:

instruments expire into cash, curbing endless rollover games. Implication: price signals stay tied to dates and deliveries, not hype.

Second, build *queuing and pacing* into exits. Instant exit is not a universal good. A periodic auction—weekly, say—can concentrate order flow, reveal true clearing prices, and reduce slippage for all. Show: a Friday auction that batches redemptions and admissions for a receivables pool, publishing a time-stamped price and fill ratio. Name: *batched liquidity*. Explain: participants plan around a calendar; the market gains rhythm rather than noise. Implication: lower churn, better discovery.

Third, align fees with patience. Show: a lower platform fee for holding to maturity than for flipping within 48 hours. Name: *anti-churn pricing*. Explain: platforms can measure holding periods and reward behaviour that funds the real economy. Implication: secondary markets that still serve primary needs.

There are limits. Liquidity can be expensive to maintain. Market-makers must be paid; audits must be done; disputes must be resolved. Too many small instruments can fragment the pool, widening spreads and raising costs—the paradox of false choice. A thousand micro-claims trade poorly; ten standardised ones trade well. Show: a dashboard with twenty near-identical tokens, each too small to attract depth. Name: *thin book problem*. Explain: fragmentation hides risk and raises execution cost. Implication: standardisation—templates for invoices by sector, jurisdiction, and payment terms—does more for liquidity than novelty.

A further limitation is *liquidity theatre*: the appearance of depth provided by wash trades or rebates that vanish when markets stress. The cure is measurement. Require venues to publish time-and-sales, depth, and effective spread; require projects to disclose redemption queues and cash buffers. Show: a monthly report comparing quoted versus realised spreads for tokens, with anomalies flagged. Name: *verifiable market quality*. Explain: transparency lets participants distinguish genuine flow from stagecraft. Implication: trust accrues to venues that measure and commit.

Short-termism is the hazard that stalks all liquid markets. It shows up as frequent re-pricing of long-duration projects, pressure to cut maintenance or community spending to hit near-term yields, and governance captured by arbitrageurs who move in and out between votes. The antidote is *temporal matching*. Show: investor classes with different rights—daily liquidity but lower yield for one; hold-to-maturity with higher yield for another—mirrored in smart contracts that respect lockups. Name: *tiered horizons*. Explain: capital with fleeting patience should not control assets that require years of care. Implication: liquidity is layered; stewardship stays intact.

A second positive example illustrates this restraint. In 2013–2019, *The International*—Valve's annual *Dota 2* tournament—used time-bound digital passes whose sales funded the prize pool. The "Compendium" created liquid, tradable cosmetics but only during a defined season; proceeds tied directly to the event's budget. Show: a live counter climbing as fans purchased passes. Name: *seasonal liquidity*. Explain: temporary, purposeful markets aligned participation with production. Implication: when the tap closes on schedule, attention returns to delivery, not flipping.

Tokenised treasuries offer a contemporary case worth framing as a scenario. Since 2019, Franklin Templeton has operated a money-market fund whose shares are recorded on a public ledger. As more issuers explore tokenised short-term government paper, secondary trading could allow treasurers to manage cash more nimbly between venues without sacrificing credit quality. The benefit is not speculation but *operational agility*: fewer intermediaries, clearer record-keeping, and fast settlement against high-grade assets. The risk, if poorly governed, is that platforms treat T-bill tokens as chips in carry trades disconnected from underlying demand. The difference, again, is the clock: are tokens a parking bay for cash until payroll, or a racetrack for leverage?

Against these examples, set a stubborn truth: liquidity cannot make a bad asset good. It can only make a claim mobile. If the invoice is fraudulent, the property encumbered, or the equipment mis-maintained, the market will distribute harm faster, not fix it. That is why the previous subchapter insisted on auditable processes.

Without clean oracles and legal wrappers, secondary markets become accelerants.

The motif of the tap returns. Who is allowed to turn it, and how far? Platforms can hard-code *circuit breakers*—halts when oracles diverge, when redemptions spike, or when spreads exceed a threshold. They can stage upgrades behind timelocks. They can require that any change to risk parameters be announced days in advance, giving holders time to adjust. These measures are not paternalism; they are acknowledgements that speed is a tool to be governed, not a good to be maximised.

So the forward test is pragmatic. If you add a secondary market to an asset, which waste does it remove, which risk does it concentrate, and which behaviour does it induce tomorrow that you actually want? Measure the answers. Compare them. Commit to the boring safeguards that keep the clock honest. Liquidity helps when it moves value to work faster than inertia can waste it; it harms when it moves attention faster than judgement can follow. The tap is there. How wide should it run, and who keeps a hand on the valve?

Fragmentation traps

On 24 June 2021 in Surfside, Florida, Champlain Towers South partially collapsed, killing ninety-eight people. The catastrophe had many causes, but one of them was mundane: years of delayed maintenance in a building governed by hundreds of flat owners who struggled to agree on repairs and the special assessments to fund them. Board minutes from 2018 record disputes over costs; assessments were approved, then stretched; contractors waited; concrete decayed. The roof still leaks. In structures where responsibility is thinly spread, consent becomes expensive. Time becomes the hidden fee.

Fractional ownership is often sold as democracy. Everyone owns a piece, everyone has a say. Yet when "everyone" is the governance model rather than the beneficiary, essential work slows. The fracture begins with the first urgent decision: replace worn membranes, fund a lift overhaul, remediate unsafe cladding. Show: a notice for a

£600,000 roof replacement circulated to 240 holders scattered across jurisdictions. Name: *governance drag.* Explain: each holder weighs a small stake against a large, immediate outlay and uncertain future benefit, and a critical mass hesitates. Implication: essential maintenance becomes a prisoner of collective action; the asset deteriorates while owners debate.

The effect is measurable in behaviour. Attendance at meetings drops below quorum. Votes roll over. Service charges go into arrears. Contractors reprice because quotes expire. Insurers raise premiums or withdraw. Each is a visible metric of fragmentation. None requires a blockchain to appear. Tokenisation can exacerbate the pattern by lowering entry thresholds and multiplying voices unless governance is designed with concentration of responsibility in mind. The motif that will recur here is the leak: a slow, predictable failure made catastrophic by delay.

To see how dilution in ownership becomes dilution in care, consider the way timeshare resorts across Spain in the 1990s and 2000s accumulated maintenance backlogs. Resorts with thousands of fractional owners struggled to pass special assessments; exit schemes trapped dissatisfied holders; reputational damage discouraged new buyers who might have refreshed the pool. Show: an annual general meeting where a simple majority is achieved only after multiple adjournments. Name: *quorum attrition.* Explain: when decisions require broad participation, fatigue replaces urgency; the marginal owner declines to engage because the effort exceeds the stake. Implication: decision-making moves from proactive maintenance to emergency response, a shift that multiplies costs by deferring them.

Now contrast that with a more tightly engineered model. In 2019, RealT began tokenising single-family rentals in Detroit. Legally, each property sits inside a dedicated limited liability company; the tokens represent membership interests. RealT does not ask hundreds of micro-holders to approve every tap washer. Instead, the operating agreement delegates day-to-day maintenance authority to a manager with fiduciary duties, while reserving only major actions—sales, refinancing—for supermajority votes. Show: a burst pipe fixed within hours because the manager holds authority and a reserve. Name: *delegated operations with bounded consent.* Explain: fractional ownership remains, but governance separates routine stewardship from existential choices. Implication: the property functions as a property, not a parliament.

The shared rental property offers a laboratory for these design choices because the failure mode is visible. Imagine a Victorian terrace in Leeds converted into four flats, then tokenised into 2,000 slices. The boiler fails in November. The agent proposes a £12,000 replacement and a two-week disruption. A proposal goes out to token holders worldwide. Many ignore it; some object; a handful cannot be reached because their wallets are unattended. Winter does not wait. Tenants withhold rent; mould spreads; the council issues a notice; lenders, if any, tighten covenants. A cost that should have been contained escalates because the decision to spend became a battleground for tiny interests.

This is not an argument against fractional ownership; it is an argument for governance that anticipates human behaviour. In corporate law, boards exist to make timely decisions under duty of care and loyalty, precisely because dispersed shareholders cannot manage operations. In commonhold or strata schemes, the law sets minimum quorums, reserve funds, and powers to levy charges. Tokenisation should not erase these disciplines; it should encode them. Show: a smart contract that enforces a monthly reserve allocation equal to 10 per cent of gross rent and releases funds for pre-authorised maintenance categories without further votes. Name: *embedded reserves*. Explain: by committing to prudent cushions in advance, the project replaces ad hoc begging with predictable provision. Implication: when the leak appears, the money exists and the authority to spend it is clear.

Two named, checkable examples illustrate the frontier between paralysis and prudence. First, the collapse of Champlain Towers in Surfside, already noted, shows how deferring assessments for known structural issues can end in catastrophe; while the building was not a tokenised asset, the governance problem—too many small stakes resisting a large, necessary spend—maps directly onto fractionalisation. Secondly, in July 2020, the Law Commission of England and Wales published a set of proposals to modernise *commonhold*—a tenure that allows flat owners to own their unit and collectively own the building's fabric—specifically to address governance complexity. The report recommended clearer default rules for decision thresholds, reserve funds, and dispute resolution to prevent deadlock. Show: a legal framework that lowers the cost of making boring, necessary decisions. Name: *Commonhold reform proposals (Law Commission, July 2020)*. Explain: when the law anticipates paralysis, it prescribes mechanisms—appointed managers, lower thresholds for urgent works, cost recovery powers—that keep buildings liveable. Implication: tokenised buildings need equivalent scaffolding in code and contract, not libertarian fantasies of pure voting.

There is a credible counter-example to consider: community land trusts (CLTs). In a CLT, a non-profit trusts holds land in perpetuity and grants long leases for homes at controlled prices. Ownership is dispersed across residents and stakeholders; yet many CLTs maintain properties well and act swiftly in emergencies. The reconciliation lies in structure. CLTs vest operational authority in professional managers and embed mission—long-term affordability—into their charters. Show: a CLT board approving a roof repair at a single meeting because reserves and mandates exist. Name: *mission-anchored centralisation*. Explain: fragmentation in ownership does not imply fragmentation in authority; where strategy is stable and management empowered, many hands need not mean many brakes. Implication: we should not confuse dispersion of benefit with dispersion of decision-making.

Metrics make this concrete. A property's maintenance health can be tracked through average days to approve work orders, variance between budgeted and actual capital expenditure, arrears rate, and reserve fund coverage (months of operating expenses). When ownership is atomised beyond a governance capacity threshold—say, more than 100 holders per asset without delegated management—these metrics degrade: approvals lengthen, capex deviates, arrears rise, reserves thin. The figures will vary by asset and jurisdiction, but the direction is consistent. You can measure a leak by the time from report to repair. You can price paralysis.

Standards from earlier sections matter. The same choice to encode predictable behaviours in ERC-style templates can be applied to property. A property token standard that surfaces mandatory fields—reserve ratio, manager authority scope, escalation thresholds—turns opaque governance into inspectable risk. Show: a wallet displaying "Reserves: 4.2 months" and "Urgent repairs threshold: £25,000" in plain text before purchase. Name: *governance disclosure at the edge*. Explain: buyers stop funding paralysis because they can see it coming; sellers who want better prices adopt stronger defaults. Implication: liquidity, as argued earlier, improves when information aligns incentives; the same is true for maintenance.

Fragmentation also invites *hold-out behaviour*. When a major improvement requires supermajority consent—say, to install energy-efficient windows or solar panels—a small minority can block action, anticipating that others will bear the cost of delay. Law addresses this through compulsory purchase of dissenting shares or court-sanctioned schemes of arrangement. Tokenised property will need equivalents: drag-along rights for essential works, expert determination for disputed scope, and pre-committed arbitration. Show: a smart contract that, upon an independent surveyor's report of urgent structural risk, lowers the consent threshold and allows costs to be levied with staged payment plans. Name: *contingent governance*. Explain: no system should require unanimity to fix a roof; threshold flexibility must be a feature, not a plea. Implication: responsiveness is not autocracy when it is bound to evidence, expertise, and appeal paths.

Fragmentation traps extend beyond bricks. Consider wind-farm cooperatives with thousands of small shareholders. When turbines age, repowering decisions demand large capital and temporary shutdowns. Projects that embedded clear life-cycle plans and delegated technical authority proceed; those that relied on plebiscites stall and bleed revenue. Or look to music catalogues sold as fractional royalty tokens: holders who expected monthly distributions may oppose reinvestment in marketing or catalogue refreshes, even when the net present value would rise. The same behavioural economics applies: people discount long-term gains when stakes are small and delays are immediate. Design has to counteract that bias.

There is a temptation in token markets to claim that mere price signals solve governance: if maintenance is underfunded, token prices will fall, disciplining managers. Prices move. Rooves do not. Market discounts cannot replace a decision to hire a contractor on Thursday. Governance is a doing discipline. It lives in the cadence of meetings, the content of agendas, the authority to sign a purchase order, and the reserve in the bank.

We should therefore be precise about where to place consent. Routine operations—repairs under a threshold, compliance tasks, insurance renewals—must sit with an accountable operator subject to audit and removal, not with a perpetual referendum. Strategic decisions—sale, refinancing, change of use—justify broader votes and higher thresholds. Between those poles, tie triggers to evidence: surveyor reports, statutory notices, expiry of warranties. Show: a manager mandated to execute any recommendation labelled "urgent" by an accredited inspector, with cost caps and post-action reporting. Name: *evidence-gated authority*. Explain: we replace opinion with qualification; disputes shift from "whether" to "whether the evidence meets the standard". Implication: the leak is fixed because a professional said so and the system trusts the certification.

Two design cautions remain. First, the *thin-ownership problem*. When the median holder's stake is below the level at which engagement pays—say, less than one month's rent—voter fatigue is inevitable. You can't educate indifference away. The countermeasure is either to raise the minimum bite or to pool representation through delegated voting, where holders pick stewards who aggregate voice for a term. Secondly, *pseudo-democracy*. Some projects maintain the theatre of votes while the operator holds all real levers. That breeds cynicism and suppresses future capital formation. The remedy is straightforward: publish what is delegated, publish what is reserved, and publish performance. If the manager fixed twenty-eight work orders in thirty days at a median time-to-repair of forty-eight hours, show it. If reserve coverage fell from six to four months, show it too. Measurement is oxygen.

We return to the leak. Not every leak is literal; some are slow losses of energy performance, tenant goodwill, or legal compliance. They all cost more later. The trap is to treat fractionalisation as a moral good rather than a tool. Democracy at the wrong layer is vandalism by delay. Concentration at the right layer is stewardship by design. The question for any tokenised property is brutally simple: when the next leak appears, who decides, how fast, with which money, and against what professional test? If the answers are vague or collective, the building will tell the truth before the dashboard does.

Operational compliance, not slogans

In June 2014, at the Port of Qingdao in China, banks discovered that the same piles of copper and aluminium had been pledged multiple times for loans. Warehouse receipts were forged or duplicated; collateral that appeared ample on paper proved illusory on site. Standard Chartered, Citigroup, and others froze financing while investigators traced custody chains across bonded warehouses and logistics firms. The scandal did not hinge on exotic derivatives. It turned on basic failures: no verifiable proof that the metal existed where the paperwork said it did, and no uncontested proof of who controlled it. Paper failed. Process failed. The lesson travels easily into token markets. If a claim about atoms cannot be audited, decorating it with code does not turn it into truth.

Tokenisation tempts issuers to speak in sweeping promises—"on-chain transparency," "24/7 markets," "disintermediated access"—as if rhetoric could do the work of reconciliation. But operational integrity lives in duller places: a stamped inspection report, a bank feed that shows cash cleared, a title search, a trustee's ledger. The grammar of trust is prosaic. It is also portable. Whether the asset is a tonne of metal, a municipal bond, a rental stream, or a shipment of machine parts, four proofs decide whether a token deserves belief: that the thing exists; that a specific party controls it; that the cash attached to it is mapped from origin to outcome; and that a legitimate pathway exists to resolve disputes when data and reality diverge. The motif here is the file: the packet of evidence that turns slogans into obligations. If the file is thin, the token is weak.

Start with the first proof. Show: a surveyor's certificate, a warehouse audit, a registrar's letter, a timestamped photo set with GPS coordinates, or all of them together. Name: proof of existence. Explain: a token that claims to represent an asset must anchor that claim in evidence a third party can verify without trusting the issuer's word. Implication: anyone contemplating purchase should ask to see that evidence and how it is refreshed. A one-off inspection is a promise with an expiry date. Measured as behaviour, projects that respect existence proofs commit to re-verification cycles—monthly, quarterly, or on event—and publish exceptions with cause. If a container is delayed at Felixstowe or a property's tenants churn, the file shows it.

Proof of control—who can move, sell, or encumber the asset—matters as much. The Qingdao scandal was at its core a control failure: several parties believed they held the same collateral because nobody could show who had a *present* power to dispose. Show: a tri-party control agreement, a trustee deed, a perfected security interest, or a custodian attestation that substitution requires co-signatures. Name: proof of control. Explain: control is not a slogan about "custody"; it is a defined, legally enforceable right with constraints. Implication: token holders are not protected by "immutability"; they are protected by a chain of documents that courts will recognise. In practice, this appears as operational habits: daily position reconciliations, dual-control procedures, separation between front-office minting and back-office control functions, and independent sign-offs recorded on an immutable log.

Cash-flow mapping brings clarity to what an investor can reasonably expect and when. Greensill's collapse in March 2021 taught this brutally: when receivables financing slides from specific, confirmed invoices into vague "future receivables," cash-flow maps blur; redemptions depend on continued issuance rather than defined settlements. Show: a schedule that ties every promised distribution to an observable event—debtor payment, coupon date, lease receipt—and to a bank account whose statements are attested and later reconciled to on-chain distributions. Name: cash-flow mapping. Explain: a token should not only say *what* cash is owed, but from *where*, *by whom*, and under *what path* it will arrive. Implication: projects that pass this test publish dashboards that match inputs and outputs: dates, amounts, variances, with explanations for delays beyond defined tolerances. Spreads tightens when explanations beat excuses.

Dispute pathways determine whether an investor's remedy is theoretical or real. When records conflict—an oracle feed says "paid," the debtor says "not received"—who adjudicates and on what evidence? Show: an escalation ladder from helpdesk to independent administrator to a nominated court or arbitration venue, tied to documents that empower each actor to see the necessary data and issue binding instructions. Name: dispute pathways. Explain: this is not a customer support email; it is a charter of recourse that turns error or fraud into a process rather than a panic. Implication: firms that take this seriously report median resolution times and win/loss ratios; they publish anonymised case studies because they expect problems and measure how they exit them.

These four proofs—existence, control, cash-flows, dispute—sound like a checklist because they are. Checklists are a discipline, not a flourish. They are how operating theatres avoid leaving swabs inside patients and why flight decks still read aloud the obvious. Checklists survive because humans forget. Token engineers are not exceptions. A "lean template" for real-world assets should hard-wire each proof into both code and contract. The form itself can be plain; the commitments are where substance lives.

Consider two named cases where this discipline manifested with measurable benefits. In September 2019, Banco Santander in Madrid issued a blockchain-settled bond and managed coupon payments on-chain. The instrument was boring by design. What mattered operationally was the reconciliation: every on-chain state mapped exactly to off-chain records; cash movements were mirrored against the bank's balance sheet; the paying agent role was explicit. The outcome was shorter settlement cycles and fewer reconciliations—efficiency born from auditability rather than marketing. In November 2022, under the Monetary Authority of Singapore's *Project Guardian*, a pilot executed tokenised assets within a governed sandbox: banks could only sell into pools with clear eligibility criteria; price discovery and settlement were observed; regulators watched the file, not the press release. The result was not a revolution; it was a tidy demonstration of how process earns permission to scale.

Set against those, a credible counter-example helps sharpen the point. In 2021, a wave of projects sold "asset-backed" tokens linked to commodities stored in informal depots across several jurisdictions. White papers promised "24/7 liquidity" and "trustless ownership." Yet when auditors requested warehouse receipts and verified stock counts, documentation proved incomplete or contradictory; where evidence did exist, it did not match the on-chain supply. Tokens continued to trade until withdrawals spiked; then the market seized and issuers disappeared. The failure mode was not a zero-day exploit. It was a null checklist. Reconciliation is dull until it is the only thing that matters.

How should a lean template appear in daily operations, without lapsing into a bureaucratic maze? In prose rather than bullet points, it amounts to pre-committing to four narratives that any outsider can read. The first narrative states: *what exists, where, under whose supervision, with what inspection cadence, and what documentary proof we hold today and will refresh when.* It names the third parties—surveyor, custodian, registrar—and defines their duties and liabilities. The second narrative states: *who controls substitution, release, and disposal; how many signatures are required; which keys can do what; and where those constraints appear in code and in law.* The third states: *which bank accounts, which payers, which oracles; how tokens accrue and distribute cash; how reconciliations occur; who certifies them and how often.* The fourth states: *when a number does not match, who asks whom for what, where evidence lives, what deadlines apply, and which court or arbitration body has jurisdiction if consent fails.* If a token cannot produce these narratives in the file, it has not been operationally designed; it has been advertised.

Metrics are the relief maps of these narratives. Setting targets turns ideals into behaviours: maximum age of existence proofs before refresh; percentage of assets with dual control; variance tolerances on cash-flow timing; median dispute resolution time; number of days between a debtor's bank credit and on-chain distribution; timelocks for governance changes. When projects publish such metrics, their "transparency" stops being an abstract noun. It becomes a table a professional can read, compare, and price. If a platform claims "institutional-grade reporting" but cannot show these numbers, the phrase means nothing.

Standards bodies have begun to translate this operational posture into shared grammar. The International Swaps and Derivatives Association (ISDA) in 2023 released documentation frameworks for digital asset derivatives that, among other things, define how disputes over valuation and settlement should be handled across venues. The benefit is not glamour but convergence: when everyone uses similar words for similar things, reconciliation speeds up and costs fall. Likewise, Ethereum's EIP-2981 royalty standard, while softer than law, shows how supply-side intent can be encoded for marketplaces to read; the point for real-world assets is analogous—publish operational intent as fields that wallets and markets can display: reserve ratios, audit cadence, control schema. A buyer should not have to fossick through PDFs to discover whether a manager can substitute collateral unilaterally.

Examples that combine on-chain verifiability with off-chain audits continue to set the pace. MakerDAO's integration of real-world collateral from 2022 onwards forced community-level habits around the file: legal opinions posted and debated, attestation reports published on schedule, risk parameters adjusted when external conditions changed. The community did not always agree, but the process was inspectable, and the arguments referred to facts rather than slogans. That is compliance as habit, not posture.

Where does this leave the rhetoric of "trustless" systems? Nowhere especially useful when atoms are involved. Oracles and legal wrappers reintroduce trust by necessity. The moral move is not to deny this, but to localise and expose it. Name the parties. Publish the contracts. Time-stamp the attestations. Admit where uncertainty sits. Then make the system resilient to that uncertainty with buffers and procedures: reserve funds for property maintenance; over-collateralisation thresholds for receivables pools; kill-switches with multi-signature control; circuit breakers tied to oracle divergence. You reduce harm not by promising that failure cannot happen, but by rehearsing what you will do when it does.

All of this sounds workmanlike because it is. The lure of slogans remains strong because they are cheap and travel well. Checklists cost concentration and, worse, create evidence that can be audited later. They also reduce the cost of capital. Markets prefer instruments whose operational stories are short, verifiable, and repeatable. If a platform can prove that 98 per cent of distributions landed within two business days of payer receipt for twelve consecutive months, that number will do more to attract patient capital than any manifesto. If custody logs show zero single-person authority over substitutions for nine quarters, that, too, is worth more than adjectives.

A lean template therefore asks issuers to make three commitments before they mint: we will not ask buyers to take our word where an independent attestation is possible; we will express operational promises in data that machines can read and humans can understand; and when we change something material, we will announce it with enough time for others to object or exit. These are not philosophical positions. They are workplace rules for money.

The unresolved tension is old and inescapable. How much procedure can a young market tolerate before it stifles experimentation, and how much looseness can it permit before it repeats Qingdao by other means? Each project must pick a point on that line and defend it with evidence. The file will tell if it chose well.

Chapter 4
NFTs and the Meaning of Ownership

In March 2021, a digital collage by the artist Beeple sold at Christie's for $69.3 million. The sale was heralded as a revolution—a JPEG commanding the price of a Basquiat. But what the buyer received was not the image itself. It was a token: a cryptographic receipt pointing to a file stored elsewhere, its value drawn not from pixels but from provenance. Beneath the hysteria, an ancient question re-emerged in a new form: what does it mean to *own* something intangible? The auction was less a triumph of art than a mirror held up to our evolving sense of possession. The medium had changed; the psychology had not.

NFTs—non-fungible tokens—were born in exuberance but will survive, if they do, through discipline. Their story is not about cartoon apes or speculative bubbles; it is about programmable uniqueness. What began as a technical quirk—the ability to distinguish one token from another—has matured into a design space for rights, access, and participation. A ticket that upgrades after three uses, a warranty that follows the object it covers, a membership that confers status only while the holder contributes value: these are not gimmicks. They are experiments in aligning digital identity with lived behaviour. The NFT, stripped of hype, is a machine for encoding relationships.

The distinction matters because ownership is not a monolith; it is a bundle of permissions and expectations. In the physical world, the bundle is bounded by law and custom: deeds, receipts, titles, and trust. Online, those boundaries blur. The NFT promises to reintroduce structure—not by dictating who may *own*, but by defining what *ownership does*. It converts the abstract right to access or participate into an object that can move, expire, or evolve. Yet this programmable ownership also reveals a paradox: control lies not in the blockchain itself but in the infrastructure around it—the marketplaces, wallets, and contracts that interpret the code. When those intermediaries toggle a royalty on or off, as several did in 2023, creators discover the fragility of promises written in code but executed by platform power.

This chapter examines how that fragility can be tamed without extinguishing creativity. We begin with what lies beyond the JPEG: the uses of non-fungibility where scarcity is not an aesthetic trick but a functional necessity. A concert ticket tied to a specific seat, an accreditation that records continuing education, a digital key that unlocks a device only for a verified owner—all are non-fungible by design, not declaration. The artistry lies in constraint. By mapping ownership to distinct experiences or histories, designers turn tokens into living artefacts, capable of earning their identity through use. In such systems, time itself becomes metadata.

From there, we move to the uneasy intersection between creators and platforms. Early NFT rhetoric promised "automatic royalties"—a dream of perpetual income enforced by code. Reality intervened. Smart contracts can *suggest* a royalty, but marketplaces decide whether to honour it. When OpenSea and Blur, two of the largest NFT platforms, switched their royalty policies in 2023, toggling enforcement to attract traders, artists faced a hard truth: programmability without enforcement is theatre. The episode exposes a wider tension in digital ownership—between decentralised ideals and centralised execution. Platforms, not protocols, still adjudicate who gets paid.

Ownership also extends beyond individual possession. Communities form around tokens not just as collectors but as co-authors of meaning. An NFT can bind hundreds or thousands of patrons into a shared project—a book, a festival, a game—turning ownership into participation. Yet collective power brings fatigue. Endless voting corrodes enthusiasm; governance becomes a chore. The most resilient communities recognise this and shift from perpetual referenda to milestone-based collaboration: holders unlock perks or access when the project hits defined targets. Governance becomes an *arc*, not a treadmill. The best NFT communities resemble guilds rather than parliaments—light in structure, heavy in continuity.

And then there is taste—the currency of cultural legitimacy. NFTs exposed how easily scarcity can be faked and meaning diluted. When every token claims to be "unique," uniqueness itself loses value. The same mechanics that empower creation also enable spam: mass airdrops, inflated collections, and social manipulation masquerading as community. Good NFT design resists this drift not by building walls but by curating context. A museum label confers more than authentication; it confers *interpretation.* Similarly, thoughtful projects constrain supply, embed narrative, and invite discernment. They understand that the human hunger for status is not the problem; it is the palette. The challenge is to make digital status signify substance rather than noise.

The NFT, then, is not a toy of speculation but a test of civilisation's oldest questions: what can be owned, what should be shared, and how value accrues to meaning rather than momentum. The technology may be new, but the debate echoes through centuries—from Roman property law to Renaissance patronage to the licensing wars of the internet age. Each era has redrawn the boundaries between ownership and access, between creator and custodian. NFTs are the latest iteration of that struggle, compressed into code and priced in seconds.

As we move through this chapter, we will see how digital ownership can mature—how programmable receipts become instruments of accountability, how communities design governance without exhaustion, and how status goods reclaim dignity through scarcity with purpose. We will also confront the limits: where ownership shades into theatre, where openness invites exploitation, and where cultural value resists tokenisation altogether.

Ownership, in the age of the token, is not about having more—it is about knowing what it means to hold something that others can see, verify, and yet never touch. It is both a mirror and a contract. The question that follows, and the one this chapter leaves open, is deceptively simple: when code writes the receipt, who writes the meaning?

Beyond JPEGs

On 8 May 2022, at the MGM Grand in Las Vegas, a small group of concertgoers bypassed the usual queues. Their tickets—NFTs minted on Polygon by the electronic artist 3LAU—did more than grant entry. They updated in real time. After each scan, the digital pass altered its metadata to record the holder's attendance history. By the third concert in the tour, the NFT had transformed into a VIP credential, unlocking backstage access and a signed vinyl. No paper ticket could have done this; no static image could have adapted to behaviour. The event offered a quiet revelation: non-fungibility was not a gimmick, but a grammar for programmable relationships.

An NFT is, at root, a receipt that *remembers*. It is proof of an encounter rather than an object—a certificate that records not only possession but participation. The first wave of NFT enthusiasm misread this potential, mistaking stillness for scarcity. JPEGs stood in for assets that might have changed over time. But the token's real power lies in its verbs: it can expire, evolve, restrict, or reward. That difference turns what might have been mere memorabilia into infrastructure for interaction. The motif here is the ticket—humble, serial, often discarded—reborn as a living instrument of access and memory.

Tickets illustrate why non-fungibility matters. Show: a general admission QR code at Wembley Stadium, identical to 90,000 others. Name: fungibility. Explain: any ticket in the same section is interchangeable; no one cares which copy you hold. But when a credential needs to trace specific behaviour—a seat allocation, a loyalty reward, a safety record—it must be unique. That uniqueness, encoded cryptographically, becomes its virtue. Implication: non-fungibility is not a philosophy; it is a tool for accountability. You can measure its effect in fewer disputes and cleaner data.

Sporting and entertainment industries have already tested this logic. In July 2022, UEFA issued over 2.5 million digital match tickets via blockchain to curb counterfeiting. The tokens tied each seat to a verifiable record of entry, deterring resale scams that plagued earlier tournaments. In South Korea, the airline T'way began experimenting with tokenised boarding passes that integrate loyalty points—each pass linked to an immutable itinerary and passenger record. The result was not a speculative market but operational hygiene. These are not JPEGs; they are receipts that behave.

Memberships push the concept further by encoding time, privilege, and history. When Starbucks launched its "Odyssey" programme in

December 2022, it turned NFTs into loyalty artefacts that tracked participation across purchases, quizzes, and events. The tokens could not be freely minted or faked; they evolved as holders engaged, unlocking benefits calibrated to genuine behaviour. Show: a customer who attends a tasting session receives an update to their NFT badge. Name: dynamic credentials. Explain: the token itself is not the coffee; it is the programmable record of relationship. Implication: non-fungibility migrates from status to service—it becomes how brands recognise and reward real people in digital spaces.

The same mechanism applies to warranties and certifications. Consider Sony's 2023 pilot project linking physical electronics to NFT-based warranties in Japan. Each registered product generated a unique token tied to its serial number. Repairs and replacements updated the metadata, producing a service log visible to both manufacturer and owner. Show: a camera's lens replaced under warranty, recorded automatically in the token. Name: proof-of-maintenance. Explain: rather than a paper receipt prone to loss or forgery, the warranty becomes a transparent chain of service events. Implication: resale markets gain credibility because buyers can audit repair histories without trusting sellers.

The thread across these cases is traceability—the ability of a digital object to mirror the life of a physical or social relationship. Non-fungibility allows that mirroring to be precise. A gym membership that locks after inactivity, a university certificate that updates with continuing education, a piece of software that recognises its authorised operator—all rely on individuality that cannot be swapped away. Yet each remains lightweight: a token on a public ledger that carries its own provenance.

There are limits. A credible counter-example comes from the glut of "utility NFTs" issued during the 2021–22 bull run. Many promised perks—event access, product discounts, exclusive drops—but lacked coherent operational design. When servers shut down or partnerships dissolved, tokens persisted as hollow shells, legally meaningless and technically inert. Show: a hospitality token that once granted hotel upgrades but now points to a dead URL. Name: the orphaned token. Explain: programmability without governance invites entropy; the code may run, but the promise expires. Implication: the NFT's durability is double-edged—if it outlives the institution that imbued it with function, its persistence becomes absurdity.

Reconciling this requires discipline rather than despair. The projects that endure treat NFTs not as speculative assets but as elements of a contract stack: code backed by enforceable terms, clear expiration rules, and auditable updates. Proof of concept lies in the ticketing pilots by Ticketmaster and Flow in 2023, where metadata automatically changed after each use and expired post-event, preventing scalping while preserving verifiable souvenirs. Show: a concertgoer re-selling a used ticket cannot reuse its privileges. Name: progressive state change. Explain: each event adds a layer of history while curtailing misuse. Implication: programmability replaces policing; control comes from logic, not gatekeepers.

Non-fungibility also redefines loyalty. Traditional programmes count transactions; NFTs can count *commitments*. A festival pass might accumulate reputation: attend three years, volunteer once, and your access tier upgrades automatically. The pattern is visible in Coachella's "Key Collection," launched in February 2022—ten NFTs tied to lifetime tickets and behind-the-scenes experiences, each tracked by unique on-chain histories. When one key was sold on the secondary market, its privileges followed automatically to the new owner, proving transferability need not erase accountability. Non-fungibility made provenance portable.

The motif of the ticket—simple, serial, personal—reappears as an organising metaphor for all these use cases. A ticket signifies permission bounded by rules: time, seat, holder. When digitised as an NFT, that permission can be reissued, modified, or extended without losing traceability. In corporate training, for instance, Accenture's 2022 trial of digital credentials let employees store verified skills as NFTs, each linked to an issuing manager's signature. The tokens could update when employees completed new certifications. HR departments no longer had to chase paper; the proof travelled with the person. The cost was not zero, but the friction fell dramatically.

The challenge, as with all programmable media, is design ethics. Each layer of automation encodes a power relationship. When a warranty auto-expires or a pass downgrades, who decides the rules? When a loyalty token embeds behavioural data, who owns the analytics? Programmability can just as easily enforce fairness as control. The frontier lies in *who writes the script.* A token that upgrades after three uses is not just a technical feat; it is a policy decision about reward and recognition.

There is also a cultural dimension. NFTs reintroduce individuality into a digital environment obsessed with scale. Every major platform trains users to behave as data points—likes, clicks, impressions, fungible acts feeding aggregate value. Non-fungibility, in contrast, insists on singularity: this ticket, this credential, this proof. It carries memory. It can change without losing identity. That quality makes it potent for communities seeking durable bonds. A digital badge earned through genuine participation has moral weight precisely because it cannot be cloned.

Still, programmability does not excuse complexity. The best systems hide their machinery. A fan at a stadium should not need to grasp cryptographic proofs to enter a gate; the NFT should simply *work*. The success of 3LAU's dynamic tickets came not from blockchain jargon but from clarity: scan, enjoy, repeat. Each scan altered the token's metadata seamlessly. The technology disappeared into the experience. Projects that replicate this humility will endure; those that demand ideological literacy will wither.

Metrics tell the same story. A well-designed NFT system can be measured by redemption rate, fraud incidence, update latency, and user comprehension. The UEFA ticketing pilot cut counterfeit attempts by 80 per cent (UEFA, 2022). Starbucks' Odyssey reported engagement levels five times higher than its previous rewards tiers within its first quarter. These are not speculative returns; they are operational outcomes. Each metric reflects a principle: that technology succeeds when it simplifies proof, not when it glorifies itself.

The quiet motif of the ticket leads us back to first principles: proof and purpose. NFTs that behave—by changing state, remembering history, or expiring with dignity—embody both. They make verification mundane, which is precisely what trust needs to scale. They also expose the boundaries between code and commitment. A concert pass can upgrade automatically, but only the organiser can decide what that upgrade means. Law and logic meet there, in the last metre between contract and experience.

The next decade will test whether non-fungibility matures into infrastructure or remains an aesthetic. The experiment is already underway in airlines, art galleries, logistics firms, and universities—all using tokens not to *sell pictures* but to *prove events*. Each must balance openness with assurance, novelty with reliability. The unresolved question lingers: how much intelligence should a receipt have before it stops being a record and starts being a ruler? The answer will decide whether NFTs become a footnote of speculation or the filing system of the programmable age.

Creators, royalties, reality

On 17 November 2022, OpenSea announced it would experiment with enforcing creator royalties through an "Operator Filter"—a smart-contract mechanism that blocked marketplaces refusing to honour fees. Nine months later, in August 2023, the company said it would retire that filter and shift to *optional* royalties, citing competition and buyer preference. The policy did not fail technically; it failed politically. Royalty logic lived in code, but power lived in platforms. During the same period, Blur, a rival marketplace launched in October 2022, surged in volume while allowing discounted or optional royalties. The lesson arrived with uncomfortable clarity. Automatic royalties are not automatic. The switch felt brutally simple.

What changed was not the meaning of "non-fungible" but the locus of enforcement. A smart contract can publish a preferred royalty (for example via EIP-2981, introduced in 2021), but payment depends on marketplaces reading—and choosing to respect—that field. When platforms compete on fees, "creator earnings" become a setting rather than a rule. Show: a collection that once earned 5% on every resale now earning pennies when traded through venues that ignore or minimise fees. Name: *platform discretion*. Explain: code suggests; marketplaces decide; the ledger records whatever decision is taken. Implication: a creator's long-term income hinges on off-chain incentives, not cryptographic intention.

Two concrete cases illustrate how quickly policy can rewrite economics. In October 2022, Solana's leading marketplace Magic Eden made royalties optional amid pressure from competitors; in December 2022 it introduced the *Open Creator Protocol*, a toolset to help *new* collections enforce royalties by restricting where they could be traded. In Ethereum's market, OpenSea's "Operator Filter" (November 2022) was conceived to do something similar—blocking non-compliant venues—but by August 2023 OpenSea announced its sunset, restoring choice to buyers and sellers. Show: the same NFT earning a royalty on one site, and none on another, on the same day. Name: *policy toggles*. Explain: enforcement is not universal; it is fragmented across interfaces. Implication: creators face basis risk—the risk that revenues vary with venue, not with demand for the work.

A credible counter-example helps. On Tezos, platforms like fxhash and objkt.com have, since 2021, treated creator royalties as cultural infrastructure, integrating them consistently across marketplaces and social norms. The sums are smaller; the community is tighter; the value of reputation is higher. Royalty integrity persists not because the code is stronger, but because the social contract is thicker. Reconcile the difference: where markets prize composability and speed above all, norms yield to incentives; where communities prize patronage and reputation, enforcement can be social first and technical second.

Royalty debates often mistake syntax for settlement. EIP-2981 provides a standardised way for contracts to *declare* royalty information—recipient address and basis points—but the standard does not compel any payment. It is a broadcast, not a bailiff. Show: a marketplace reading royaltyInfo(tokenId, salePrice) and then either honouring or ignoring the response. Name: *advisory standards*. Explain: the interface stabilises expectations and reduces integration friction, but it cannot deputise platforms as tax collectors. Implication: standards shape behaviour only when business models align; otherwise, they become polite suggestions.

The real determinant is *where value accrues.* Markets that court professional traders optimise for low fees and high throughput; platforms courting creators optimise for downstream income and reputation. In early 2023, Blur incentivised traders with token rewards, effectively subsidising trading costs and squeezing space for creator earnings. Trading migrated rapidly. Show: a collection's floor price holding steady while royalty receipts fall as a share of value transacted. Name: *royalty compression.* Explain: competition reallocates surplus from creators to traders and buyers when platforms treat royalties as optional frictions. Implication: long-run production suffers if creators cannot forecast income from secondary markets; fewer works justify high-effort production.

If automatic royalties depend on off-chain enforcement, what can creators and platforms design to reduce fragility without shutting the market? Three patterns have emerged. The first is *access gating*: tie privileges to proof of payment. A project can publish perks—discord roles, airdrops, allowlists—that are unlocked only for wallets with a provable royalty payment history (detected through marketplace receipts or proprietary claim flows). Show: a collector who flips without paying royalties loses eligibility for future drops. Name: *utility-conditioned earnings.* Explain: rather than litigate behaviour on resale, projects *price* behaviour into future benefits. Implication: incentives migrate from punishment to preference; conscientious buyers become first-class citizens.

The second is *royalty-aware liquidity.* Protocols and pools can enforce minimum royalties at the smart-contract level for trades that occur within their rails. In 2022–23, several AMM-style NFT exchanges experimented with pool parameters that escrowed a creator fee on each swap. Trades could still occur off-pool for less, but liquidity inside the pool obeyed the rule. Show: a swap function that routes 2.5% to the creator address before executing. Name: *in-protocol remittance.* Explain: payment becomes a property of the venue, not a preference of the user. Implication: creators favour venues that encode their economics; over time, liquidity can cluster where rules are predictable.

The third is *project-level design.* Some creators shifted from "royalties forever" to hybrid models: higher primary prices with explicit service commitments; subscriptions that bundle updates and community services; or periodic buy-backs funded by primary sales to support secondary floors. Show: a studio committing to quarterly updates and support in lieu of relying on secondary cuts. Name: *upfront value, explicit service.* Explain: replace uncertain downstream income with priced, deliverable promises. Implication: creators regain budgeting clarity; collectors know what they are paying for.

Even with these adaptations, risk persists where *platform switches* reside. The motif of the switch—on, off; enforced, optional—captures the asymmetry. Artists design for decades; platforms optimise for quarters. When incentives shift, the toggle flips. You can see the fragility in behaviour: creators posting lists of "approved marketplaces," contracts hard-coding block-lists, communities urging boycotts. None of this prevents unilateral policy moves; it merely declares preference.

Law has entered cautiously. Jurisdictions recognise that a smart contract calling something a "royalty" does not make it legally enforceable across marketplaces or borders. In the UK and EU, moral rights and resale rights exist in narrow contexts (the Artist's Resale Right), but they apply to physical art and regulated intermediaries, not to global P2P token markets. Attempts to import those doctrines onto blockchains run headlong into jurisdictional variance and anonymity. The sober implication is that "automatic royalties" is a marketing phrase for a private-rule ecosystem. Platforms write the rules. They can also rewrite them.

Metrics help separate sentiment from structure. A creator's health can be tracked by the share of revenue from primary versus secondary sales, average royalty realised per trade (not just nominal), variance across venues, and concentration risk (how dependent receipts are on one platform). After policy shifts in 2023, many collections saw realised royalty rates fall materially relative to stated rates, even when unit sales rose—a sign that volume substituted for earnings. Designers who publish these metrics invite accountability and adapt faster; those who hide behind slogans lose planning power.

There are ethical choices too. Royalty enforcement can become censorship when it relies on block-lists that exclude entire classes of venues or buyers. It can also create perverse incentives, such as wash-trading to farm future perks. A better lens is *reciprocity*. Do scheme rules reward genuine patronage and creative labour, or do they merely tax movement? Do they price in services—support, updates, curation—that the creator can control, or do they free-ride on marketplaces as involuntary tax agents?

The strongest royalty systems therefore look less like toll booths and more like *contracts of care*. A musician can issue passes that entitle holders to periodic stems, behind-the-scenes sessions, or priority tour seats—benefits that only the musician can deliver and revoke. A visual artist can tie conservation services and authenticity checks to tokens that must ping a registry for updates, creating touchpoints where patron and creator meet across time. In both, royalties become a subscription to provenance, not a fee for flipping.

Still, we should not romanticise workarounds. Some collectors will route around any rule that costs them basis points; some platforms will always chase those traders. Optionality is sticky. The unresolved tension is whether secondary markets can sustain creator income without coercion. The forward test is simple and demanding: if a platform toggled royalties off tomorrow, would your project still have a reason for patrons to pay? If not, the problem is not the switch. It is the design.

Communities as co-owners

In February 2021, the band Kings of Leon released their album *When You See Yourself* as an NFT through the platform YellowHeart. Each token granted the buyer not only a copy of the album but also access to exclusive artwork, lifetime front-row seats to their concerts, and future perks determined collectively by holders. Within weeks, the drop had raised over $2 million. Yet what made it significant was not the revenue but the structure: fans became stakeholders in the band's ongoing narrative. They were not investors in equity, but participants in continuity. Each holder owned a fragment of a living relationship—part collectible, part commitment. The sale revealed a shift in cultural gravity: from audience to co-ownership.

NFTs excel not at creating speculative tribes, but at codifying shared arcs. A well-designed collection binds its patrons to a project's evolution, giving them tangible markers of belonging without overburdening them with bureaucratic governance. That distinction—between ownership and administration—is critical. Show: a DAO that requires constant votes on trivial proposals. Name: *voter fatigue*. Explain: when engagement becomes an obligation, attention evaporates. Implication: communities need rhythm, not noise. They must structure participation as chapters, not chores.

Early crypto communities often mistook voting for vitality. In 2020, the DeFi protocol Compound pioneered on-chain governance, allowing token holders to propose and vote on system parameters. It was democratic in form, but exhausting in practice: hundreds of minor votes, few of which engaged the broader community. Participation dropped below 10% by mid-2021. The mechanism had become a procedural treadmill. Compare this to *Nouns DAO*, launched in August 2021, which issues one unique NFT each day, each conferring a vote in treasury decisions. Here, simplicity and cadence sustain attention: one noun per day, one clear rhythm of growth. But even Nouns faces the same structural question—how to balance inclusion with coherence.

The NFT as community bond need not mimic corporate governance. It can express alignment through milestones rather than motions. Show: a film project whose supporters receive updates and new rights as funding thresholds are met. Name: *milestone-based perks*. Explain: decisions are pre-programmed around objective events—production begins, prototype ships, exhibition opens—rather than left to constant referenda. Implication: governance becomes episodic, predictable, and tied to delivery. The result is trust through performance, not through votes.

A striking example emerged with the *Ethereum Name Service (ENS)* governance airdrop in November 2021. Instead of relying on continuous open voting, ENS used a constitution ratified once by token holders, setting long-term principles that future delegates could interpret. The broader community delegated their votes to representatives, focusing their attention on key inflection points rather than day-to-day decisions. The pattern—delegation anchored by milestones—mirrors how healthy democracies function. It turns participation into punctuation: strategic, finite, and meaningful.

Cultural projects have followed similar logic. *Friends with Benefits* (FWB), a social DAO founded in 2020, discovered that cultural cohesion requires curation. Instead of every member voting on every partnership or event, the community introduced workstreams—small, rotating committees empowered to act within defined budgets. The NFT membership signals belonging, but execution rests with trusted contributors. Behaviour, not noise, becomes proof of alignment. FWB's continuity rests less on direct democracy than on reputation cycles: contribute, rest, return.

The motif here is the *arc*—a narrative curve binding creators and patrons through time. Each milestone marks progress, and each NFT serves as a ledger of participation. Consider *Zora's* experiment in open editions tied to project updates. Artists mint dynamic NFTs that evolve with each completed phase—new artwork layers, access unlocks, or commemorative variants. Show: an artwork's metadata updating when its corresponding mural is installed in a physical space. Name: *evolving token identity*. Explain: the NFT functions as both proof and witness of progress. Implication: community engagement aligns naturally with creative cadence, avoiding procedural fatigue.

Metrics confirm the difference. Projects that use milestone-based updates maintain significantly higher holder retention and secondary-market value stability than those reliant on frequent governance votes (Messari, 2023). Retention behaves like trust—it compounds when participation feels coherent. In contrast, DAOs with constant referenda see engagement drop sharply after the first 60 days, signalling cognitive overload. The lesson: attention is finite. Systems that respect it endure.

Yet we should not romanticise simplicity. The counter-example is instructive: in 2022, the *ConstitutionDAO* famously raised over $47 million in days to bid for a rare copy of the U.S. Constitution at Sotheby's. Thousands of small donors coalesced around a single purpose. But when the bid failed, the project stalled. The community had no plan beyond the moment of purchase. Show: a treasury full, a mission complete, and no framework for continuity. Name: *post-event entropy*. Explain: shared excitement is not the same as shared structure. Implication: without milestones beyond the initial goal, collective energy dissolves.

Reconciling these models requires acknowledging that *ownership* is not synonymous with *control*. In cultural production, creative direction must remain clear, but stakeholders can be invited into defined chapters. A musician may grant holders early access to demos after a tour milestone; a publisher may unlock revenue shares once pre-sales cross a target; a research collective may release findings progressively as experiments replicate. These are not tokenomics; they are narrative mechanics. They transform the community from an audience into a chorus.

This design philosophy echoes the cooperative movements of the 19th century, where co-ownership meant shared benefit, not endless deliberation. The Rochdale Pioneers of 1844 structured their cooperative so members earned dividends from purchases, not voting sessions. The mechanism scaled because it balanced principle with practicality. NFTs can revive that tradition, embedding distributive logic in code without collapsing under procedure.

The real frontier is not technical—it is dramaturgical. Communities flourish when their ownership feels like a story they help tell. Milestones create tempo; perks provide cues. A governance-lite design does not remove participation; it scores it like music. When members anticipate the next verse rather than the next poll, engagement becomes voluntary and joyful. The NFT, in this sense, is a modern libretto—a token that synchronises expectation and memory.

Still, the balance remains delicate. Too little participation, and communities ossify into brands with customers, not co-owners. Too much, and they decay into noise. The unresolved tension is therefore one of rhythm: how often should a community be called to act? The forward test is deceptively simple. If every holder must vote weekly, fatigue is certain. If no one is ever asked to engage, apathy follows. Somewhere between lies the cadence of durable collaboration—a beat that invites participation without demanding it. The NFT can keep time, but only the humans can play in tune.

Status, taste, and spam

In March 2021, Christie's sold Beeple's *Everydays: The First 5000 Days* for $69.3 million. The transaction, executed partly in Ethereum, marked a cultural threshold: a digital file authenticated by an NFT entered the same price bracket as a Monet or a Basquiat. Yet within months, the same NFT market that had briefly seemed a temple of taste began drowning in noise—millions of tokens minted daily, many automated, few curated. The paradox was immediate: a technology built to prove originality had made imitation effortless. When everything can be owned, ownership loses meaning.

Status goods have always relied on scarcity that feels earned. The 18th-century collector sought rarity through geography; the 20th-century connoisseur, through gatekeepers and galleries. NFTs briefly promised a more democratic route to status—anyone could verify provenance—but soon revealed the same ancient truth: taste is social before it is technical. The capacity to discriminate between signal and spam defines the new elite. Show: an open marketplace flooded with unsolicited "airdrops." Name: *context collapse.* Explain: when objects appear without narrative or selection, value fragments. Implication: the architecture of curation must be rebuilt in code and community alike.

The NFT's early euphoria mistook abundance for vitality. Open minting platforms like OpenSea and Rarible enabled anyone to create a token with minimal cost. By mid-2022, over 80% of NFTs minted on OpenSea were flagged as spam, plagiarised, or fraudulent (OpenSea Transparency Report, July 2022). The same openness that encouraged experimentation also eroded trust. A flood of tokens promised prestige but delivered clutter. This is the digital equivalent of a luxury brand leaving its logo unprotected—status dissolves when replication is frictionless.

Contrast that with the curated model pioneered by *Art Blocks*, launched in November 2020 in Houston. Each generative artwork is vetted, its algorithm verified, and its edition capped. Collectors know both scarcity and authorship. The platform's success—over $1 billion in cumulative sales by 2023—shows that constraint, not freedom, sustains value. Show: a 500-piece edition of *Fidenza* by Tyler Hobbs selling for over 1,000 ETH each at its peak. Name: *curated scarcity*. Explain: by limiting supply and verifying process, Art Blocks transformed code into pedigree. Implication: scarcity alone is insufficient; provenance must carry aesthetic legitimacy.

Curation, then, becomes infrastructure. Platforms act as cultural filters, transforming raw minting into social signal. In June 2022, *SuperRare DAO* restructured itself to decentralise curation: galleries and artists vote to admit new participants, blending peer review with collective taste. This model mirrors the academic journal more than the open bazaar. It trades friction for integrity. The result is slower, but it restores the semiotics of distinction—the difference between art and asset.

Not all scarcity is noble. In 2021, thousands of projects attempted to engineer exclusivity through gimmicks: limited drops, gated Discords, artificially scarce avatars. Many succeeded briefly, then collapsed as their cultural context vanished. The *Bored Ape Yacht Club* (BAYC), minted in April 2021, remains the canonical survivor. Its 10,000 cartoon apes became social tokens for entry into a club of celebrities, investors, and digital tastemakers. Yet even BAYC's creators recognised that scarcity must evolve; by 2023 they had shifted focus from mere collectibles to "Otherside," a metaverse project promising interactive experiences. Show: static images turned into participatory assets. Name: *narrative continuity*. Explain: sustained value demands ongoing cultural production, not numerical rarity alone. Implication: curation is temporal as well as selective—it must keep meaning alive.

The counter-example arrived just as vividly. In 2022, *LooksRare* tried to outcompete OpenSea by issuing massive airdrops—free tokens to users who had traded NFTs elsewhere. The campaign generated spectacular short-term volume but was later revealed (Chainalysis, 2022) to consist largely of wash trades designed to farm rewards. Here was status by spam: attention extracted through quantity. The metric was not cultural relevance but transaction count. When everything is airdropped, nothing feels chosen.

The motif that threads these examples is *attention as capital.* Status goods function by filtering access to limited cognitive and social space. NFTs, being programmable, can express these filters explicitly. A well-designed NFT defines its boundaries: who can mint, how many can exist, when they can evolve. Limiting supply is not elitism; it is a defence against entropy. The question becomes: how to constrain abundance without suffocating creativity?

One approach lies in *contextual metadata.* Projects like *Bright Moments*, which stages live minting events where collectors witness generative art being created on-site, tether digital assets to social rituals. In a London or Berlin gallery, an NFT minted in real time carries not just code but memory: "I was there." Show: the audience scanning QR codes as art emerges on screen. Name: *proof of presence.* Explain: tying minting to context transforms ownership into participation. Implication: status derives from narrative embedded in process, not price alone.

Metrics confirm the pattern. Collections with constrained supply (fewer than 10,000 tokens) and active curatorial oversight maintain floor-price stability 40–60% higher than open-mint projects over a 12-month horizon (NonFungible.com, 2023). Meanwhile, airdrop-heavy schemes see rapid attrition: user engagement falls below 10% after the first reward cycle. Behaviour follows psychology: what costs nothing commands no care.

Yet curatorial discipline introduces its own tension: who curates the curators? A closed system risks ossification and exclusion, replicating the gallery gatekeeping the NFT movement once sought to escape. The *Tezos* ecosystem offers an instructive middle ground. Platforms such as *objkt.com* and *fxhash* operate open entry but rely on social sorting—visible transaction histories, collector follow-lists, and community-driven tagging—to elevate signal. The system self-organises taste rather than dictating it. Scarcity arises emergently, not imposed.

Taste, after all, is not static. What confers prestige today may bore tomorrow. The NFT's programmability allows for *living scarcity*—tokens that evolve or expire, refreshing cultural attention. Consider *Async Art*, launched in 2020, where owners of different "layers" of a digital artwork can alter its composition. Scarcity here is relational: multiple participants hold interdependent rights, shaping the piece collectively. Show: an image shifting as contributors adjust colours or text. Name: *dynamic authorship*. Explain: status derives from stewardship, not stasis. Implication: cultural value migrates from possession to participation.

Spam, by contrast, is the death of context. Airdrop culture, which peaked during 2022's speculative frenzy, flooded wallets with unsolicited tokens—often scams linking to phishing sites. For collectors, the experience resembled digital littering. Platforms like OpenSea introduced *hidden* folders to quarantine these unwanted tokens, an implicit admission that frictionless distribution breeds contamination. The aesthetic economy depends on filtration.

This dynamic mirrors earlier media histories. The printing press empowered pamphleteers and propagandists alike; the internet multiplied voices and misinformation in equal measure. Each revolution of access creates a counter-revolution of curation. NFTs are no different. Their legitimacy will depend not on their novelty but on the quality of the filters—human, algorithmic, or hybrid—that preserve meaning amid surplus.

The quiet motif of *signal and noise* resurfaces here. Every collector becomes an editor; every wallet, a gallery. Status, once anchored in physical provenance, now hinges on discernment. The digital elite will not be those who own the most, but those who select best—who can navigate abundance without drowning in it.

Still, the field faces a lasting dilemma. If curation restores exclusivity, does it also re-entrench inequality? The forward test asks this: can a network design scarcity that rewards taste rather than privilege? Can it make quality discoverable without turning discovery itself into a gated commodity? The answer will decide whether NFTs mature into cultural institutions—or remain a cautionary tale of infinite noise dressed as art.

Chapter 5
Fractional Investment, Democratised (and Disciplined)

In September 2022, a start-up called Rally sold 0.0001% slices of a 1985 pair of Nike Air Jordan 1s worn by Michael Jordan during his rookie season. The total valuation—just over $1 million—was justified as "cultural price discovery." Each buyer owned a tokenised fraction, complete with digital certificate and secondary trading rights. It sounded revolutionary: shared ownership of icons, open to anyone with a smartphone. But six months later, trading had stalled, liquidity evaporated, and the platform quietly adjusted valuations downward. What began as access had curdled into speculation. The story captures a tension that defines the age of fractionalisation: the promise of inclusion, and the peril of illusion.

The idea of shared ownership is not new. It echoes the joint-stock companies of the 17th century, when the Dutch East India Company first allowed citizens to buy and sell shares representing fragments of trade expeditions. That innovation fuelled global commerce—and occasional mania. What is new is the speed and scale with which tokenisation turns everything from property to pop culture into investable fragments. A vineyard in Bordeaux, a Picasso sketch, even a song catalogue can now be split into thousands of tradable tokens. Each fraction claims a share of future value, yet too often that claim rests on vibes rather than verifiable rights. When substance fails to match symbol, the market becomes theatre.

The discipline of fractional investment begins with evidence. A slice should connect directly to measurable cash flows or enforceable claims, not to mere proximity to glamour. The technology can anchor trust, but only if the data trail connects token to reality. An NFT representing royalties from a 1990s hit song must be backed by audited statements showing payments from streaming platforms. A share in a tokenised building should trace rent receipts through a regulated custodian. This linkage—the *last metre* from code to cash—is where legitimacy lives or dies. Without it, fractional ownership devolves into collectible theatre, and democratisation becomes marketing gloss.

Liquidity is often sold as a virtue, yet it behaves like a mirage. Many platforms promise "24/7 trading" of fractional assets but neglect the simplest economic fact: liquidity only exists when someone wants to buy. Thinly traded markets disguise fragility as freedom. In 2021, several tokenised real estate platforms in the United States reported daily trading volumes of less than $10,000 despite multimillion-dollar assets listed. Those slices could be bought instantly—but not sold. The architecture of access without exit invites disillusionment. Meaningful liquidity requires structure: scheduled auctions, periodic redemptions, or standing market-makers who commit capital to stability rather than hype.

Democratisation also demands discipline in how access is framed. Lowering minimum investment thresholds expands participation; it does not erase responsibility. When fractional investment is marketed as a lottery—"get rich from a £10 share of a Ferrari"—it erodes trust for the very audience it claims to empower. Transparent gating mechanisms can help: clear disclosures of asset class, valuation methodology, lock-up periods, and use-case suitability. A well-designed platform invites participation for use and understanding, not for gambling. The difference is moral as much as mechanical.

Fees, too, hide in the cracks of enthusiasm. A fractional platform may boast zero-commission trades while embedding spreads, custody fees, or opaque exit costs. The fairness test is simple: if a retail investor cannot trace one pound of investment through its full lifecycle—entry, management, and exit—the design has failed. Transparency here is not cosmetic; it is the foundation of trust. Imagine a vintage car fund where each investor sees, line by line, insurance costs, maintenance expenses, and administrative margins before any yield is distributed. The code can automate disclosure; only the will to expose it is missing.

Fractionalisation, at its best, aligns finance with participation. It can open doors long closed—allowing teachers to share in music royalties, or students to invest in fine wine without the cellar. But democratisation without guardrails reproduces the same inequalities it seeks to dismantle. The paradox is that true inclusion requires friction: limits on leverage, cooling-off periods, audited cash-flow reporting. Discipline, not dazzle, defines mature access.

The chapter that follows explores how to distinguish signal from spectacle in the age of fractional ownership. It examines the anatomy of credible evidence, the mechanics of liquidity that works, and the economics of fairness when millions share the same asset in microcosm. Behind every tokenised Picasso or song lies a simple test: does this fraction confer real rights, or merely reflect reflected light?

The question remains deliberately unresolved. Shared ownership can either become the most transparent financial architecture in history—or another speculative hall of mirrors. The deciding factor will not be the elegance of the code but the courage of the design. The new frontier of democratised investment demands not fewer rules but better ones—crafted for participation that endures when the novelty fades.

Slices with substance

On 11 January 2022, the platform Royal—co-founded by the producer 3LAU—offered tokens linked to streaming royalties from two Nas tracks, "Ultra Black" and "Rare." The sale, hosted in the United States and publicised as a first for a major artist, sold out within minutes. Holders were promised a defined share of future streaming income, paid as distributions when the rights administrator remitted cash. Months later, those holders began receiving small but real payouts tied to the songs' actual performance, not social media heat. The statement arrived, and the numbers were not vibes. The statement decides what counts.

Fractional investment earns legitimacy when the slice maps cleanly to a measurable cash flow or enforceable right. Anything looser collapses into memorabilia with a price ticker. Show: a token that entitles its holder to 0.157% of publisher's share on a named track for a defined term. Name: *royalty-bearing fraction.* Explain: the claim references a specific asset (ISRC, writer share, administrator), a payment source (e.g., PRS, ASCAP, or a label's account), and a timetable for statements keyed to industry cycles. Implication: the cash movement can be audited, disputed, and corrected; the token is a receipt that behaves, not a poster with punctuation.

Use music because it exposes the core distinction. Royalty Exchange in Denver has, since the 2010s, auctioned slices of songwriter and producer royalties recorded against collecting society ledgers; buyers receive quarterly statements that reconcile to PRO distributions and label remittances. In London, Hipgnosis Songs Fund, listed on the LSE in 2018, built an institutional version of the same principle: catalogues are valued against audited revenue, with dividends funded by known inflows. Neither is "web3," but both provide a standard: cash has sources; rights have registries; statements are evidence. Token projects that wish to be more than theatre should match this discipline, then exceed it with programmable disclosure.

Three questions sort substance from spectacle. What exactly is being sold? From where will the money arrive? Who can enforce the promise if it fails? Pair each with a behaviour. The "what" demands identifiers: ISRC codes for tracks, registry IDs for artworks, parcel numbers for property, VINs for cars. The "from where" demands bank-reconciled sources: administrator names, account references, and historic payment schedules. The "who" demands a legal wrapper and a venue: an SPV with a governing law clause, a transfer agent, and a nominated arbitrator or court. These are boring questions. They are also the only questions that decide whether a fraction is an investment or an anecdote with a checkout button.

Return to the Nas case to see the mechanics. The token's claim was not to "Nas's brand," but to a defined share of streaming income on two tracks. Cash originated at services (Spotify, Apple Music), flowed through labels and administrators, then reached the platform, which disbursed pro rata to token holders. Show: a remittance advice that lists a period, a service, a territory, and an amount; an on-chain record that shows the matching distribution. Name: *two-sided reconciliation*. Explain: on-chain transparency is necessary but insufficient; off-chain statements must align. Implication: if the ledger and the ledger lines disagree, the token is a pane of glass over fog.

A second example, in property, clarifies the cross-domain pattern. From 2021 onwards, fractional rental platforms in the United States began issuing tokens representing membership interests in LLCs that each held a single house. Rent landed in a bank account; service providers deducted maintenance and insurance; net income was swept to token holders in stablecoins. The trustworthy ones adopted rhythms familiar from REITs: monthly reporting packs, reserve disclosures, and third-party bookkeeping. Show: a dashboard that ties each payout to a tenant ledger, a bank statement, and an on-chain transaction hash. Name: *cash-flow triangulation.* Explain: each number must have two mirrors—one legal, one technical. Implication: when tenants churn, the statement shows vacancy; when boilers fail, reserves fall; when rent rises, distributions follow with lag and explanation.

Now a counter-example that reveals the cliff's edge. In February 2022, the site HitPiece attempted to sell "music NFTs" that referenced songs and artwork without licences from rights-holders; takedown notices followed and the platform apologised. The episode was not a quirk; it was a category error. Tokens pointed to assets the issuer did not control. Show: a listing for a track whose writer and publisher never consented. Name: *non-consensual minting.* Explain: the blockchain did its job—it recorded a sale. The law did its job—it disputed the right. Implication: a slice without control is not a slice; it is a liability with graphics.

The motif through all of this is the *statement.* It arrives on a cadence, it names sources, it reconciles parts. Projects that respect the statement behave predictably. They publish cash-flow maps: which accounts receive money, which fees are retained, which dates trigger distribution. They adopt reporting periods and stick to them. They present variance with reasons: "June's payment was 11% below forecast due to a DSP adjustment in Germany; clawback posted in July." Language like this signals a mature operation, and it can be encoded: a metadata field for "variance reason," an oracle that ingests administrator PDF statements and anchors hashes on-chain, a rule that blocks new mints when arrears pass a threshold.

Evidence is not an aesthetic; it is a stack. At the base sits *proof of existence* (the asset or right is real and identified). Above it sits *proof of control* (the issuer can commit the right). Above that sits *proof of cash flow* (money has moved in the past and has a path to move again). At the top sits *proof of remedy* (if something breaks, who compels whom?). You can measure this stack. For music: number of consecutive periods with on-time distributions; mean absolute percentage error between forecast and actual; percentage of cash reconciled within five business days. For property: occupancy, arrears ageing, reserve coverage, median days-to-repair. For any asset: the ratio of narrative to numbers in investor communications. When numerators shrink and denominators swell, substance decays.

Fees sit directly on the statement and must appear there, not in footnotes. A credible platform breaks out collection fees, administration fees, currency conversion, custody charges, and slippage if secondary trades occur. It publishes *effective take* as a percentage of gross receipts, not just headline fees. It reports *time to cash*, measured door-to-door from payer to holder. It names *who can change fees* and *how long notice must be*. Investors then price what matters: not promise, but friction.

Rights clarity belongs on the statement too. A share of *writer's* performance royalties behaves differently from a share of *master* recording income; mechanical, performance, and sync revenues move on different cycles and can be clawed back when disputes arise. Show: a distribution note that splits cash by source with standard labels (performance/mechanical/master/sync) and cites the administering societies. Name: *source taxonomy*. Explain: when rights are sliced, they must retain their identity; otherwise, "royalties" becomes a single bucket that hides risk. Implication: platforms that teach this taxonomy earn durable trust; those that blur it will raise cheap money once and then pay for it with reputation.

A further example from institutional practice shows the attainable bar. When Banco Santander issued a blockchain-settled bond in Madrid in September 2019, coupon flows reconciled to the bank's own ledger and were posted to holders automatically. The novelty was plumbing; the virtue was audit. Fractional music or property should copy this stance: automation is a means to reconciliation, not a substitute for it. The mature move is not to promise 24/7 liquidity, but to promise 12/12 statements that close on time.

The temptation, especially in culture, is to sell proximity rather than participation: "own a piece of a moment." That is a souvenir, not a security. If a project cannot produce a 12-month pro forma with conservative assumptions, a policy for reserves, and named third-party attestations, it is selling a feeling. Feelings can be fine; they are not income. The discipline here is to price sentiment as sentiment—cheap, capped, and separate from revenue claims—while reserving "slices" for items that can be counted.

None of this denies that many legitimate slices pay little. Streaming pennies are real but small; single-family rentals can run flat after maintenance; net income fluctuates with macro cycles. The point is not to maximise yield; it is to *expose* it. A defender of vibes might object that the romance is the draw. Fair enough—then call it patronage and remove words like "share," "yield," and "royalty" unless law, accountancy, and the postman agree.

Designers can encode this honesty. Set thresholds that forbid using "royalty" in metadata unless the contract references an identified right and a named administrator. Require that every distribution call a function with a hash of the off-chain statement attached. Display a *coverage ratio* on the token page: rolling twelve-month cash actually received divided by cash forecast a year prior. Publish a *silence clock* that turns red when no distribution has occurred within an expected window. These are small moves. They turn marketing into monitoring.

Two reconciliations bring the thread home. First, a Nas token that pays £6 this quarter is not a failure if the statement shows why and the upstreams match; the fraction is doing its job—measuring cultural cash as it is, not as we wish it to be. Secondly, a fractional sneaker or car fund may be fine *if* it states plainly that returns rely on resale and storage, not income, and that cash flows in the interim are zero by design. Silence then is a feature, not a bug. The harm begins when silence pretends to be song.

So the forward test for any slice is blunt. Before you mint, fill the page a cautious auditor would fill: identifiers, control, sources, schedule, fees, venue, remedy. Before you buy, read the page and ask one question the statement must answer without poetry: *where will the next pound come from, and who can make it move if someone stalls?* If that answer is cloudy, the fraction is light. If it is crisp, the slice has weight.

Access vs speculation

In July 2021, Robinhood went public on the Nasdaq at a valuation of $32 billion. Within its first week of trading, the app that had once promised to "democratise finance" saw its shares spike 80% in a single day, fuelled by the same retail traders it had empowered. For many, the irony was unmistakable: a platform built to grant access had created another lottery. Some early users gained spectacularly; most did not. The pattern echoed a deeper truth that fractional ownership now faces: access can widen opportunity, but without discipline it degenerates into speculation.

The distinction is not moral but structural. True access allows smaller investors to participate in real economic flows—to own a slice of a wind farm, a rental property, or a song's royalties—and to hold it long enough for the underlying asset to deliver returns. Speculation, by contrast, rewards speed over substance. It is the flash trade, the flip, the short-term game disguised as inclusion. The challenge is to build systems that invite participation without feeding the dopamine loop of volatility.

Show: a user buying £50 of a tokenised property, hoping to earn rental yield over months. Name: *participatory access.* Explain: the investor accepts illiquidity as the price of legitimacy; their goal is use, not resale. Implication: if liquidity is instant, attention shifts from what the asset does to what its price might do next. Democratisation without pacing becomes chaos with branding.

One way to see this is through *crowdfunding's second act.* In 2012, the U.S. JOBS Act loosened securities rules to let ordinary investors back early-stage companies online. By 2020, over 1,200 firms had raised through platforms like SeedInvest and Crowdcube. But the most successful campaigns, regulators later noted, shared a feature: they limited resale. Investors had to hold their shares for at least a year before trading. This cooling-off period turned enthusiasm into commitment. When tokenised platforms erase such constraints, they invite not partnership but speculation disguised as participation.

Token-based investing often mistakes *access* for *availability*. Access is structured entry—guarded, timed, informed. Availability is raw openness. In 2021, several tokenised art and music marketplaces discovered this difference painfully. OpenSea, for instance, saw a surge of fractionalised NFTs as collectives split artworks into millions of low-cost shares. Prices soared, then collapsed when traders realised the underlying rights were undefined. Holders owned exposure, not entitlement. The platform's openness had made entry easy but due diligence optional. The access was cosmetic.

To repair this, credible projects have started designing *gating mechanisms*—rules that slow participation just enough to filter intent. A simple version is minimum holding periods; a more sophisticated one ties ownership to use. For instance, *Rally*, a U.S. platform for fractional collectibles, limits withdrawals for 90 days after a trading window closes. This friction preserves market integrity by discouraging flipping and ensuring valuations respond to asset performance, not speculation. It is an old idea rendered in new code: *access with apprenticeship*.

A contrasting example reveals why restraint matters. In 2022, *Loot Project*, an Ethereum-based NFT experiment, offered "bags" of randomised text as game assets. Because they were free to mint and instantly tradable, demand exploded. Within a week, average resale prices reached 14 ETH, then collapsed below 1 ETH within a month (Dune Analytics, Sept 2022). There was nothing inherently wrong with the concept—creative, open-ended, communal—but without structure it became a frenzy. Flipping replaced building; attention replaced purpose. The episode became shorthand for a generation's speculative reflex: everyone wanted the ticket, not the concert.

The motif that runs through these examples is *the door and the lock*. Access opens the door; speculation removes the lock. Without locks—time locks, disclosure locks, utility locks—the architecture collapses. The key is to design gates that educate as they guard. Disclosure is one such gate. When fractional platforms present standardised, comparable data—cash-flow projections, fee breakdowns, and secondary-market conditions—they shift attention from short-term price to long-term performance. Transparency does not slow speculation by itself, but it raises the cost of ignorance.

The United Kingdom's Financial Conduct Authority (FCA) recognised this tension in 2023 when it tightened promotions for high-risk investments. Platforms offering tokenised or fractional assets must now provide "clear, fair, and not misleading" risk summaries, including probability-weighted outcomes. The effect is subtle but powerful: by quantifying uncertainty, disclosure rebalances attention. Investors begin to ask, "What is this asset doing?" instead of, "What might someone else pay for it?" Gating becomes cognitive rather than mechanical.

Still, the discipline must be embedded in design, not merely regulation. Consider *RealT*, a Detroit-based platform tokenising rental properties. Each investor receives ERC-20 tokens tied to an LLC that holds the deed. Yet these tokens cannot be traded freely; transfers are restricted to whitelisted wallets compliant with U.S. securities laws. This gate preserves both compliance and stability. The investor's experience is slower but more tangible: quarterly rent distributions, annual tax forms, and a real address. Contrast this with platforms that promise "instant liquidity" and "no paperwork." The former invites stewardship; the latter, speculation.

A credible counterpoint comes from *StepN*, a "move-to-earn" platform that rewarded users with tokens for physical activity. For months in 2022, StepN's model seemed to balance access with engagement: users had to walk to earn, and tokens had in-app use. Yet as secondary markets ballooned, speculative demand overwhelmed utility. Players began minting accounts solely to resell shoes; activity became proxy, not participation. The economy imploded once new entrants slowed. It was a microcosm of the access paradox: a product built on use was consumed by trade.

The problem is not trading itself; it is trading untethered from use. A healthy fractional market can accommodate secondary sales—indeed, liquidity attracts users—but only when the sale reflects underlying value. A resale of a tokenised rental unit at a premium after rent rises is rational. A resale of a tokenised sculpture minutes after minting, with no new information, is noise. The distinction can be coded: require ownership thresholds before certain rights vest, or link transferability to milestones (for example, dividends received). Behavioural design achieves what slogans cannot.

Platforms are experimenting. *Artrade* in France now segments users into tiers: "collectors" who stake for longer periods gain early access to drops, while short-term traders pay higher fees. The model echoes the loyalty schemes of traditional finance—reward patience, penalise churn. Similarly, *Cooperative DAO* projects in Singapore have begun testing "usage scoring," where investor influence increases with participation in product-related activity (such as visiting a property or attending a performance tied to the asset). These are not paternalistic gates; they are scaffolds for durable culture.

The tension remains unresolved because speculation performs a seductive function. It draws liquidity, attention, and early adoption. To eliminate it entirely would be to sterilise energy from the system. The aim, then, is equilibrium: access that enables discovery, not distortion. The guiding question for designers should be, *what behaviour does this token reward after the first week?* If the answer is "selling," the gate has failed.

Trust will not come from slogans about inclusivity, nor from regulatory checklists alone, but from the slow choreography of behaviour—earn, hold, learn, repeat. True access is cumulative. It is earned through time spent, data shared, and rights exercised. When platforms measure participation as carefully as they measure volume, the speculative fever cools into a sustainable rhythm.

The forward test for fractional democratisation, then, is simple and unforgiving. Open the door, but weigh every hinge. Who may enter, how long they stay, and what they do once inside decide whether the architecture becomes a school or a casino. The design of the gate, not the marketing of the key, determines which future takes hold.

Fees, frictions, fairness

In 1976, in Valley Forge, Pennsylvania, John C. Bogle launched the first retail index fund at Vanguard. Its innovation was not glamour but cost: a lower expense ratio than actively managed peers. The argument was austere—basis points shaved annually compound into real money—and forty years later it proved decisive. Billions shifted. Basis points compound into destinies. Fees that were once treated as trivia became the main event because their gravity was visible on a statement. The lesson holds for tokenised and fractional markets: value arrives in drips, while costs often leave in a stream.

The great confusion in access investing is that "zero" fees at the front door rarely mean zero costs inside. Platforms trumpet free minting or commission-free trades, then extract value through spreads, custody charges, settlement frictions, and punitive exits. The bill hides in the plumbing. Show: a user buys a £100 slice and sees no commission line. Name: *total cost of ownership*. Explain: between buy and sell, that investor may pay a 3–5% spread, 1–2% annual administration, insurance or storage, network fees, data access charges, and an exit toll at auction—or worse, a price-impact cost because the order book is thin. Implication: fairness demands that all those drips appear on one page, at purchase, in words a non-specialist can understand.

Two cases anchor the point. First, the December 2020 settlement in which the U.S. Securities and Exchange Commission fined Robinhood $65 million for failing to disclose that its "commission-free" model relied on payment for order flow that worsened execution prices relative to peers; customers saved fees but lost on price. The platform's posted fee was zero; the real fee hid in the spread. Second, the auction world's timeless arithmetic: a vendor's commission plus a buyer's premium at houses like Christie's and Sotheby's can total well over 30% on a hammer price, once catalogue, insurance, and shipping are included. The art market never pretended otherwise; it itemised the bite. Token markets must rise to that level of candour.

A credible counter-example clarifies the limits of "free." Some decentralised exchanges do charge near-zero explicit fees on swaps, because automated market makers set prices algorithmically and charge a small liquidity fee. But the spreads widen when pools are shallow, and slippage becomes the hidden cost. The fairness test is not whether a fee exists; it is whether the platform measures and displays the cost that does. Reconcile the tension this way: transparency about price impact earns trust even when prices move; opacity breeds suspicion even when fees are low.

The motif throughout this chapter is the bill. The bill you see. The bill you don't. In mature systems, the two converge. In immature systems, they diverge badly.

To make that convergence tangible, consider a transparent fee storyboard for a hypothetical *Vintage 12 Fund*—a tokenised collection of twelve mid-century sports cars held through an SPV, with quarterly reporting and a secondary market for slices. The fund buys, stores, insures, maintains, and eventually exits cars at specialist auctions. The storyboard shows when and how value is removed from the investor's pocket.

Entry. Show: an investor subscribes £1,000 at a posted net asset value (NAV) of £10.00 per token. The primary issuance fee is 0.75% to cover KYC and onboarding; the blockchain settlement (gas) fee is passed through at cost and displayed in currency terms. Name: *stated entry cost.* Explain: the platform converts percentage into pounds before the click. Implication: price salience curbs sticker shock later.

Spread at purchase. The fund lists a continuous two-sided quote on a venue. The best ask is £10.20, the best bid £9.85. Show: the investor pays £10.20; the quoted spread is 3.55%; the *effective spread* after execution is reported on the trade ticket. Name: *spread disclosure.* Explain: the platform must say "you paid £X above NAV, of which £Y went to liquidity providers." Implication: buyers learn quickly that "zero commission" can still be dear.

Ongoing custody and care. Vintage cars consume money standing still. The SPV holds legal title; the fund pays storage, insurance, and maintenance. Show: a monthly line item for storage (£22 per car per week), insurance (agreed value, premium disclosed), and scheduled maintenance (OEM parts at cost + 5% procurement fee). Name: *care charges*. Explain: the platform itemises in cash and in percentages of NAV, with a running twelve-month total. Implication: token holders see that "real assets" are living budgets, not inert storehouses.

Administration and reporting. The fund charges a 1.0% management fee on NAV, paid monthly in arrears, plus actual audit and legal fees. Show: the manager's fee in pounds; the auditor's invoice attached; the company secretary's cost, not an estimate. Name: *admin transparency*. Explain: investors can click through to invoices; hashes anchor PDFs on-chain. Implication: narrative shrinks; evidence grows.

Incidental frictions. Transport to concours events, preservation detailing, and compliance inspections. Show: a per-mile transport fee; the contracted rate; variance against budget. Name: *event frictions*. Explain: glamorous photos sit beside receipts. Implication: marketing cannot outrun the ledger.

Exit. Two avenues exist: periodic redemptions at NAV (quarterly windows) and external auction sales. For redemptions, the fund allocates a cash pool; requests beyond the pool queue pro rata. Show: a queue length, a fill ratio, and a forecast date to cash. Name: *redemption mechanics*. Explain: investors know exactly how "liquid" liquidity is. Implication: confidence rises because process beats promise.

For auction exits, the bill is blunt. If the fund sells a 1962 Ferrari at £2.4 million hammer, the seller's commission is 10%; the buyer pays a 26% buyer's premium; storage and catalogue fees apply. Show: net proceeds after each toll and after VAT where applicable, reconciled to bank statements. Name: *exit toll disclosure*. Explain: holders see the bite before headlines of "record price." Implication: they price exits with adult eyes.

Now embed two external, named comparators to discipline the storyboard. First, the UK's Stamp Duty Reserve Tax (SDRT) of 0.5% on most share purchases: a statutory, unavoidable toll that appears at trade and teaches investors to treat taxes as part of the all-in price. Second, Vanguard's decades-long campaign to publish *ongoing charge figures* for funds—one number that captures recurring costs. The token market's equivalent is a *Total Cost Indicator* (TCI) that blends spreads, admin, custody, and exit tolls into one rolling twelve-month figure, refreshed monthly. Show: TCI this year 3.4%, five-year average 3.1%, with sparkline. Name: *single-number honesty*. Explain: it is not perfect but it is portable. Implication: investors can compare venues without forensic work.

The bill motif returns in behaviours that platforms can measure and publish. *Execution quality*: average effective spread by hour and by size bucket. *Time to cash*: median days from redemption request to wallet receipt. *Slippage on auction exits*: difference between pre-sale estimate median and net proceeds. *Custody incidents*: number of days of lapsed insurance or missed storage SLAs (target: zero). These are not marketing KPIs; they are operational truths. When published, they become competitive pressure points that push costs down and disclosures up.

Where does friction properly live? Not all friction is unfair. A 90-day holding period reduces churn that widens spreads. An exit fee that reflects external auction tolls is honest if it matches invoices. A cold-storage fee for a gold token is legitimate if the bar sits in a named vault with inspection rights. The unfairness begins when fees bear no relation to delivered services or when costs are hidden in fine print or hard-to-observe venues like liquidity rebates. The measure is simple: does the platform link each pound charged to a service performed, evidenced, and priced against the open market?

Two further examples—one from traditional finance, one from tokens—seat the argument. The London Stock Exchange's official list transparently reports *turnover velocity* and *spread statistics* for equities; retail brokers that gamify churn without showing these costs do their users a disservice. In token markets, OpenSea's 2.5% marketplace fee (widely cited in 2021–22) was explicit; the controversy erupted not over the fee but over how royalties were enforced or not enforced elsewhere, shifting costs between creators, traders, and platforms. Again, the cost existed; the fairness fight centred on who bore it and whether the rules were visible in advance.

We should also admit the counter-case: sometimes explicit fee-heavy platforms deliver better all-in outcomes than "free" venues. A specialist car broker charging 7% might net the fund more after marketing, reputation, and bidder curation than a DIY sale with nominal fees but thin demand. Fairness here is comparative: show net, not gross; show alternatives considered; and record why a dearer route was chosen. That is how trustees speak. Token platforms entering serious asset classes should adopt the same voice.

The storyboard ends where investors care most: with exit paths that do not punish the small. If a platform routes small sellers into a permanent discount because market makers quote wider spreads to them, that is a regressive tax. Fixable, too. Design can pool small orders into periodic auctions where price discovery is fairer and spreads narrower. Design can cap platform take across the life of an investment so success fees shrink as holding periods lengthen. Design can build *fee holidays* when errors occur—if a redemption misses its SLA by ten days, the admin fee waives for that period automatically. Fairness is a verb.

So the forward test for any fractional venue is stark and practical: place the full bill—spreads, custody, care, exits—on one honest pane of glass, then live by it. Will you measure effective spreads and publish them? Will you reconcile auction tolls to invoices? Will you show time-to-cash by cohort and commit to improve? If the answers hesitate, costs will migrate from view into shadow. If the answers are plain, costs become choices that adults can price. The difference decides whether democratised investment becomes a school with a clear fee schedule or a casino where the house always wins and never prints the receipt.

Exit paths matter

In March 2020, at the height of the pandemic panic, the £3.7 billion M&G Property Portfolio—one of the UK's largest open-ended real estate funds—froze redemptions. Investors could not withdraw their money for nearly eighteen months. The assets were real: offices, logistics parks, retail parks. The cash was not. The fund simply could not liquidate properties fast enough to meet daily withdrawal requests. The episode was not fraud; it was physics. The mismatch between the liquidity promised and the liquidity possible had been exposed. In tokenised markets, where liquidity is a headline feature, the same tension looms larger still.

Liquidity feels modern, but its failures are ancient. The South Sea Bubble of 1720 imploded when buyers vanished; Lehman's bankruptcy in 2008 was, at heart, a liquidity freeze; and now, digital platforms offering 24/7 trading face the same test: what happens when everyone wants out and no one wants in? A token can be traded in microseconds, but the asset beneath—a car, a property, a debt claim—moves on the scale of weeks or months. The question is not whether liquidity exists, but *when* and *for whom.*

To navigate this, fractional platforms must design exit paths that reconcile speed with solvency. Show: three mechanisms—periodic redemptions, auctions, and market-makers. Name: *liquidity architectures*. Explain: each model defines not just how cash leaves the system, but how trust enters it. Implication: the exit is the proof.

Begin with periodic redemptions—the least glamorous but often the most honest. Funds such as UK Authorised Property Trusts or Luxembourg-based RAIF structures use *gated liquidity*: investors can redeem quarterly or annually, subject to notice periods and caps. This rhythm allows managers to sell assets in an orderly way, preserving price integrity. In digital form, this translates to *liquidity windows*: fixed dates when holders can submit redemption requests, with transparent rules for queueing and pro-rata fills. Show: a tokenised farmland fund that opens redemptions on the first business day of each quarter, publishes pre-funding levels, and confirms settlement within ten working days. Name: *windowed liquidity*. Explain: investors can plan exits without forcing fire sales. Implication: fairness replaces fantasy.

A parallel can be found in the British peer-to-peer lending sector. After the 2019 collapse of FundingSecure and Lendy, the Financial Conduct Authority mandated clearer disclosure of "liquidity assumptions." Platforms such as Assetz Capital adopted rolling redemption queues, showing expected exit times. The change was unglamorous but effective: it restored partial withdrawals and investor confidence. In token markets, similar discipline could anchor "DeFi yield" products that often tout instant exits but rely on volatile secondary pools.

Auctions, by contrast, turn illiquidity into theatre. They work when assets are heterogeneous and buyers are motivated. Classic car funds, fine wine vaults, or art-backed tokens often rely on scheduled auctions—digital or physical—to set reference prices and distribute cash. Show: a tokenised whisky fund listing casks quarterly through Bonhams in Edinburgh, proceeds distributed on-chain to token-holders within five days of sale. Name: *periodic price discovery*. Explain: auctions expose price uncertainty but confine it to a predictable calendar. Implication: investors face market truth, not constant noise.

The strength of auctions lies in their punctuation. They concentrate liquidity into moments that attract attention. The weakness is downtime. Between auctions, nothing trades. When sentiment cools or lots fail to meet reserve, holders endure long deserts of inactivity. In 2022, several digital art platforms that adopted constant micro-auctions found themselves flooded with unsold works; each failed sale eroded perceived value. Liquidity became self-cancelling. A mature platform therefore designs reserve policies, disclosure of bidder numbers, and minimum participation thresholds to ensure auctions clear or postpone cleanly.

Then come market-makers—the dream of frictionless exits. In theory, a market-maker stands ready to buy and sell at posted prices, narrowing spreads and ensuring continuous liquidity. In practice, few decentralised projects can sustain them. Automated market-makers (AMMs) like Uniswap provide algorithmic liquidity, but they need deep pools and constant rebalancing. For unique or thinly traded assets, that depth rarely exists. Show: a hypothetical car fund token trading on an AMM. A single £10,000 buy pushes price up 4%; a £10,000 sell pushes it down 5%. Name: *price impact*. Explain: liquidity is not a yes/no condition but a curve—thin at the edges, costly at scale. Implication: continuous liquidity is only as reliable as the weakest counterparty.

A credible real-world attempt to combine these methods came from Switzerland's Mt. Pelerin in 2021. The firm tokenised its own equity under Swiss law, listing shares tradable peer-to-peer via a compliant marketplace. Liquidity was provided by an internal market-maker quoting daily prices derived from external valuations. The model worked while demand outpaced supply; spreads widened sharply when volumes thinned. Show: bid–ask spread expanding from 2% to 10% in low-volume weeks (company filings, 2022). Name: *adaptive liquidity*. Explain: algorithms can simulate order books but not conjure counterparties. Implication: exit paths depend less on code than on community depth.

The counter-example is instructive. When FTX collapsed in November 2022, tokenised assets listed on its exchange—ranging from stocks to prediction markets—became untradeable overnight. Blockchain records persisted; liquidity vanished. It was not a bug; it was absence of buyers. Tokens are receipts; markets are relationships. The paradox is that digital markets promise self-sufficiency but rely heavily on human appetite.

So, what makes an exit path *reliable*? Three traits recur. First, *predictable timing*: investors know when liquidity will next be available. Second, *transparent mechanics*: they can observe queues, bids, and execution prices. Third, *circuit-breakers*: mechanisms that slow panic without confiscating choice. The best designs publish liquidity coverage ratios—cash on hand versus expected redemptions—and automatically throttle withdrawals when coverage falls below thresholds. In tokenised systems, this can be enforced by smart contracts that queue redemption calls based on timestamp and priority rules, removing discretion and emotion.

Consider an example in Singapore. ADDX, a regulated digital securities exchange, offers quarterly redemption for certain private funds and limited secondary trading in between. Its published "liquidity statistics" show completed trades, average time to exit, and price dispersion. This disclosure does not increase liquidity by itself, but it transforms perception: investors see illiquidity as managed rather than concealed. That shift—visibility over velocity—is the foundation of durable trust.

By contrast, some NFT-based "fractional ownership" projects tried to mimic stock market liquidity without volume. In 2022, platforms like Fractional.art allowed users to trade shards of high-profile NFTs, such as CryptoPunk #8104. Initial trading volumes were brisk, but as enthusiasm waned, the shards became stranded; holders discovered there was no exit except through coordinated buyout. The mechanism lacked a secondary audience. Show: daily trading dropping from 200 ETH in October 2021 to under 10 ETH by February 2022 (Dune Analytics). Name: *evaporated liquidity*. Explain: when exit depends solely on hype, time becomes the only solvent. Implication: true markets require depth, not just doors.

A sustainable exit path may therefore resemble a hybrid. Periodic redemptions give predictability; auctions give price discovery; market-makers give continuity. The optimal mix depends on the asset's nature. Real estate wants quarterly windows; collectables want spectacle; revenue-generating tokens can sustain liquidity pools. The designer's job is not to promise instant liquidity, but to declare its shape and frequency.

The motif here—the *door that opens outward*—captures the trade-off. The more easily investors can leave, the less stable the structure becomes unless inflows match outflows. Traditional funds solve this by keeping cash buffers; token platforms must do the same, perhaps through automated reserve ratios. When redemption requests exceed reserves, systems can convert them into queued claims tradable among investors—a secondary layer of liquidity within the redemption queue. This mirrors the structure of money-market funds after the 2008 crisis, when regulators introduced gates and fees to absorb shocks.

There is also a cultural dimension. Retail investors raised on 24-hour markets may expect perpetual liquidity, forgetting that markets are social contracts, not vending machines. Education matters. If a fund states: "Liquidity windows open quarterly; early exits incur a 1% fee; all requests published on-chain," that is not friction—it is fairness. Illiquidity becomes part of the story rather than a surprise.

A quieter lesson emerges from cooperative finance. The John Lewis Partnership in Britain, founded 1929, pays profit shares annually to its partners, not daily. The rhythm enforces patience and community. Tokenised projects could learn from that cadence: align exit opportunities with performance cycles, not with the twitch of the secondary market. Liquidity tied to productivity sustains trust longer than liquidity tied to sentiment.

The forward test for any fractional investment is not *can investors exit fast*, but *can they exit fairly*. Platforms must model buyer-of-last-resort scenarios: if all sellers queue, who clears the book? Is it an internal fund, a periodic auction, or a redemption pool? How is price discovered, and what is the investor told when bids fall short? Liquidity is a verb; it must be practised, not proclaimed.

The next time a prospectus or white paper trumpets "instant liquidity," the intelligent reader should ask one unglamorous question: *who, precisely, is buying on the other side when sentiment turns?* Until that answer is concrete—timed, priced, and auditable—the exit path is marketing, not mechanism.

Chapter 6
Legal and Governance Foundations

On 10 May 2022, Singapore's High Court froze the sale of a yacht. It was sleek, digital, and oddly intangible: the *Arianee* NFT attached to the vessel's title had been minted, sold, and then used as collateral for a loan. When the borrower defaulted, the lender expected to seize the token. Instead, they discovered the yacht's physical papers still listed a different owner. Code had promised possession; law disagreed. For months, lawyers, insurers, and engineers circled a single question that now defines the frontier of tokenisation: *when ownership is digital, where does authority live?*

Tokens were supposed to simplify ownership—cleaner ledgers, faster settlement, fewer middlemen. Yet as markets mature, the inverse has happened. Every smart contract leads back to a legal contract, every claim of "decentralisation" to a jurisdiction. The myth of borderless assets is dying the same slow death as the myth of stateless money. Behind every wallet address stands a person, a platform, and a court. The future is not post-legal—it is *post-naïve.*

That is where this chapter begins: at the junction where code meets courtrooms, and governance stops being an aspiration and becomes an operating system. Law, far from the enemy of innovation, is the soil in which durable systems take root. When we examine what happens when tokens meet law, we are not asking how to slow progress; we are asking how to make it real enough to survive contact with the world.

Property, consumer protection, and securities law were never designed for tokens, but they are not powerless against them. The same principles that govern a lease, a warranty, or a share apply, albeit through new wrappers. Ownership, after all, is not a database entry; it is the right to exclude, the right to benefit, and the right to transfer. Those rights must be enforceable somewhere. In the chapters before this, we traced how tokenisation creates participation and exchange; here, we uncover the invisible scaffolding that makes those exchanges credible: rights, remedies, recourse, and governance.

Consider the case of *DAOstack* in 2018. It launched with high ideals of decentralised coordination—hundreds of token-holders voting on every proposal. Within months, participation collapsed. The most active five wallets made over 60% of decisions; quorum targets were rarely met. What failed was not technology but scope. People do not want to govern everything—they want to govern meaningfully. The lesson would be repeated across the decade: *minimal viable governance* works better than maximal democracy. A smart system delegates daily operations and reserves collective attention for milestones that shape direction.

That principle applies equally to traditional corporations and DAOs. The most effective boards and communities share three traits: clarity of scope, traceability of action, and the capacity to reverse mistakes without erasing accountability. Blockchain can aid all three—if we design for it consciously. Multi-signature wallets, time-locked upgrades, and audit trails are not abstractions; they are modern equivalents of signatures, ledgers, and minutes. Yet they work only when paired with human judgment and clear documentation.

This interplay between automation and oversight defines the legal future of tokenised systems. Regulation is evolving fast: the European Union's *Markets in Crypto-Assets Regulation* (MiCA) now treats certain tokens as transferable securities; the UK's Law Commission has clarified that digital assets can constitute property under English law; and U.S. courts are increasingly ruling that NFTs tied to revenue streams fall within existing securities frameworks. The message is consistent: tokens do not float above the law—they sink into it. Every designer must now ask not, *"Is this compliant?"* but *"Which regime governs this?"*

Still, legality is only half the equation. Governance gives law its rhythm. A perfectly compliant system can still collapse through poor decision-making. The rise of decentralised autonomous organisations was an attempt to fuse both—law encoded in code, governance executed by consensus. But as the *MakerDAO* saga showed, decentralisation without delegation is paralysis. In 2021, Maker's community spent months debating collateral types and risk parameters. The process was open but exhausting. The lesson was harsh but invaluable: democracy must be designed to *scale down* as well as up.

A new generation of governance models has learned that lesson. They use *scope slicing*: operational tasks are automated or assigned to professional stewards, while token-holders intervene only at defined checkpoints—profit distributions, policy shifts, or emergency votes. In effect, governance becomes a heartbeat, not a constant buzz. It is the difference between participation and fatigue.

This chapter therefore unfolds along four dimensions. First, *Tokens meet law*—the frameworks that already exist and the decision tree for placing any token within them. Second, *Rights, remedies, recourse*—the paths by which wrongs are made right, from smart-contract bugs to fraudulent disclosures, and the documentation that turns chaos into claim. Third, *DAOs without delusion*—what collective governance can achieve when ambition meets structure. And finally, *Designing for accountability*—the technical and procedural safeguards that make trust measurable.

At its core, this is a chapter about power. The power to assign, to decide, to reverse. Legal systems encode centuries of power-balancing; governance systems must now learn to do the same in code. The objective is not to replace law but to let technology inherit its discipline. When platforms embed audit trails and reversible windows, they are not hedging—they are honouring an old truth: that power, once granted, must be traceable.

The motif running through these pages is *the ledger and the mirror*. The ledger records what happens; the mirror shows who is responsible. Together, they form accountability—the only real currency of trust. A system that records every transaction but hides every decision is still opaque. A community that votes endlessly but enforces nothing is still lawless. The synthesis of the two—traceable, enforceable, proportionate—is the true foundation of tokenised ownership.

Legal design is often dismissed as bureaucracy, yet it is the craft that makes every claim enforceable and every promise believable. When a token represents a share in a company, a royalty stream, or a right to access, what matters most is not its price, but its *path of recourse* when something fails. Who compensates? Under which jurisdiction? Using what evidence? Those are the questions that separate systems from slogans.

The broader cultural moment is one of reckoning. After the speculative booms and algorithmic collapses of the early 2020s, the digital asset sector is discovering maturity. The survivors are not the flashiest experiments but the most disciplined ones—the platforms that can prove who owns what, who decides what, and who answers when something breaks. In short: law is the new luxury, and governance is its infrastructure.

This chapter stands as both map and manifesto. The map traces how property, consumer, and securities principles still hold sway even in digital space. The manifesto insists that good design can turn those principles into code, culture, and contract. The path forward is not regulation versus innovation, but regulation *as* innovation—a recognition that systems become robust only when they can be held to account.

As you turn the page, consider a simple question that threads through the arguments ahead: if ownership is programmable, what else should be? Rules? Rights? Remedies? Perhaps the next evolution of tokenisation is not technical at all, but moral—a reprogramming of how responsibility itself is shared, proven, and enforced. The code may be new, but the question is ancient: *who governs the governors?*

Tokens meet law

On 28 July 2022, the High Court of England and Wales declared, for the first time, that non-fungible tokens could be recognised as *property*. The case, *Osbourne v. Persons Unknown*, arose when digital artist Lavinia Osbourne alleged that two of her NFTs—*Boss Beauties #680* and *#691*—had been stolen from her MetaMask wallet and resold through OpenSea. The court granted an injunction freezing the assets and authorised disclosure orders against the exchange. In a single judgment, the blockchain myth that "code is law" met the older, sterner reality that *law is law*. The ruling did not elevate tokens above jurisdictions; it pulled them firmly within. Ownership in digital form, the court made clear, carries the same obligations and protections as ownership in physical form.

That moment was quiet but revolutionary. It proved that centuries-old doctrines—property, contract, equity—could stretch to cover digital artefacts without breaking. The NFT, once hailed as an escape from legal complexity, found itself bound by it. Yet this was not regression; it was integration. The legal system was not strangling innovation but giving it a spine. Without enforceability, ownership is theatre. With it, ownership becomes reality.

The motif that threads through this discussion is *gravity*. Tokens may appear weightless—bytes on a ledger—but law supplies the gravitational pull that keeps them from drifting into irrelevance. The point is not whether tokens *should* be regulated, but *where* they already are. Property law, consumer law, and securities regulation each assert jurisdiction through the practical question: *what is this token doing?* The triage begins there.

Show: a token that merely proves access to a concert. Name: *utility*. Explain: it grants a right to enter a venue, no different in principle from a paper ticket. Implication: it sits under consumer law, not financial regulation; refunds, cancellations, and misrepresentations are the relevant duties. Show again: a token representing revenue share from a music catalogue. Name: *investment*. Explain: it embodies rights to future cash flows, making it a regulated financial instrument under securities law. Implication: its issuer must disclose, audit, and register, just as if it sold shares. Show a third: a purely collectible token, a work of art. Name: *property*. Explain: ownership is protected by tort and equity, not market regulation, but theft and misappropriation remain actionable. Implication: civil remedies, not hype, anchor value.

This is the decision tree every project must climb: *what does the token confer?* Access, income, or control? Each path leads to a distinct legal ecosystem. The art is not to invent new law but to map the right one.

Property remains the oldest and most flexible branch. When the UK Law Commission reported in June 2023 that digital assets "meet the criteria of things in action," it formalised what judges had already begun to practise. Ownership of a token is now a matter of evidence: who controls the private key, what contractual promises underpin the ledger entry, and whether the transfer was authorised. Courts have frozen tokens, granted injunctions, and even recognised off-chain claims where keys were lost. The behaviour of law has adapted, not capitulated. The *gravity* motif returns here: law follows possession because possession can be proven, however digital its form.

Yet property rights alone do not solve the harder problems of consumer protection. In 2021, the UK's Advertising Standards Authority banned multiple crypto adverts for misleading claims about "guaranteed returns." In one case, the promotion by Arsenal Football Club for its "fan token" was censured for failing to disclose financial risk. The incident revealed that once tokens touch the public, consumer law awakens. Misrepresentation, unfair terms, and negligence are timeless categories. The medium—blockchain—does not confer immunity.

Across the Atlantic, the same logic took a sharper form. The U.S. Securities and Exchange Commission's lawsuit against Ripple Labs, filed December 2020, alleged that its sale of XRP tokens constituted an unregistered securities offering. The *Howey* test—originating from a 1946 Supreme Court decision on orange groves—decided the fate of a twenty-first-century token. The principle endured: if investors expect profits primarily from the efforts of others, the instrument is a security. The asset's digital wrapper could not disguise its economic substance. When a federal judge in July 2023 held that certain XRP sales qualified as securities while others did not, she underscored a practical reality: classification depends not on the technology but on *context of sale.*

That distinction—between code and context—is the essence of the legal decision tree. Regulators examine *function*, not form. A governance token that confers voting rights over a revenue-generating protocol may cross into the domain of collective investment schemes. A loyalty token redeemable for merchandise stays within consumer regulation. The dividing lines are not arbitrary; they rest on established doctrines of inducement, expectation, and control.

The counter-example, though, deserves attention. Decentralised finance (DeFi) protocols often claim to be "non-custodial" and "community-run." When something fails—an exploit, a flash loan attack—who bears liability? If the code was open-source and the deployer anonymous, enforcement collapses. Law's gravity thins at the edges of anonymity. In August 2022, the U.S. Office of Foreign Assets Control sanctioned the crypto mixer Tornado Cash, treating its code as an entity. Critics called this absurd, likening it to sanctioning mathematics. But the logic was regulatory necessity: where accountability cannot attach to a person, it attaches to a mechanism. The limitation is clear—law can reach code but cannot yet reason with it.

This tension defines the decade ahead. The next generation of tokenised systems will succeed only if they design *for* jurisdiction rather than against it. That means encoding disclosures, contractual metadata, and dispute mechanisms directly into token structures. Some projects already experiment with "legal wrappers": smart contracts linked to traditional corporate entities that anchor rights in recognised law. In Switzerland, *DAURA AG* has issued share tokens under Swiss Code of Obligations since 2021; holders are registered as shareholders in the commercial register, bridging code and court seamlessly. This model—hybrid, transparent, enforceable—will likely become the template for credible digital assets.

Meanwhile, the European Union's *Markets in Crypto-Assets Regulation* (MiCA), passed April 2023, brings a continental coherence. It defines three token categories—asset-referenced, e-money, and utility—and demands clear white papers, capital reserves, and consumer recourse. It is not innovation's enemy but its scaffolding. Without it, platforms drift between regulatory islands; with it, they can plan, raise, and scale. Law gives tokens the same foundation that accounting gave corporations: predictability.

To see how this plays out, imagine a simple triage map. Step one: identify *use*. Is the token consumptive, speculative, or representational? Step two: map *promises*. Are profits, governance, or redemptions offered? Step three: anchor *jurisdiction*. Where are issuers domiciled, servers located, or investors targeted? The intersection of these three determines the governing regime—property, consumer, or securities law. This "decision tree" is not theoretical. It is the same structure regulators now use to classify token projects. When builders internalise it early, they avoid the legal purgatory that so many startups discover too late.

At the frontier of property and code stands one further test: enforcement. Courts can freeze wallets but cannot compel blockchains to reverse transactions. That gap will not close through legislation alone; it requires design. Programmable "pause" functions, escrow locks, and multisig controls can align code with court orders. Far from undermining decentralisation, these mechanisms clarify accountability. A reversible window—say, 48 hours before settlement—mirrors the cooling-off periods of consumer contracts. The principle is continuity: law adapts when design allows it to act.

The quiet revolution, then, is not in statutes but in systems. Each time a platform embeds legal clarity, it converts volatility into legitimacy. Property doctrines safeguard possession; consumer rules protect participation; securities law disciplines speculation. Together they form a lattice that prevents digital markets from collapsing under their own exuberance.

Still, the gravitational metaphor holds a warning. Too much legal weight can stifle innovation; too little, and assets drift into vacuum. The challenge is calibration. Jurisdictions must learn to enforce without smothering, and developers must learn to respect without retreating. As precedents multiply—from Singapore's recognition of digital assets as property in 2022 to the UK's forthcoming Digital Assets Bill—the convergence accelerates. Tokens will not escape the orbit of law; they will define its new terrain.

So the unresolved question, the one that hovers over every project from NFT platform to decentralised exchange, is this: if every token must answer to a jurisdiction, which jurisdiction do you trust to answer for it? The future of tokenisation will hinge less on technology than on that act of choosing—where to plant its legal flag, and how much gravity it is willing to accept.

Rights, remedies, recourse

On 2 August 2022, the Solana-based wallet service Slope was hacked. Around 9,000 user wallets were drained of funds, totalling roughly $4.5 million. Panic spread through Telegram groups and Twitter threads; victims demanded refunds, explanations, and lawsuits. But the company had no direct contractual relationship with most users. Transactions were self-custodied. The attackers were anonymous. The blockchain recorded the theft immutably, yet offered no mechanism for restitution. The episode exposed a quiet truth of the token economy: when things break, the public record endures, but responsibility dissolves.

That moment crystallised the new frontier of digital ownership. In traditional finance, loss triggers a predictable chain of remedies—banks reverse charges, insurers assess claims, courts enforce restitution. In tokenised systems, the line between service and user, platform and product, is blurred. Code executes transfers automatically, but accountability remains human. *Who fixes what* becomes not a rhetorical question but a structural fault line.

The motif that threads through this inquiry is *the chain of care.* Each link—contract, platform policy, insurer, court—represents a possible path of recourse. The strength of the chain depends on how clearly those links are defined *before* something fails. When a project promises "trustless" systems, the word often conceals the absence of trust's replacement: liability.

The law, for all its bureaucracy, begins from clarity. In conventional commerce, contracts allocate risk. If a courier loses a parcel, the sender's contract governs refunds; if a company misrepresents returns, consumer law provides remedies. Token platforms too often skip this foundation. Many rely on "terms of use" buried in small print that disclaim all liability, while simultaneously advertising safety and transparency. The contradiction is not just moral; it is legal. Under UK and EU consumer regulations, such disclaimers can be void if they mislead. The token economy's first maturation, therefore, lies not in smarter code but in *plainer contracts.*

Show: a case where the absence of a clear contract forced costly improvisation. In April 2021, the NFT marketplace Nifty Gateway suffered unauthorised account breaches. Users lost high-value assets—some pieces worth over $100,000. The company argued that its platform had not been compromised, only user accounts. Because the NFTs themselves lived on an external blockchain, traditional refund mechanisms did not apply. Eventually, Nifty Gateway reimbursed selected users as a "gesture of goodwill." Name: *discretionary restitution.* Explain: compensation arose from reputational pressure, not legal obligation. Implication: without enforceable documentation, recourse depends on brand optics, not rights.

Contrast this with a case of structured recourse. Since 2020, Singapore's Monetary Authority has licensed certain digital-asset custodians under its Payment Services Act, mandating segregation of customer assets and requiring insurance or guarantees against operational loss. When a licensed custodian fails, courts can trace segregated funds and prioritise clients as creditors. Here, *recourse* is not improvisation; it is infrastructure. Regulation builds a predictable hierarchy of remedies before failure occurs.

Between those poles—discretion and discipline—lies the most interesting frontier: *platform policy as proto-law.* Exchanges and NFT marketplaces increasingly function as micro-jurisdictions. OpenSea's dispute-resolution mechanism, for instance, freezes disputed assets upon credible claim, pending investigation. In early 2022, when several stolen *Bored Ape Yacht Club* NFTs were flagged, OpenSea blocked their resale. The measure protected buyers but angered holders who claimed ignorance. The company was neither judge nor regulator, yet its policy shaped outcomes faster than courts could. These platform-level decisions illustrate the emergence of "code-adjacent law": policies with real economic impact, enforced algorithmically but crafted by human teams.

However, such policies are double-edged. They provide swift response but limited due process. Users cannot easily appeal a freeze, and platforms can unilaterally define "credible claim." The risk is procedural opacity. When private intermediaries act as quasi-regulators, accountability must follow. This is where documentation re-enters the scene—not the white paper or tokenomics deck, but legal-grade *user agreements* that state how disputes escalate, how evidence is assessed, and what jurisdictions apply. The clearer those documents, the shorter the dispute.

An instructive example comes from the insurance sector. Nexus Mutual, founded in London in 2019, operates as a decentralised mutual providing smart-contract cover. When the *Yearn Finance* protocol suffered a loss in February 2021, Nexus processed claims through a voting mechanism. Holders of the mutual's governance token assessed evidence and voted on payouts. Some claims were accepted; others rejected, citing ambiguous event definitions. The process was transparent but emotionally bruising—policyholders felt peers, not professionals, judged them. The episode highlighted that even decentralised insurance must adopt standardised definitions, loss reports, and audit logs. Without them, community voting replaces evidence with sentiment.

At the heart of every remedy lies documentation: contracts, records, and correspondence that prove what was promised and what was performed. In tokenised ecosystems, these materials often scatter across chat threads, GitHub commits, and JSON files. When disputes reach arbitration or court, reconstructing intent becomes forensic archaeology. That is why forward-thinking platforms now embed documentation *on-chain*—digital signatures, hashed agreements, and transaction-linked receipts. The purpose is not publicity but provenance: to show, unambiguously, who owed what to whom at the moment of failure.

Legal systems are adapting to these evidentiary shifts. The Singapore International Arbitration Centre in 2022 introduced clauses for smart-contract disputes, allowing parties to submit blockchain evidence directly. The UK Jurisdiction Taskforce's Digital Dispute Resolution Rules (2021) go further: they permit arbitral awards to be executed by code, including automatic fund transfers. Here, the *chain of care* becomes literal—the same ledger that recorded an obligation can now enforce its resolution. Such developments shrink the gap between contract and consequence.

Still, not every failure warrants litigation. Many can be resolved through structured mediation or insurance. Consider Lloyd's of

London's partnership with Coincover (2020), which offers digital-asset theft insurance backed by traditional underwriters. The product blends algorithmic monitoring with conventional claims processes. When losses occur, payouts follow verifiable breach data, not user testimony. It represents a pragmatic hybrid: blockchain for evidence, institutions for enforcement.

The counter-example is telling. During the collapse of the algorithmic stablecoin TerraUSD in May 2022, investors sought compensation through courts in South Korea, Singapore, and the U.S. The claims spanned misrepresentation, negligence, and breach of securities laws. Yet because Terra operated through opaque jurisdictions and pseudonymous foundations, most plaintiffs found no accountable counterparty. Billions were lost, but recourse evaporated. Gravity, again: without a defined anchor—contract, policy, or insurer—law cannot apply its pull.

The larger implication is cultural. Many in the digital-asset world equate decentralisation with independence from traditional remedies. But independence without accountability breeds fragility. Systems that can absorb failure gracefully—through refund, arbitration, or insurance—earn legitimacy faster than those that promise perfection. Recourse is not a burden; it is a selling point.

So how should designers build it in? The emerging best practice is a *tiered approach*. At the base: contracts specifying obligations, jurisdiction, and evidence standards. Above them: platform policies that handle routine errors—fraudulent listings, double transfers, or key loss—through predefined processes. Beyond that: optional coverage—escrow services, insurance pools, or third-party guarantees. Finally, at the apex: access to courts or arbitration for exceptional cases. Each tier narrows the dispute, saving time and cost before escalation.

This structure mirrors how financial markets evolved. Stock exchanges began as private clubs with rules enforced internally; over time, public law codified those norms. Token markets are tracing the same arc. The transition from "community guidelines" to enforceable terms marks their passage from experimentation to infrastructure. The platforms that survive will be those that treat documentation not as legal theatre but as operational architecture.

The *chain of care* motif returns one last time. When a wallet is drained, or a smart contract fails, or a marketplace freezes, the path to remedy should be as visible as the path that caused the loss. The buyer should know: first, which contract governs; second, which platform policy applies; third, whether insurance or compensation exists; and finally, where judicial recourse begins. Absent that chain, even the most advanced blockchain is a one-way ledger—a record of pain, not restitution.

The unresolved tension remains this: how much responsibility can decentralised systems absorb without re-centralising power? If every layer of recourse requires a named entity, have we circled back to the institutions tokenisation sought to escape? Yet the alternative—pure autonomy without repair—is untenable. The mature future of digital ownership will not eliminate failure; it will make recovery legible. The next breakthrough may not be technical at all, but procedural: a world where when something breaks, everyone knows, precisely, *who fixes what.*

DAOs without delusion

On 27 June 2022, MakerDAO's governance forum crashed under its own earnestness. Hundreds of posts debated collateral types, oracle risks, and parameter tweaks; delegates scrambled across calls while markets whipsawed. The vote barely cleared quorum. A protocol entrusted with billions in stablecoin guarantees had, for a moment, looked like a town hall after a storm—crowded, loud, and indecisive. Technology had scaled coordination; it had not scaled judgment. Out of that stress came an unglamorous insight that now shapes the strongest decentralised organisations: collective decision-making works when the *scope* is clear. Everything else becomes noise.

DAOs began with an old promise in new code—ownership becomes participation, and participation becomes power. The early years mistook maximal democracy for accountability. They learned, quickly, that attention is finite and that the work of running systems is procedural before it is philosophical. The practical question is not whether token-holders should decide; it is *what* they should decide, *when*, and *at what resolution*. The answer, learned the hard way, is minimal-viable-governance: delegate routine operations to competent stewards, bound by budgets and audits, and reserve collective votes for milestones that change the organisation's path.

Show: an over-broad agenda. Name: scope creep. Explain: when everything is votable, nothing is prioritised; when every routine configuration requires a proposal, calendars fill and throughput drops. Implication: apathy grows; a handful of hyper-engaged wallets capture the process by sheer persistence. Healthy DAOs invert the premise. They define a narrow "constitutional" layer—mission, treasury policy, emergency powers—and push everything else into chartered teams and templated processes. Votes punctuate, not saturate.

Two concrete examples demonstrate the pattern. ENS DAO launched in November 2021 with a written constitution that stated principles once, then empowered token-holders to delegate votes to representatives who focus on policy and funding. Most operational work—running resolvers, maintenance, partnerships—sits with working groups on defined mandates renewed each term. Participation stabilised. Crucially, the constitution functions as scope: it says what the DAO is *for*, so proposals outside that remit rarely waste time. MakerDAO, bruised by 2022's governance overload, moved towards a similar architecture by expanding "core units" into more accountable "endgame subDAOs," each with budgets, deliverables, and elected leadership; macro parameters and risk appetite remained at the top. The aim was identical: put day-to-day levers in professional hands, keep existential levers in the community.

A credible counter-example shows the cliff edge. Nouns DAO, launched in August 2021, issues one unique Noun daily, with treasury governed by token-holders. The cadence is elegant. Yet in September 2023, a large faction executed a "rage quit" fork, exiting with a pro rata share of the treasury. Why? Drift in mandate and expectations. Many holders preferred cash over culture. The mechanism worked as designed; the social contract had frayed.

Reconcile this to our thesis: even beautifully engineered voting rhythms fail when the DAO's *purpose* is ambiguous. Minimal governance depends on maximal clarity of mission.

The motif that will guide this piece is the *brief*. Every effective team knows that good briefs prevent bad meetings. DAOs need briefs at three layers: the constitutional brief (why we exist), the mandate brief (what this unit must deliver), and the decision brief (what *this vote* changes in the world). Without these, votes become expressions of taste rather than instruments of policy.

Begin with the constitutional brief. It should name scope, not slogans. A media DAO might write: "We fund and publish open research on digital property; we do not speculate in assets; we maintain public registries." Short. Specific. Testable. Then lock it with a high threshold—say, 67% for amendments after two weeks' notice—and a time-lock on execution. Show: a proposal to add trading activities is ruled out of order by a neutral secretary because it violates scope. Name: scope guard. Explain: process protects purpose; where human moderation feels risky, encode it—allow proposals only from whitelisted templates that check against scope fields. Implication: the chain of decisions stays taut; fewer digressions, fewer theatrics.

Move to mandate briefs. Here, the minimal-viable-governance pattern is simple: create small executive teams ("pods", "core units", "workstreams") with three ingredients—budget, KPIs, and kill-switches. The DAO approves a budget and a set of outcomes for a term (e.g., six months) and appoints stewards with the authority to act. Performance is measured by a *proposal-to-ship ratio* (how many funded initiatives delivered), mean time to decision for operational changes, and budget variance. If metrics slip outside defined bands, a pre-authorised "review motion" triggers. Show: the protocol risk pod misses SLA on parameter updates twice in a quarter; a review motion pares budget by 20% and demands corrective actions. Name: bounded delegation. Explain: authority flows down; accountability flows up. Implication: token-holders monitor *results*, not tactics.

The third layer—the decision brief—lives on each proposal page. The best DAOs enforce a two-page rule. Page one: the change, the cost, the risk, and the reversible window. Page two: the test for success and the rollback plan. That second part is often missing. It matters. If a fee change fails, how fast can the DAO revert, and who executes? Show: a fee parameter increase with a 72-hour time-lock; if slippage rises above a threshold, a multi-sig can revert within the window. Name: reversible governance. Explain: speed without safeties invites regret; safeties without speed invite sclerosis. Implication: the DAO learns without gambling the treasury.

Evidence beats enthusiasm. So measure governance like operations. Track *quorum attainment time* (median hours to quorum), *delegate concentration* (share of votes across top ten wallets), *agenda density* (proposals per week), and *decision yield* (percentage of passed proposals that ship). If quorum time lengthens, delegates dominate, agendas bloat, and yield falls, the DAO is in governance debt. Reduce the scope of what reaches chain. Consolidate votes into "milestone bundles" rather than micro-changes. Ship quarterly "omnibus" proposals that roll up routine items, freeing attention for strategy.

Two further case studies underscore this logic. Gitcoin's Grants programme (2020–2023) migrated from a single monolithic round to domain-specific workstreams with dedicated stewards, each running quadratic funding under standard playbooks. The community still sets broad parameters, but operational discretion sits with workstream leads. The result: less performative voting, more consistent outcomes; fraud detection improved because responsible teams owned the brief. Contrast with SushiSwap's governance turbulence in 2021–2022, where lack of clear mandate and disputes over compensation paralysed execution; the lesson was eventually encoded in a more conventional corporate wrapper and a trimmed governance perimeter. Show: the DAO that writes contracts after drama. Name: institutional backfill. Explain: law and structure arrive late but necessary. Implication: better to design the backfill early.

Delegation deserves precision. Not all token-holders have time or context to vote well. Delegate models work when three elements exist: transparent delegate platforms, term limits, and conflict-of-interest disclosures. ENS, again, provides a useful benchmark: delegates publish statements of priorities and activity; the community can reassign voting weight; stewards rotate on fixed calendars. Introduce *delegate KPIs*—attendance, position statements posted within 72 hours of major votes, and response time to community questions. Pay delegates stipends tied to these metrics, not to token price. Show: a delegate who misses two cycles loses stipend automatically. Name: performance-tethered legitimacy. Explain: representation becomes accountable; legitimacy is earned, not presumed. Implication: fewer spectators, more stewards.

Minimal-viable-governance is not minimal *law*. Most durable DAOs anchor their on-chain processes in off-chain wrappers—foundations, LLCs, or cooperative associations—so they can sign contracts, hire staff, and face courts when necessary. The wrapper does not "centralise" the DAO; it localises legal duties. The governance brief should state what the wrapper can and cannot do without a vote. For example: "The foundation may execute vendor agreements up to £250,000 within the approved budget; material changes to treasury policy require token-holder approval." Show: a vendor contract challenged by a community member; the secretary cites the mandate and declines to escalate. Name: procedural clarity. Explain: fights shrink; decisions stick. Implication: energy returns to building.

Security is governance. Time-locked upgrades and multi-signature treasuries are not belt-and-braces; they are the braces. A pattern worth standardising: 2-of-3 multi-sig for routine spend, 4-of-7 with geographically and institutionally separated signers for large transfers, and a 48–72 hour delay on contract upgrades, during which monitors can flag anomalies. Add a *pause council*—a small group with narrow emergency powers to halt specific functions upon predefined triggers (oracle failure, price deviation, known exploit). Publish incident runbooks and practise them. Show: a drill twice a year where paths to pause and revert are executed on testnets. Name: governance fire drill. Explain: crisis competence is trained, not improvised. Implication: when it matters, no one fumbles.

Culture completes structure. DAOs thrive when the default posture is *do, then document*. Strong teams post weeknotes; they publish budgets as living ledgers; they link every vote to an execution artefact—a pull request, a contract address, a signed invoice. They avoid vibe wars by insisting on artefacts. If a proposal lacks a brief, it is bounced. If a debate lacks data, it waits. This is not bureaucracy; it is craft. Show: a treasury dashboard that explains every outflow with a link; disputes shrink because evidence is ambient. Name: documentation gravity. Explain: records pull arguments into orbit. Implication: trust accrues to the organisation, not to personalities.

The limits are real. Minimal-viable-governance can slide into rubber-stamping if mandates ossify or metrics game. A DAO that delegates too much risks drifting into managerialism; one that votes too much drifts into populism. The correction is regular *mandate renewal.* Every term end, the unit must present a short case: what we did, what we missed, why we're still needed. The vote is binary. Renew or retire. Sunsets are healthy. Show: a marketing pod failing to justify renewal after two poor quarters; funds reallocated to protocol security. Name: planned attrition. Explain: resource allocation adapts; stagnation loses oxygen. Implication: the DAO remains dynamic without constant churn.

Then there is the ever-present problem of plutocracy. Token-weighted voting skews power to wealth. There are mitigations: quadratic voting for non-financial decisions, capped influence per address for community grants, or bicameral models where a "citizen chamber" of contributors must ratify major moves. None is perfect; all are better than fatalism. A realistic synthesis uses token-weighted votes for budget ceilings and risk parameters, and contribution-weighted votes for programme design and grants, separating money control from content curation. Show: a grant slate passing both chambers; if either vetoes, the brief returns for revision. Name: dual-key governance. Explain: incentives align across capital and labour. Implication: legitimacy widens without paralysing speed.

Finally, align incentives with time. Require *vesting votes*: to participate in milestone decisions, tokens must be staked for a minimum duration. This filters for commitment. Couple it with *evidence-gated proposals*: only units that hit prior milestones may propose new spend above a threshold. These are simple circuits. They reward care. They penalise noise.

The brief motif returns, as promised. Before you design forums or tokenomics, write the briefs. What must the community decide? What must stewards own? What is the cadence? What are the brakes? Put those on a single page and live by it. The rest is mechanics.

The unresolved tension remains by design. How lean can governance get without hiding power, and how participatory can it be without bleeding energy? The forward test is practical and merciless: pick a recent decision, trace it from idea to execution, and count the days, the posts, the wallets, and the pounds. If the path is long, noisy, and unclear, cut scope or cut steps. If the path is fast but invisible, add briefs and brakes. Minimal-viable-governance is not anti-democratic. It is a promise: to spend collective attention only where it changes the arc.

Designing for accountability

On 30 September 2021, a software upgrade at Compound Finance misfired. A single function, deployed without a guarded delay, began dispensing tens of millions of dollars' worth of COMP to random users. The protocol worked technically; governance failed operationally. Two days of frantic triage followed, capped by public pleas from founder Robert Leshner for the windfall recipients to return funds (Compound Labs, Oct 2021). Some did. Many did not. The lesson was plain even through the panic: systems without brakes turn small mistakes into cascading losses. Accountability is a design choice.

A year later, in March 2022, Sky Mavis disclosed that the Ronin Bridge for *Axie Infinity* had been compromised. Attackers used five private keys to approve withdrawals totalling roughly $620 million (Sky Mavis, 2022). The multi-signature scheme existed but was shallow; signers were concentrated and the process lacked independent checks. Again, the pattern rhymed. Where controls were cosmetic, loss became structural. Trust requires a trail.

The motif that runs through these pages is the *flight recorder*. Aircraft survive not because pilots never err but because systems anticipate failure and preserve forensic truth. Tokenised systems can do the same: encode logs that cannot be edited, stage upgrades behind time locks, and require multi-party sign-off for actions that move money or change rules. Each measure shifts accountability from virtue to architecture. The aim is not to slow everything down. It is to make reversals boringly possible.

Show: a protocol introduces a seven-day delay before any governance-approved contract upgrade can execute. Name: *time-locked upgrades*. Explain: the elapsed time allows independent monitors, auditors, and users to inspect the exact bytecode scheduled for deployment and to simulate its effects. Implication: an error becomes an alert, not an exploit. The behaviour that matters is simple: during the lock, publish a diff, run a testnet dry run, and open a public review window with signed attestations from at least two auditors. Measure it: percentage of upgrades that shipped with complete diffs and auditor sign-offs; average review time used versus available; number of issues caught pre-deploy. Numbers are the flight recorder's heartbeat.

Multi-signature releases translate dual control into code. The point is not mystique; it is mundane separation of duties. Show: routine treasury transfers require 2-of-3 signatures; large movements require 4-of-7 with institutional and geographic distribution, plus a 48–72 hour timelock. Name: *tiered multi-sig*. Explain: thresholds scale with risk; no single person can drain funds or force upgrades. Implication: insider threats become containable; courts can recognise roles; insurers can price risk. The visible behaviour is rotation: signers are rotated on a schedule, with public keys announced and retirement procedures documented. Metrics help: average time to assemble signatures, signer participation rates, and frequency of emergency bypasses (target: zero). If these numbers are opaque, accountability is performative.

Now the first worked example. In September 2019, Banco Santander issued a blockchain-settled bond from Madrid, managing coupon flows on-chain under bank-grade controls. No "DAO mysticism"; just process. Upgrades moved behind change windows; cash movements reconciled to bank ledgers; internal audit logged each step. The concrete outcome was fewer reconciliation breaks and predictable settlement. Name: *audit-integrated automation*. Explain:

systems earned trust by design behaviours—time windows, dual control, parallel logs. Implication: tokenised finance is not a street performance; it is a taped rehearsal.

Second example: MakerDAO's evolution after 2020. Early incident reviews highlighted how parameter changes and oracle updates could ripple into systemic risk. The community formalised *emergency shutdown* procedures and later introduced *circuit breakers* for specific collateral types. Time locks and multi-sig councils did not eliminate risk; they made it legible. Show: a collateral's debt ceiling increase scheduled with a delay and kill-switch; abnormal volatility triggers a pause on that market alone. Name: *granular pausing.* Explain: brakes are precise, not blanket. Implication: interventions protect solvency without freezing healthy subsystems. The relevant metrics—pause frequency, scope, and mean time to unpause—turn slogans about "prudence" into evidence.

A credible counter-example clarifies the stakes. The Nomad bridge exploit (August 2022) allowed hundreds of copycat transactions to siphon roughly $190 million because a trusted root was set to an all-zeros value. No time lock, no staged rollout, no flight recorder robust enough to stop contagion. The post-mortem begged for what good design would have provided in advance: change controls that catch dangerous defaults, simulation harnesses, and a reversible window that quarantines abnormal outflows. Reconcile it to the thesis: openness without guardrails is not decentralisation; it is negligence in public.

Logs are the flight recorder's memory. They must be *structured, signed, and surfaced.* Structured: events use consistent schemas so machines and auditors can parse them. Signed: off-chain attestations—board minutes, audit letters—are hashed and anchored on-chain to prevent disputes about wording later. Surfaced: dashboards display key events with human-readable explanations and links to the raw data. The visible behaviour is housekeeping: weekly digests that map actions to logs, not to personalities, and changelogs that link every governance vote to an execution artefact. A system that moves billions should publish a *change ledger* no less rigorous than a regulated exchange's release notes.

Audits are necessary, not sufficient. Push beyond the badge. Require auditor accountability tied to scope and time. Show: an upgrade with two independent reviews, each stating the commit hash, test coverage attained, and known residual risks. Name: *attestation clarity*. Explain: a PDF that waves at "best practices" is not an audit; a signed attestation that binds an auditor's reputation to specific code is. Implication: insurers and courts can read it; the public can price it. Track the audit's hit rate: issues found per thousand lines, proportion of criticals mitigated pre-deploy, and re-opened issues after incidents. A declining hit rate without other controls may signal complacency.

Reversible windows should not be universal; they should be *scoped*. Money-moving actions get shorter windows; rule-changing actions get longer ones. Show: transfers above £500,000 post to an escrow contract with a 24-hour cancel function accessible to a defined emergency council; parameter changes affecting solvency lock for 72 hours. Name: *graduated reversibility*. Explain: not all consequences are equal; neither should the brakes be. Implication: speed lives where it helps; caution lives where it must. Publish the *reversal rate* and reasons; high rates may reveal governance churn, low rates with high incident counts may reveal hubris.

Observability reduces argument. If a project claims "99.9% uptime," show your *time-to-detect* and *time-to-mitigate* across a rolling window. If you claim "institutional-grade custody," publish signer distribution, key ceremony procedures, and recovery drills with dates. Practice the drills. Twice a year, run a full-lifecycle incident simulation: inject a mock oracle failure, trip the pause, gather signatures, post the logs, revert safely on a testnet. Time it. Record it. Share a redacted timeline. The metric—mean time to safe state—belongs on the homepage, not in a grant proposal.

Good accountability design extends to the human layer: permissions, procurement, payroll. Encode budgets with *circuit breakers*: when a cost centre overshoots by 10% in a month, disbursements require an extra signature. Encode *conflict-of-interest* attestations into delegate dashboards; a vote that benefits a signer's firm shows a flag. Record minutes. Publish them. Logs keep leaders honest and critics precise. The flight recorder cuts both ways.

Sometimes, the right brake is procedural. Introduce "cold staging" for risky features: deploy to a dark contract with no public hooks, let auditors and monitors observe live state changes for a week, then atomically switch pointers after the lock. Pair it with "canary releases": route 1% of flows through the new logic; auto-revert if anomaly metrics tip. Behavioural design heals techno-optimism: ship less drama.

Privacy and accountability are not opposites; they are complements. Sensitive signer identities can be masked while publishing *roles* and *locations* at a high level—jurisdiction, institution type, service-level commitments. Use zero-knowledge attestations where feasible: a signer proves they are part of an approved set without revealing which one. The behaviour that matters is disclosure with restraint: enough for external assurance, not enough for attackers.

There is a governance dividend too. When communities see logs, reversals, and drills, rhetoric recedes. Debates move from "trust the team" to "read the tape." Proposal quality rises because proposers must prepare rollback plans and commit to metrics. The *flight recorder* becomes a cultural artefact. It disciplines tone. It anchors memory. It outlasts influencers.

Two final patterns deserve a place on every serious project's checklist. First, *separation of keys and knobs*: the people who can move money should not be the people who can change rules, and vice versa. Demonstrate it in org charts and Gnosis Safe roles. Second, *open incident promises*: commit in advance to publish an incident report within, say, 14 days of material events, with root cause, blast radius, user impact, and corrective actions. Measure adherence to that promise. Missing it without explanation is itself a breach of accountability.

None of this is free. Time locks slow heroics. Multi-sigs create scheduling friction. Audits cost money; drills cost energy. The trade-off is strategic: modest drag today buys resilience tomorrow. The Compound and Ronin episodes show the price of skipping the spend. They are not morality plays; they are budget lines.

The unresolved tension persists. How much brake can a young protocol bear before it loses speed, and how much speed can it seek before it loses control? Pick a recent change. Trace it end to end. Was there a diff? A delay? Independent eyes? A clean log? A defined rollback? If any answer is *no*, you are flying without a recorder. The forward test is blunt and fair: encode enough memory and mercy that when—not if—something breaks, your system can show the tape, take the blame, and cleanly reverse the harm.

Chapter 7
Consumer Adoption: Trust by Design

In May 2021, the British Museum launched a limited collection of digital artworks through a blockchain-based platform. The campaign was cautious, almost modest—prints of Hokusai's *Great Wave* translated into non-fungible tokens. Yet what captured attention was not the novelty of ownership but the clarity of the experience. Each buyer was guided step by step: what they were purchasing, what they were entitled to, how to store it, and even how to resell it. There were no cryptographic riddles, no wallet jargon, no friction disguised as freedom. The museum's name lent cultural weight, but its design lent confidence. Adoption began not with speculation but with comprehension.

The digital economy loves to declare revolutions; consumers prefer working systems. Tokens, wallets, and decentralised services promise empowerment but often deliver confusion. The paradox is brutal: technologies built for transparency are frequently opaque to their users. Interfaces speak in hashes and keys rather than in rights and responsibilities. What millions understood intuitively about bank cards or mobile apps—what it does, what can go wrong, who to call—becomes obscure when translated into code. The next leap in adoption will not come from faster chains or cheaper fees; it will come from *trust by design.*

Trust is not a mood. It is an outcome of structure, language, and responsiveness. Consumers trust systems that anticipate error, translate complexity, and offer remedies. This chapter begins with a simple proposition: people adopt what they can *see* and *explain.* When value, risk, and recourse are legible, participation follows. The blockchain world has spent a decade optimising proof; it must now optimise understanding.

Consider the analogy of a museum pass. It is more than a ticket; it is a compact. The holder knows what doors it opens, what benefits it confers, and for how long. A well-designed digital asset should feel the same. The act of onboarding—the first interaction where a user receives a token or joins a platform—defines the boundary between fascination and frustration. Transparent language about fees, limits, and rights builds dignity into participation. Hiding complexity does not simplify it; it merely defers panic.

The most effective consumer systems do not demand trust—they *earn* it through defaults that protect. In financial technology, that means setting sensible transaction limits, prompting confirmation before irreversible actions, and designing recovery flows for lost credentials. In digital ownership, it means *progressive disclosure*: revealing advanced functions only when a user is ready, never sooner. People are not failing to understand; they are failing to be understood.

At its best, trust design resembles urban planning. Streets need clear signs, not lectures on traffic theory. A newcomer should not crash before learning the rules. Sandboxed first transactions—small, reversible trials that teach mechanics—can replace the current industry habit of throwing users straight into markets with irreversible consequences. Good defaults protect not just funds but dignity.

Trust also flows sideways—from peers, not platforms. Reputation systems, when built carefully, serve as bridges between anonymity and accountability. Verified profiles, service histories, and visible dispute rates provide social proof where regulators have yet to tread. Airbnb learned this lesson long before blockchain: credibility online begins with traceable behaviour. Token markets must now absorb it. When newcomers see that a marketplace discloses seller records, resolution times, and refund ratios, fear turns into engagement. A system that measures reliability as carefully as it measures liquidity becomes self-stabilising.

Yet the industry's loudest actors have too often mistaken slogans for support. "Be your own bank" is stirring until a password is lost or a transfer misfires. Consumers do not crave slogans; they crave systems that answer emails, refund errors, and document processes. Human support remains a differentiator, not a weakness. When Coinbase introduced 24-hour live help in 2022, complaints fell sharply despite market volatility. The gesture was mundane, but it signalled something vital: professionalism is the ultimate innovation.

The quiet motif that threads through this chapter is visibility. Trust arises not from blind belief but from being able to *see*—to see fees, to see processes, to see accountability. Visibility transforms cryptography into comprehension. It bridges the psychological distance between consumer and code.

Across the sections ahead, we examine how value can be made visible without dumbing down: how interfaces translate cryptographic actions into meaningful promises; how defaults can prevent loss before law arrives; how off-chain reputation systems can anchor digital commitments; and how support structures—documentation, live agents, and refund paths—complete the social contract. Each theme advances a simple truth: if token economies want mass adoption, they must feel as safe and legible as public libraries or transport cards.

There is a moral undertone to this project. Designing for trust is designing for inclusion. Complexity has long functioned as a gatekeeper; clarity can be an equaliser. The first generation of blockchain tools served insiders fluent in code and risk. The next must serve citizens—people who expect fairness, recovery, and explanation.

The unresolved tension, of course, is how to balance empowerment with protection. Every safeguard adds friction; every freedom adds hazard. Too much automation breeds complacency, too much caution breeds stagnation. The art lies in defaults that teach before they constrain. The forward test is clear: when a new user enters, can they *see* the value, understand the cost, and recover from a mistake without reading a white paper?

Consumer adoption is not a marketing problem. It is a design philosophy rooted in empathy, transparency, and responsibility. Trust will not be granted to the next wave of digital products; it must be built, inspected, and maintained. The age of speculation made tokens exciting. The age of trust will make them ordinary—and only then, truly transformative.

Make value visible

In September 2021, the British Museum became the unlikely face of a digital experiment. Partnering with LaCollection, a blockchain-based platform in Paris, it issued limited-edition NFTs of Katsushika Hokusai's *The Great Wave off Kanagawa.* The project could have easily descended into the same speculative frenzy that tainted many early NFT launches. Yet the opposite happened. The museum framed each digital token not as an "investment opportunity" but as an extension of its ticketing and membership model—clear provenance, tiered access, defined benefits. Buyers understood what they were acquiring, what rights it conferred, and where the boundary of ownership lay. No promises of riches, only a guarantee of clarity. The drop sold out within hours. It worked because people could *see* the value.

This case illustrates a fundamental rule of adoption: comprehension precedes conviction. Consumers cannot trust what they cannot explain. The blockchain world has often mistaken transparency for legibility—publishing code while neglecting comprehension. A ledger may be open, yet still unreadable to those who are meant to benefit from it. *Visibility* here does not mean exposure; it means translation. The technical must become social. Keys, fees, and rights must be expressed in language that a museum visitor, a commuter, or a schoolteacher could repeat without hesitation. The motif throughout this essay is *the museum pass*—a simple, familiar object that makes ownership, access, and privilege tangible without a single line of code.

Show: a user downloads a digital wallet and is asked to store a 24-word recovery phrase. Name: abstraction failure. Explain: the wallet assumes literacy in cryptography rather than in consequences. Most users do not fear technology; they fear embarrassment. When asked to "secure private keys," many do not know what they risk losing. The implication is brutal: adoption stalls not because technology fails but because *interfaces humiliate.* Every complex action that requires explanation drives away potential participants.

To correct this, design must teach through metaphor, not instruction. The museum pass does this effortlessly. A pass signals duration ("valid for one year"), scope ("all exhibitions included"), and value ("priority entry"). It does not lecture on authentication protocols or ticketing architecture. Translating that sensibility to digital assets means making ownership a story, not a riddle. When a person acquires a token—whether for an artwork, a concert, or a service—they should see its economic and experiential boundaries at a glance: *what it grants, for how long, under what rules.* The right to transfer, the duty to pay fees, and the scope of access can all be visualised in one elegant interface.

In 2022, London start-up Vaulted Art applied this principle. It offered fractional digital ownership of physical artworks, displaying each buyer's rights as a "digital pass" rather than a "token balance." Users could see the percentage they owned, the income they were entitled to, and the schedule of exhibitions where the physical piece was shown. The interface did not conceal the blockchain; it humanised it. Users interacted with clarity, not code. Result: higher retention, fewer support tickets, and a measurable increase in referral purchases. Visibility, in this sense, became usability.

Contrast this with a counter-example: the 2021 launch of NBA Top Shot, by Dapper Labs. Despite early hype, many users struggled to understand what they had bought. Were they collectors of licensed clips or speculators in tradable rights? When withdrawals were delayed and secondary markets froze, outrage spread not because systems failed, but because expectations had never been articulated in plain language. A collectible became a liability. Reconcile this with our thesis: consumers forgive risk, not confusion. Systems collapse when the story of value fractures.

The museum pass motif reveals a deeper truth: value is not inherent in data but in the confidence to describe it. Show: a visitor holds a pass marked "premium member." Name: contextual privilege. Explain: the artefact gains meaning from social cues—others recognise its legitimacy. In digital design, this social signalling must be engineered through transparency. When a digital asset displays its provenance, terms, and usage rights within the interface, it builds context into code. Implication: visibility is not decoration; it is social infrastructure.

Two elements anchor this principle—*rights articulation* and *cost legibility*. Rights articulation ensures that ownership feels like agency, not obligation. A well-designed onboarding flow reveals three things at once: what you can do, what you cannot do, and where to seek recourse. For instance, the Australian start-up Synthetix redesigned its staking interface in 2023 to display potential yield alongside lock-up periods and risk exposure, linking every metric to audited data sources. Users reported higher trust and longer holding periods. This was not a victory of marketing; it was literacy.

Cost legibility, meanwhile, separates participation from exploitation. A system that hides fees breeds cynicism. Binance's user research in mid-2022 found that 38% of new retail users abandoned their first trade when confronted by gas fees they hadn't anticipated. Visibility, here, is not a regulatory obligation; it is behavioural engineering. When users can simulate outcomes—"If you stake £100, your likely cost is £1.20, your withdrawal lock-up is 48 hours"—participation rises because surprise vanishes. Transparency saves attention.

The core of this chapter's argument is not technological; it is psychological. Human beings adopt what they can explain to others. Richard Thaler's research on behavioural economics shows that perceived fairness drives usage more than absolute value (Thaler, *Misbehaving*, 2015). When a system shows its logic—why this fee exists, why this delay protects—the mind relaxes. The invisible ceases to feel arbitrary. Visibility is not mere education; it is pre-emptive empathy.

The best onboarding flows already practice this. Coinbase's "learn and earn" modules, introduced in 2020, rewarded users for completing short lessons explaining each asset's function. Simple, quantifiable literacy. In contrast, many decentralised applications still greet users with a wallet prompt and a hexadecimal address, assuming prior fluency. Show: an interface that requires trust before it earns it. Name: cognitive toll. Explain: adoption slows as users retreat to what they already understand. Implication: abstraction does not scale without translation.

We can measure visibility. Track *time to comprehension*—the minutes between a user's first interaction and their first confident transaction.

Track *self-reported understanding*—how many can articulate what their asset represents. Track *support dependency*—the number of tickets per 1,000 users in their first month. These are not vanity metrics; they are design diagnostics. A system that claims "mass adoption" without reducing these numbers is simply performing accessibility, not achieving it.

Yet even visibility has limits. Too much explanation can breed overwhelm. The art lies in *progressive disclosure*: start with meaning, layer detail as curiosity grows. The first screen shows "You now hold a one-year museum pass. Tap for details." Only upon tapping do advanced users see transaction hashes, signatures, and expiration schedules. Visibility must respect hierarchy. Not every truth deserves top billing.

There is also a cultural layer. Clarity depends on language that aligns with social context. A museum pass in London conveys prestige; a festival pass in Goa conveys community. Both are access artefacts, but their narratives differ. When digital systems ignore context, their metaphors fail. Wallets should speak the language of the communities they serve—artists, gamers, philanthropists—not that of engineers. The blockchain may be universal, but comprehension is local.

Consider a small but telling example: in 2022, the Estonian government launched NFT-based digital residency certificates. The certificates did not promise citizenship; they granted verifiable access to e-services. The interface emphasised "rights of use" rather than "ownership," averting legal confusion. It worked because it matched user expectations with administrative honesty. This is visibility at the civic level: citizens could see what they owned and what they did not.

The paradox of visibility is that it often hides effort. The smoother an onboarding experience feels, the harder it has worked behind the scenes—mapping flows, staging explanations, and translating cryptography into clarity. That invisible labour is the mark of serious design. It acknowledges that comprehension is not a feature; it is a right.

The unresolved tension lies in how much visibility a system can afford. Full transparency may expose users to overload or competitors to replication. Partial transparency risks mistrust. The test is pragmatic: if a newcomer cannot describe, within one sentence, what they have just bought and why it matters, visibility has failed.

The museum pass remains the quiet motif—a reminder that technology's most radical act is to make the invisible comprehensible. A pass is proof not of ownership alone but of narrative: this is yours, for now, under these terms. Make value visible, and the revolution will not need persuasion. It will need only tickets.

Defaults that protect

In 1959, in Gothenburg, Volvo engineer Nils Bohlin patented the three-point seatbelt and the company made the design freely available. They understood something quietly radical: safety should not rely on perfect behaviour. Design should carry the load. The belt became a default. Lives were saved because protection was opt-out, not opt-in. That lesson, born on Scandinavian roads, matters in token economies. Defaults quietly decide outcomes. They always have.

Digital ownership promises control, then exposes novices to irreversible clicks, opaque fees, and brittle recovery. A single mis-signed transaction can drain a wallet faster than you can say "confirm". The paradox is glaring: we have systems able to settle value worldwide in seconds, yet many first interactions are booby-traps masquerading as freedom. Sensible defaults are not paternalism; they are infrastructure. They reduce regret at scale.

What does a protective default look like? Start with behaviour, not slogans. Show: the first time a user sends value, the interface caps the amount to £10 and routes it through a simulated environment with real fees disclosed. Name: *sandboxed first transaction.* Explain: the user learns the sequence—review, confirm, finality—without catastrophic risk. Implication: comprehension rises; support tickets fall; trust compounds. The seatbelt quietly clicks.

Consider a bank that already treats defaults as policy. In 2018, Monzo in London launched a "gambling block" that customers could enable; switching it off required contacting support and waiting out a cooling-off period. It was deliberately inconvenient. The design worked because friction was placed *before* harm, not after. Token systems can adapt the pattern: a "high-risk action" block that requires a timed delay and extra confirmation to send funds to a fresh address or to sign permissions for an unknown contract. It is a brake. It prevents messes.

Now turn to wallets and signatures. In 2022 and 2023, hardware and software providers began disabling "blind signing" by default and promoting human-readable EIP-712 messages. Show: a device that refuses to approve an opaque blob, insisting on a structured prompt—token, amount, contract, expiry. Name: *transaction clarity.* Explain: the default reframes power; the user inspects meaning, not hex. Implication: scams lose their favourite trick—hiding intent in gibberish. Seatbelt, secured.

Protective defaults begin with *limits.* A wallet can cap outbound value for the first 72 hours after creation, raising ceilings as the user demonstrates fluency. A platform can default to withdrawal address whitelists with a 24-hour cooling period for new entries. A DAO can default to time-locked upgrades so that any change sleeps before it strikes. Limits are not mistrust; they are cadence. Systems that move quickly must also brake predictably.

Alerts are the second pillar. Not the shrill pop-ups that users learn to ignore, but layered signals tied to genuine risk. Show: a push notification that fires when permissions are requested for "unlimited spend"; an email when a new device logs in; an on-screen banner when gas spikes fivefold. Name: *risk-weighted alerts.* Explain: the system measures context—new counterparties, abnormal sizes, altered routes—and surfaces what matters. Implication: attention is conserved for moments that count.

Recovery closes the triad. People forget. Devices fail. Keys get lost. A system that celebrates self-custody must provide graduated paths back from error. Social recovery—assigning a set of trusted contacts whose combined approvals can restore a wallet—should be opt-in but discoverable. Hosted recovery—a vaulting service that can reissue access after rigorous checks—should be available without shame. The default here is *plurality*: no single lost factor should mean total loss, and no recovery path should be hidden behind jargon. Good systems make the painful path visible before pain appears.

The museum pass, our motif from the previous section, translates beautifully here. A pass has dates. It has zones. It has rules on the back. In a digital pass, limits, alerts, and recovery *are* those rules. "You can enter this wing three times per month." "You will be warned if you try to enter a restricted area." "If you lose this, go here with identification." The clarity is pre-emptive. The default is instruction, not mystique.

Two concrete examples show the craft. Kraken's Global Settings Lock (GSL) allows users to freeze critical account settings; any change triggers a 24-hour hold and alerts. It is a default for discipline: opt in once, then sleep better. A second example lies outside pure crypto but belongs to the same family: Apple's Screen Time "Ask to Buy" makes purchases by minors require approval; its genius is posture—it assumes protection first, and makes exception a deliberate act by an adult. Both designs encode a principle: *delay beats regret*. The visible outcome is fewer surprises and predictable processes when something goes wrong.

A credible counter-example, and a painful one, is the Wintermute exploit in September 2022. The London market maker lost around $160 million after an attacker exploited a weakness in the Profanity vanity-address tool. The failure was not only in code; it was in defaults. The system allowed address generation with insufficient entropy and no warnings that the choice carried structural risk. No "Are you sure?" No time-lock on moving newly generated keys to production. No obvious belt. Reconciling this to our thesis: when systems leave safety to individual vigilance under stress, they outsource fragility. Defaults should absorb it.

Progressive disclosure turns these mechanics into a humane experience. A first-time user sees meaning: "Send £5 to this friend." Only upon tapping "Details" do they see nonce, gas, chain ID. The second time, the limit rises and advanced toggles appear. The third time, the user may opt into power features: spending caps per dApp, fee-saving modes, custom alerts. The pattern respects learning curves. It avoids "expert mode by accident." It teaches without testing patience.

Sandboxed first transactions are the training wheels for irrevocable ledgers. Design the sandbox as a real path with fake stakes. Charge the real fee—tiny, disclosed—so the user experiences cost honestly. Display the result as if it were production: "You just sent 0.0001 ETH. Here's the hash. This is final." Then unwind it automatically to a faucet address and annotate the feed with "trial." The behaviour it drives is confidence. Measure it: *trial completion rate*; *drop-off before first real send*; *error rate after sandbox*. If designers cannot show these numbers improving, the sandbox is theatre.

Defaults that protect must be honest about trade-offs. Limits frustrate power users. Alerts can numb. Recovery can be abused if identity checks are lax. The remedy is not to remove safety, but to make it *graduated*. Show: three tiers of security—Basic, Standard, Advanced—with clear differences. In Basic, small limits, loud alerts, hosted recovery. In Standard, higher limits, quieter alerts, optional social recovery. In Advanced, high limits, terse alerts, no hosted recovery, hardware enforced. Name: *security tiers*. Explain: users choose friction knowingly, moving between tiers with cool-down periods, not on a whim. Implication: customisable safety avoids one-size-fits-none.

Metrics turn principles into practice. Track *false-positive rate* for alerts; if it climbs, tune thresholds. Track *time-to-notify* when a risky action is taken; every minute counts. Track *successful recovery rate* and *recovery time*; publish them. Track *first-transaction success rate*; redesign until novices succeed without help. A design claim without a number is a wish. The seatbelt metaphor survives because crash data did.

Language is a default too. "Seed phrase" terrifies; "recovery words" instructs. "Blind signing" confuses; "signing without seeing what you agree to" warns. "Gas" is jargon; "network fee" clarifies. We do not infantilise users by choosing clear words; we enfranchise them. Each word is a small belt across the laps of the uninitiated. Choose well.

Support absorbs the rest. Defaults reduce harms; support cleans what leaks through. Protective systems publish a clear answer to three questions before trouble starts. Who can reverse a mistake? How fast will they try? What evidence must a user provide? The defaults should route users to human help for high-risk moments. Live support is a cost. It is also a moat. Platforms that underwrite their defaults with competent people turn adoption into retention.

Designers must also encode *consent to friction.* It is easier to protect when the protected agree. Ask at the right time. After onboarding, not at the first screen, present a short pact: "To keep you safe, we'll limit your first send to £10, warn you about untrusted permissions, and require a 24-hour delay for new addresses. You can change this later. Agree?" The pattern reframes friction as care. Users accept belts when they understand the crash.

We can bring the museum pass motif back as a diagnostic. A pass is legible even when language fails—colours for tiers, icons for rights, dates for scope. Digital defaults should be equally visible. The send screen should show the belt: a small padlock icon for a cooled-down payment, a yellow triangle for an out-of-limits attempt, a blue badge for insured balances. Visual language carries memory.

The limits of defaults remain. Over-zealous controls may push experienced users to riskier tools. Under-built controls may invite endless "education" campaigns that blame victims for design. The balance is a craft. It will vary by audience, asset, and jurisdiction. But the test endures. Pick a new user. Watch their first ten minutes. Count unnecessary choices. Count surprise costs. Count moments where the system could have stopped a mistake and didn't. Then move defaults until the counts drop.

One last seatbelt click. The three-point design succeeded because it worked with bodies, not against them. It anchored at the right places. Protective defaults must do the same—anchor at the right moments:

before large transfers, before granting unlimited permissions, before changing destinations, before disabling protections. Put friction at the doors, not in the corridors. Make the safest path the path of least resistance.

The unresolved question is a live one. How much friction can a mass-market token system impose before users defect, and which protections should be *unskippable* regardless of preference? The forward test is blunt: if you removed your warning banners tomorrow, would losses spike, or would users stay safe because the important brakes live in code, not decoration? When the answer is the latter, the defaults are doing their job. The belt is worn. The ride continues.

Reputation and reviews

In October 2014, a modest apartment in Paris became a landmark for trust design. Airbnb, then six years old, faced a growing backlash over property damage and fraud. Its response was neither technological nor legal but reputational. The company introduced host verification, mandatory profile photos, and public reviews that linked behaviour to identity. Within a year, bookings recovered, complaints fell, and an invisible asset—credibility—was rebuilt. Airbnb did not discover trust; it operationalised it. A stranger's home became a product because reviews made risk legible.

Digital asset markets now face their own Airbnb moment. Tokens promise transparency yet trade in anonymity. Smart contracts enforce execution but cannot enforce character. A ledger can show what happened, not *why*. The gap between verified transaction and verified intent is the fault line where fear lives. Newcomers hesitate not because they doubt the technology, but because they doubt *people*. Off-chain reputation—histories, attestations, reviews—can stabilise on-chain promises. It converts code's rigidity into social confidence.

Show: a user contemplates buying a digital artwork for £1,000. Name: asymmetry. Explain: the seller is an alias, the smart contract is flawless, yet the buyer's comfort hinges on invisible cues—profile age, prior sales, dispute history. Implication: technology without context is sterile. The blockchain's greatest challenge is not engineering but sociology.

Reputation systems act as bridges between worlds: machine-verifiable events and human-meaningful assurance. A verified profile, linked to an established identity or attested by peers, offers a foundation. When OpenSea introduced verified badges in 2022 for high-volume creators and collections, fraudulent listings dropped sharply. The visible signal—blue check, green tick—compressed uncertainty. In contrast, platforms without verification suffered cascading scams as impostors exploited visual ambiguity. Visibility, once again, proved to be the truest form of security.

Yet reputation is not static data; it is living memory. Platforms such as eBay understood this decades ago. Its feedback score, introduced in 1996, transformed anonymous auctions into functioning markets by tying each transaction to a traceable identity. A single red mark could tank a seller's prospects. But the same rigidity that built confidence could also create tyranny. One unfair rating could haunt indefinitely. The system taught a crucial lesson: reputation must be auditable and, occasionally, forgivable.

Token markets can adopt that insight. Immutable ledgers need not imply immutable stigma. A fair reputation model distinguishes between *fault* and *noise*—between malicious behaviour and honest error. A protocol might, for example, weigh reviews by verified transaction volume or age of account, introducing gravity to experience. Gitcoin, a funding platform for open-source software, began weighting contributor reputations by peer endorsements rather than simple counts in 2021. The quality of attestation mattered more than its quantity. As a result, sybil attacks fell, and projects could identify reliable contributors without heavy KYC.

The motif threading through this piece is *memory with context.* A review alone is noise; a review anchored in provenance is narrative. Show: a marketplace displaying not just five-star averages but dispute resolution rates and median refund times. Name: *contextual credibility.* Explain: users see not a reputation score but an accountability pattern. Implication: the system converts past performance into present reassurance.

Metrics anchor these abstractions. A credible reputation protocol can measure *resolution latency* (average time to settle disputes), *reversal rate* (percentage of transactions later contested), and *verified participation ratio* (share of users with completed attestations). These numbers reveal health. For instance, in a 2023 audit of the decentralised freelance marketplace Braintrust, contracts with verified worker histories closed 35% faster and had 40% fewer conflicts. Reputation functioned as lubricant, reducing transaction friction without legal overreach.

But reputation, mishandled, can ossify into exclusion. Consider the Chinese social credit system—an extreme illustration of totalising trust metrics. By aggregating behavioural data into a single score, it collapses nuance into authority. It punishes context-free deviation. That dystopian version of visibility teaches a necessary restraint: reputation must empower choice, not dictate access. In token economies, decentralised identity frameworks must protect pluralism—the right to rebuild, to compartmentalise, to start fresh under new terms.

A credible limitation comes from DeFi governance tokens. In 2020–2022, projects such as Compound and Aave experimented with "reputation voting," giving greater influence to addresses with long participation records. It seemed logical—commitment equals credibility—but it privileged incumbents and discouraged newcomers. When Aave's governance review in August 2022 found stagnation in proposal diversity, it reversed course, introducing delegated representation to balance experience with renewal. Reputation had to breathe.

Reputation systems also intersect with dispute resolution. A marketplace that publishes transparent dispute metrics creates a feedback loop of deterrence. In 2021, NFT platform Rarible introduced public arbitration outcomes: when a buyer challenged a sale, the case and verdict were posted (with redacted identities). Fraud attempts dropped by 30%. The simple act of making enforcement visible replaced fear with foresight. Review culture, at its best, is a civic tool—a distributed ombudsman.

The quiet power of reviews lies in their narrative density. A string of text from a previous participant communicates more than a dashboard ever could. The difference between "arrived late" and "resolved fast" is tone; tone is trust. Natural-language feedback, when paired with cryptographic verification, humanises code. It reminds users that value flows through relationships. Tokens represent assets, but reviews represent *experience.*

There is also a pragmatic tension between privacy and proof. A verified review requires some disclosure, yet anonymity is a core appeal of decentralised systems. One emerging compromise is *zero-knowledge reputation*: users prove they meet certain conditions ("I have completed ten trades without dispute") without revealing specific identities. Projects such as Proof of Humanity and Sismo are exploring these architectures—where reputation becomes portable yet pseudonymous. It's memory without exposure. The implications are vast: systems that remember without naming can scale trust without surveillance.

Reputation's future is modular. A musician's token sale might rely on streaming royalties and fan endorsements; a lending protocol might weight repayment history; an NFT marketplace might blend peer ratings with off-chain identity verification. What unites them is a shared grammar of reliability. Whether expressed as stars, badges, or attestations, each form is a social prosthetic—compensating for what code alone cannot see.

The motif returns: memory with context. When a user inspects a marketplace profile, they should glimpse a living map of accountability—proofs, disputes, resolutions, endorsements. The goal is not perfection but predictability. The user's question—*can I trust this person?*—should meet structured evidence, not faith.

The challenge, of course, is equilibrium. Too little reputation breeds chaos; too much breeds caste. A healthy system must allow redemption and decay. Reputation should age, not ossify—like food with an expiry date, signalling freshness, not permanence. Designers can encode decay curves so that older events fade unless reaffirmed. It restores forgiveness to systems otherwise bound by eternal memory.

Off-chain reputation stabilises on-chain economies because it reintroduces humanity where automation removed it. Verification and history make digital trade legible to the cautious. Reviews transform statistical probability into social comfort. The unresolved question is timeless: how much of ourselves must we reveal to be trusted, and how much must systems forget for us to stay free? The test for token economies is not whether they can record everything, but whether they can remember wisely.

Support, not slogans

On 10 November 2021, Coinbase announced round-the-clock phone support for retail customers in the UK and US, after months of public frustration about unresolved account holds and slow responses during volatile trading days. The company's move was pragmatic, not ideological: when retail money is at stake, a human voice at 2 a.m. is not a luxury. It is table stakes. The announcement didn't change the code. It changed confidence. Support is a product. And in tokenised markets, where mistakes can be irreversible and vocabulary alien, the handrail matters as much as the stairs.

There is a paradox at the heart of decentralised services. They sell independence, then abandon users to cryptic error codes, Discord channels, and forum threads. The industry's rhetoric—be sovereign, be early, be brave—too often substitutes for engineering the calm, boring rituals of care that consumer finance has spent decades refining. People do not need pep talks. They need to know what will happen when something goes wrong, who will do what, and when. The motif for this section is the *handrail.* It must be there, sturdy, obvious, and used without drama. A handrail does not preach. It prevents falls.

Show: a customer's card is charged, the token never appears, the wallet shows nothing, and the gas meter ticks. Name: support gap. Explain: the platform has no single page that ties payment IDs to on-chain transaction hashes, no published service levels for crediting assets, and no clear route to a refund. Implication: even if the back-office fixes the issue, the experience teaches the user to fear the staircase. By contrast, when support is designed alongside the product, value feels visible at the moments of greatest stress.

Documentation is the first handrail. Not FAQs padded with marketing, but living operational manuals that map rights, fees, exceptions, and remedies. PayPal's Buyer Protection, formalised in the mid-2000s, became a growth engine not because of its logo but because its policy pages were surgical: eligible items, proof required, timelines, and outcomes. Amazon's A-to-Z Guarantee operates with similar clarity. Digital asset platforms can translate that ethos. A clean documentation set should tether every user action to a clear result and a named evidence artefact. "If a token you purchase does not arrive within X minutes, submit the payment reference and destination address here; our system will reconcile automatically; refunds are issued in Y hours to the source method." No flourish; just choreography.

Now the second handrail: live help. Not everything is solvable in text. In 2021–22, several major exchanges, including Coinbase and Kraken, expanded staffed channels—chat, phone, and dedicated incident lines—precisely because outages and identity checks were clogging email queues. The lesson is architectural. Complex issues do not queue well. They escalate well. Platforms that triage to human agents at the right moment—identity verification failure, suspected account compromise, frozen withdrawals—cut total resolution time because context travels faster by voice. A token transfer lost to a stuck nonce is not a ticket; it is a conversation.

Refunds and reversals form the third handrail, and the most contested. Blockchains settle as designed, but businesses settle as promised. A museum pass can be refunded even if the turnstile logs say "admitted". The friction in digital assets is not the chain's finality; it is the industry's reluctance to publish rules that let ordinary people recognise fairness. The practical route is to separate *token settlement* from *commercial settlement*. Platforms can commit to refunding fiat or stablecoin when failures are attributable to their systems—mispriced fees, misapplied limits, incorrect smart-contract parameters—while disclaiming responsibility for user-signed external approvals. The distinction is not legal advice; it is design clarity. It aligns expectations with the locus of control.

Two named examples show how handrails shift behaviour. First, after the NFT theft controversies of early 2022, OpenSea instituted a process to freeze flagged assets and strengthened its stolen-items policy, guiding users towards police reports and providing structured forms rather than ad hoc email exchanges. The outcomes were imperfect and contested, but the direction was correct: a visible procedure replaced public appeals. Second, UK challenger bank Monzo's 2018 "gambling block"—a toggle that adds deliberate friction and a cooling-off period to high-risk spend—demonstrated how support can be designed as a feature. Users do not read sermons; they use switches. Token platforms facing approval scams and signature traps can adopt the same posture: off by default is ideology; off with a named switch and a time delay is support.

A credible counter-example clarifies the limits. During the collapse of Celsius in June 2022, withdrawals were halted and support channels were quickly overwhelmed. The platform's terms of use, fee schedules, and risk disclosures existed, but the handrails were ornamental; they led nowhere a user could stand. The lesson is not that centralised services are doomed, but that support theatre—policies without power, dashboards without actions—becomes reputational kerosene during a crisis. Reconcile this to our thesis: support must be empowered by cash, authority, and process. Otherwise, it is a slogan waiting to burn.

What does serious support look like under the hood? Start with *tracing*. Every inflow and outflow should be reconciled through a single internal ledger that links three IDs: the payment reference, the wallet transaction hash, and the user account. Give users a "where's my asset?" tracker that renders those joins in human language. "We received your £250 at 14:03. We broadcast your on-chain transaction at 14:05. Average confirmation time on this network is nine minutes. If you see nothing by 14:20, click to open a refund investigation." Support staff should see the same timeline plus machine-generated anomaly flags—gas too low, nonce conflict, pool congestion—so they can act, not apologise.

Next, *service levels*. Publish them, meet them, and pay when you miss them. If a platform claims to credit deposits within fifteen minutes 99% of the time, it should back the claim with an SLA: when it fails, users receive a fee credit or a small goodwill payment automatically. This is not largesse; it is a commitment device that turns reliability into contract. Airlines learned long ago that on-time performance feels real when compensation is automatic. Digital finance can do the same.

Third, *dispute handling*. Token markets will attract grifters for as long as assets have prices. The way to protect newcomers is not to infantilise them but to stage disputes cleanly. Publish a two-tier model: a rapid, internal review based on logs and receipts with a 72-hour decision target, followed by an optional independent arbitration route for material sums. The UK Jurisdiction Taskforce's Digital Dispute Resolution Rules (2021) offer a blueprint for code-linked arbitration; they permit awards to be executed by smart contract. Add transparency without doxxing: publish anonymised dispute stats—rate of disputes per 1,000 trades, median resolution time, percentage upheld versus rejected. Numbers calm nerves. They show that the handrail is bolted into a wall.

Support must also reach beyond tickets. Good documentation and live help rely on *diagnostics* that product teams maintain. Runbooks for common failure modes—stuck transactions, stale oracles, failed NFT mints—should be written in the same tone as consumer pages and referenced by support. Link each to a real-time status dashboard that shows incidents, impact, and steps taken, with clear timestamps. The first effect is practical: fewer duplicate tickets. The second is cultural: a platform that narrates its own failures earns permission to recover.

The handrail metaphor extends to identity recovery. People lose keys. Devices break. The absolutist line—"lose your seed, lose your funds"—may be technically pure, but it is economically naïve for mass markets. A layered posture is possible without centralising the world. Offer *graduated recovery*: hosted recovery (rigorous identity checks; slow but available), social recovery (pre-designated guardians who can help restore access), and recovery-resistant modes (for users who opt out). Explain each choice plainly at onboarding and let users switch tiers after cool-down periods. Support teams then operate playbooks: documents needed, checks performed, timeframes promised. Publish completion rates and median times. Treat recovery as a capability, not a confession.

Language is support. "Seed phrase" intimidates; "recovery words" instructs. "Blind signing" mystifies; "sign without seeing what you agree to" warns. Move jargon down the page. Put meaning first. A surprising share of "support" is the labour of translation. Platforms that invest in words lower their total ticket volume because users repair their own confusion. Every screen is a leaflet; write it that way.

There is also an ethical dimension. Some of the most harm-reducing support is invisible: pre-emptive warnings and nudges that cost conversion in the moment and save reputations over months. Flag first-time users attempting high-risk approvals with an interstitial that forces a scroll through *what this permission means* in plain English, with a link to revoke later. Add a "call me back" button on any screen that touches identity or large withdrawals; staff it properly. Audit the drop-offs and the complaints. If the numbers are stable and trust improves, keep the friction. If they are punitive without benefit, adjust. Support is an experiment with a ledger.

A consumer business earns the right to minimalism only after it has proved it can resolve messes. That proof is empirical. Track *first contact resolution* (what percentage of issues are solved in a single interaction), *time to first human* (minutes from opening a high-risk ticket to speaking to a person), *refund issuance time* (median hours for eligible cases), and *post-incident satisfaction* (a short, single-question survey three days after resolution, not immediately). Post the numbers quarterly. They are not marketing. They are the constitution of care.

Two more named sketches show how support builds moats. In 2020, Singapore's regulated exchange ADDX built a "concierge onboarding" for first-time investors, mixing guided calls with screen-sharing. The compliance lift paid back in lower abandonment and fewer KYC back-and forths. Fewer tickets. Faster funds. In 2019, Dyson's no-quibble returns policy for online sales—plainly documented, fast, and generous—turned a high-consideration purchase into a predictable experience. Both cases demonstrate the same principle: when customers can anticipate the downside, they commit to the upside.

Token platforms often protest that such systems are costly. They are. So were seatbelts, call centres, and clear returns policies when first introduced. But they compound value in the only currency that keeps consumer businesses alive: earned forgiveness. A platform that resolves one crisis well retains tens of quiet customers who never tweet. The alternative—ideology as customer care—earns applause from insiders and silence from the mainstream.

The handrail motif returns. Good support is not loud. It is obvious, polished, and sturdy; it blends into the staircase. Users touch it without thinking, trusting that it will hold. The unresolved question is how far to go. How much human help should a protocol promise before it becomes a company in disguise? Where should refunds begin and end in a world of final settlement? The forward test is simple and merciless. Pick the last five material failures. For each, ask: who wrote to whom, what was promised, how long it took, and what the user would say now. If those answers are crisp and boring, the handrail is in place. If they are vivid, emotive, and unresolved, you have slogans where support should be.

Chapter 8
Web3 Business Models That Endure

In April 2021, when Beeple's *Everydays: The First 5000 Days* sold for $69 million at Christie's, headlines claimed the arrival of a new creator economy. Yet within months, the market that had inflated around token drops and speculative hype began to hollow. Prices crashed. Discords quietened. The paradox was plain: blockchains had given artists permanence, but not livelihoods. The infrastructure was sound; the business models were brittle. The problem was not technology. It was imagination—an excess of novelty and a deficit of endurance.

The oldest rule of commerce still applies: any market that cannot support maintenance will collapse into theatre. From tulips to tech stocks, speculation has always outpaced utility. The question that drives this chapter is not how to mint the next token, but how to make value persist after the first sale. How do digital economies earn the slow revenue that funds continuity—hosting, updates, support—when everything else trades at light speed? How does a decentralised system prove that sustainability can be more radical than hype?

Endurance begins when token economies start behaving like real businesses. It starts with recurring revenue, clear costs, and honest service. The platforms that survive the next cycle will not rely on token drops or viral spikes. They will pair digital assets with subscriptions, analytics, curation, and care. We have seen the first prototypes already. Mirror's *writing NFTs* linked publishing with patronage, but its longer-term strength lay in offering creators analytics and distribution tools—a tools-plus-membership model disguised as a marketplace. The token was a receipt, not the product. Value emerged not from scarcity but from sustained service.

Two-sided markets must grow out of the adolescent phase where they reward extraction and call it alignment. Tokens can beautifully synchronise incentives between creators and fans—when fees are capped, discovery rotates, and governance is transparent. When they are not, they reproduce the worst of Web2: pay-for-visibility loops that exhaust both sides. The stronger platforms will impose discipline, not libertarian purity. Fee caps act as trust signals. Rotating discovery slots mirror fair-trade markets, ensuring that attention—like liquidity—circulates rather than concentrates. These are not anti-capitalist moves. They are anti-rentier ones.

A subtler evolution is unfolding in how value compounds. Data, once fenced behind corporate APIs, is being reconceived as a commons. The proof is visible in projects such as Lens Protocol and OpenSea's open metadata repositories. Shared registries let independent developers build extensions and analysis tools that, in turn, reinforce the parent ecosystem. Instead of lock-in, they achieve depth. Open data transforms a single product into a platform and a platform into a field. It turns interoperability into a moat. In the Web3 economy, defensibility will not come from secrecy but from participation.

Enduring models also understand time. Too many token roadmaps read like press releases disguised as plans—grand gestures, unclear sequencing, no cadence of delivery. The market punishes them the same way it punishes theatrical IPOs that fail to ship. The alternative is mundane but powerful: ship in increments. Test nets, pilot cohorts, staged unlocks. Every milestone becomes a social contract between builders and holders. The discipline is measurable: timelines met, updates verified, expectations managed. Projects that respect this rhythm reduce "sell-the-news" cliffs because they build a habit of progress, not a hope of miracles.

The motif that runs through all these ideas is *maintenance as meaning*. Durable business models make maintenance visible. They reward it, report it, and ritualise it. In the service economy, continuity is currency. In decentralised economies, it is salvation. The logic of Web3 must mature from "mint and exit" to "serve and stay." That shift will define which tokens become tools and which fade into footnotes.

The chapters ahead map this maturation. We explore how sustainable Web3 ventures pair tokens with service revenue, how two-sided markets can balance creation and discovery, how open data compounds ecosystem value, and how honest roadmaps rebuild trust. The thread connecting them is not ideology but responsibility—the recognition that decentralisation without durability is self-defeating.

By the end of this chapter, a pattern emerges: the businesses that endure do not promise revolution; they practise reliability. They treat users not as speculators but as stakeholders in a continuing service. The promise of Web3, once stripped of slogans, is simple and old. Build something worth paying for twice: once to join, and again to stay. The rest is noise.

Revenue beyond token drops

In March 2022, the artist collective *PleasrDAO* raised over $4 million to purchase the unreleased Wu-Tang Clan album *Once Upon a Time in Shaolin* and tokenised fractional ownership among its members. The spectacle made headlines. Yet by year's end, most secondary trades had stalled, and the collective shifted focus from trading to curation, archiving, and building a platform for rights management. The episode distilled a hard truth: a token drop can ignite attention, but it cannot sustain a business. Once the crowd disperses, maintenance begins. The difference between a fleeting sale and an enduring enterprise lies in whether tokens are paired with services that create recurring value.

The first generation of Web3 projects mistook monetisation for business modelling. A token drop mimicked revenue but acted more like a one-time crowdfunding campaign: cash up front, liability deferred. Without a structure for ongoing delivery—updates, analytics, community moderation, or user support—the proceeds became a mirage. As the 2021–2022 cycle proved, capital raised through token offerings often evaporated faster than it accrued because it lacked the discipline of recurring demand. The essential lesson was not financial but operational: the token is a receipt, not the product.

The more sustainable pattern emerging across Web3 resembles a hybrid: a *tools-plus-membership bundle.* Instead of selling exposure to volatility, creators and platforms sell access to enduring capability. A platform issues tokens as access credentials to services—data analytics, creative tools, curated discovery channels—and then monetises ongoing usage. This is not ideology. It is customer retention through value that repeats. When Mirror, the decentralised publishing platform, introduced its *Writing NFT* model in 2021, it quietly coupled the token with tangible utilities: content analytics, distribution feeds, and collaboration tools. The token certified authorship, but the subscription funded continuity. The model blended symbolic ownership with service-based revenue—the old economics of software-as-a-service translated into the language of blockchain.

Show: a digital artist wants to fund long-term archiving and community interaction. Name: *service wrapping*. Explain: instead of a one-off NFT sale, they issue a tiered membership token granting holders storage, analytic dashboards, and curated exhibitions updated monthly. Implication: their revenue now aligns with ongoing delivery. Each renewal becomes a proof of relevance. The motif here is *maintenance as value*. Maintenance is not overhead; it is product.

History offers analogues. When Adobe shifted from perpetual licences to Creative Cloud subscriptions in 2013, many predicted a backlash. Instead, recurring revenue rose from $4 billion to over $17 billion by 2021 (Adobe Annual Report, 2021). The logic was simple: creatives do not buy software; they rent reliability. The same psychology applies to decentralised services. Tokens that confer identity or ownership are static; tokens that bundle dynamic utility—storage, updates, analytics—sustain trust through predictability. Subscription logic is not antithetical to decentralisation; it is its stabiliser.

Two recent examples show this trajectory. First, *Zora*, a protocol for minting and auctioning digital media, introduced Zora Network in June 2023 as a layer-two solution that subsidises minting fees. Revenue now flows from infrastructure fees and API access for developers—a steady service base—rather than from hype cycles. Second, *Royal*, the music-royalty marketplace founded by DJ 3LAU, began bundling its tokens with data dashboards that show streaming analytics and royalty forecasts to holders. The value proposition shifted from speculation on resale to participation in transparent accounting. Both platforms learned the same discipline: serve the activity, not the asset.

A credible counter-example clarifies the limits. *LooksRare*, launched in January 2022, distributed large token incentives to attract traders from OpenSea. For a few months, its daily volume surpassed $400 million. By June, 95% of that traffic had vanished. The rewards farmed activity but not loyalty; the model mistook cash flow for commitment. Its failure was diagnostic: rewards attract velocity, but only service retains gravity. Reconcile this to the thesis: enduring business models reward usage, not presence.

What, then, constitutes a healthy revenue architecture for tokenised enterprises? First, transparency around service tiers—how much a user pays, for what, and when. Second, continuous delivery: regular updates, measurable reliability, public uptime. Third, contextual analytics—tools that tell users not only what they own but how it performs. Consider *Sound.xyz*, the music platform that pairs NFT releases with fan data dashboards. It treats listening as engagement, not speculation. Artists learn where their audience is, which tracks convert, and which collectors return. That intelligence is the subscription's value. Tokens become passports to insight, not casino chips.

A practical pattern is emerging: the *creator stack*. Creators anchor revenue around three concentric layers—token ownership (proof of belonging), tools and analytics (proof of improvement), and community curation (proof of attention). The bundle mirrors the evolution of Patreon and Substack, which grew not by amplifying scarcity but by scaffolding consistency. The Web3 analogue adds programmable incentives but keeps the economic logic intact: subscriptions outlive hype.

Metrics matter. A sustainable platform can measure recurring transaction ratio (percentage of revenue from renewals versus one-off drops), active-to-passive holder ratio (how many token holders use associated services monthly), and churn rate (percentage of members lapsing within a quarter). These are old instruments from SaaS, but they discipline token projects into realism. A creator economy that treats retention as its heartbeat becomes antifragile. The platform that publishes its retention rate signals maturity; the one that hides behind token price signals fragility.

The motif of maintenance returns. Maintenance, properly designed, compounds. Each update—whether a software patch, an analytics improvement, or a curated drop—reaffirms trust. It also widens the moat. Users accumulate workflow dependency, not ideological loyalty. When *Canva* added AI-powered design suggestions in 2023, its users did not need convincing; they had already built habits. Web3 tools can achieve the same stickiness by making tokens an instrument of service continuity: a key that unlocks evolving capability.

Yet there is tension. Subscriptions introduce recurring costs that challenge the decentralised ethos of one-time ownership. Critics argue that recurring fees recreate rent-seeking. The response is structural: transparency and proportionality. If fees fund visible maintenance—open-source development, audits, or uptime guarantees—they become a social contract. When *Arweave* introduced its "permanent storage fee" model in 2020, it blended one-off payments with a treasury that funds perpetual hosting. Users pay once; the system manages forever. It is not "free," but it is fair.

Another design question is governance. When revenue shifts from drops to service, who controls pricing and quality? Some projects experiment with token-holder councils that approve feature releases or pricing adjustments. Others maintain central stewardship with periodic audits. The most promising hybrid appears in decentralised service networks like *Livepeer*, where operators earn fees for streaming bandwidth, but protocol parameters—like inflation and fee splits—are voted on collectively. The model mirrors a co-operative utility: distributed ownership, unified standards, predictable income.

This new discipline also reshapes marketing. A business sustained by subscriptions must justify value every month. That accountability curbs hype. Token drops may sell the future; subscriptions must serve the present. The result is a healthier relationship between narrative and reality. The platforms that survive the next decade will not promise revolutions; they will demonstrate routines. Their pitch decks will show renewal rates, not Discord growth. Their core users will be customers, not "community."

A quiet but profound cultural shift is underway. As speculation fades, creators rediscover the oldest joy in commerce: building relationships that last longer than the first sale. The Web3 movement, once intoxicated by novelty, is maturing into service economies that sound almost traditional—billing, maintenance, customer care—but executed through transparent, programmable ledgers. The glamour of tokenisation gives way to the dignity of continuity.

The unresolved tension remains philosophical. Can a decentralised economy sustain itself through the very mechanisms—subscriptions, contracts, updates—that once defined centralised platforms? Or must it invent entirely new rhythms of obligation and reward? The answer will determine which Web3 ventures endure. The token drop was the spark. The service is the fire. The question now is who will tend it.

Two-sided markets

In February 2023, Blur overtook OpenSea as the largest NFT marketplace by trading volume, pulling over $400 million in weekly transactions. Its rise was not driven by better design or cheaper minting. It was fuelled by reward points—tokens distributed to traders for activity. For a few weeks, the strategy looked like genius. Then, the metrics turned hollow. As analytics from Nansen showed by April, 70% of Blur's trades came from a handful of "farmers" flipping assets back and forth to harvest rewards. Volume was up; value was not. The marketplace had succeeded in building activity but failed to build an economy. The problem was not liquidity—it was alignment.

Two-sided markets, whether in art, rides, or code, live or die by how they balance their sides. When one side extracts too much, the other withers. This equilibrium problem has existed since 1633, when Amsterdam's first tulip traders tried to stabilise prices through capped commissions. It resurfaced in 2007, when Apple's iTunes Store set its standard 30% revenue share—a number both resented and stabilising. In Web3, where creators and collectors interact through programmable tokens, the stakes are sharper. The promise is that incentives can be designed into the system itself; the risk is that they can also be gamed at scale. The quiet motif here is the *market mirror*: tokens reflect the values of their platform design. What they reward, they reproduce.

Show: a marketplace introduces a creator token that grants early supporters fee discounts and access to drops. Name: incentive mirroring. Explain: every incentive—staking yield, royalty split, visibility algorithm—broadcasts a moral signal about what behaviour counts. Implication: when trading rewards dominate, speculation replaces curation; when discovery and engagement rewards dominate, quality compounds. The task of Web3 business models is to engineer this mirror so that it reflects contribution, not extraction.

Fee design is the first mirror. Platforms that cap fees at sustainable but humane levels—typically between 2% and 5%—signal fairness to both sides. OpenSea's 2.5% commission became a market standard precisely because it was low enough to encourage participation yet high enough to sustain operations. When Blur cut fees to zero during its incentive wars, it gained market share but lost trust. Fees are not taxes; they are trust contracts. They tell participants how the house sustains itself. Cap them transparently, publish their use, and rotate their beneficiaries, and the marketplace becomes legible again.

Rotating discovery slots are the second mirror. Every platform—Spotify, YouTube, TikTok, or Zora—controls an invisible currency called *attention allocation*. In 2022, the music platform Audius experimented with rotating feature slots based on token-weighted votes. The results were uneven but instructive. Rotation forced diversity; it surfaced mid-tier artists and reduced the power of incumbents. The broader implication is profound: algorithmic curation can be treated as a governance domain, not a black box. In a decentralised environment, rotation restores fairness without flattening merit.

Name another case: the NFT platform *Foundation* introduced "Collections" in 2021, where curators earned a share of transaction fees from artworks they onboarded. This turned discovery into labour, not luck. Yet even here, concentration appeared—top curators captured most fees. The counter-example demonstrates that even well-meant alignment mechanisms can harden into hierarchies. The reconciliation lies in rotation again: limit how long curators or collectors can hold privileged slots. Design expiry into power. The old problem of gatekeeping becomes a question of cadence.

A healthy two-sided market, whether tokenised or not, functions as a flywheel: creators attract collectors; collectors reward creators; and both grow the platform. But in tokenised systems, that flywheel spins faster—and can overheat. The speculative era of 2021–2022 showed what happens when both sides mistake liquidity for loyalty. Projects that relied solely on transaction mining, like LooksRare, inflated volumes but failed to cultivate repeat buyers. By contrast, slower systems—like *SuperRare's* invite-only artist model—sacrificed initial scale for curatorial quality. They capped minting rights and limited exposure windows. It was not democratic, but it was sustainable. The contrast underlines the moral physics of markets: attention must circulate, not concentrate.

The design levers available to Web3 architects are unusually rich. Tokens can carry programmable royalties that split revenue between creator, curator, and collector. They can encode caps on resale frequency or require a time delay before re-listing—mechanisms that slow down speculation and emphasise holding. Imagine a "cooling period" NFT, which must be held for seven days before resale, or a rotating discovery algorithm that reweights visibility daily across new creators. These features sound mundane but perform a political function: they embed equilibrium into code.

Metrics again reveal integrity. A fair two-sided market should track the *creator-to-collector revenue ratio* (what proportion of total value accrues to the original makers) and the *repeat buyer rate* (percentage of collectors who purchase from the same creator more than once). These are not aesthetic numbers; they are health indicators. A marketplace with 80% of value flowing to traders and only 20% to producers is extractive, however lively its Discord.

The *market mirror* motif reappears here. Each fee schedule, reward programme, and discovery rule reflects the moral assumptions of its designers. If they treat users as arbitrageurs, users will behave that way. If they treat them as patrons, patronage emerges. A well-built marketplace must therefore cultivate scarcity of exposure, not of content. Scarcity of attention—engineered through deliberate pacing and rotation—creates a rhythm where discovery feels earned, not auctioned.

One can trace this logic back to older markets. In 1840s Paris, the Salon's jury rotated its members every two years to prevent artistic monopolies. In 1950s Tokyo, the Kabuki theatres introduced rotation of headliners to balance fame and freshness. These systems did not abolish hierarchy; they refreshed it. The same pattern belongs in Web3: rotate curators, rotate visibility, and treat fairness as a renewable resource.

There is, however, a counter-tension worth naming. Too much rotation risks instability. Algorithms that over-randomise discovery frustrate both creators and collectors, eroding the sense of meritocracy. Predictability, not perfect equality, sustains trust. Spotify's own attempts to equalise discovery through algorithmic serendipity in 2019 briefly depressed engagement because listeners felt disconnected from taste cues. The lesson applies directly: rotation must be bounded by coherence. Fairness without relevance collapses into noise.

A further frontier is collective governance over market rules. DAOs and protocol-based marketplaces can experiment with dynamic fee caps—adjusting rates based on transaction volume or user tenure. For example, a marketplace could set fees at 5% for the first trade, declining to 2% after a certain number of repeat transactions. This structure rewards loyalty without undermining revenue. Similarly, discovery slots could rotate through a transparent randomiser seeded by wallet participation rather than token weight, ensuring small collectors and new creators have an equal shot. These are not utopian tweaks; they are incremental mechanisms that formalise fairness.

What remains constant is the need for *symmetry*. A two-sided market that earns trust does so through visible reciprocation. Every action by one side must generate benefit for the other, not merely for the platform. That principle differentiates patronage from speculation, and marketplaces from casinos. Fee caps, rotation, and disclosure rules are instruments of this symmetry. They make fairness inspectable.

The unresolved question—the forward test—is whether the architects of Web3 marketplaces can resist the gravity of extraction once capital flows in. Token systems promise alignment, yet every alignment mechanism is vulnerable to its own parody. Reward loyalty too heavily, and you breed entitlement; rotate too frequently, and you erode continuity. The design challenge is to craft markets that breathe—concentrating attention just long enough to create value, then dispersing it before it ossifies.

In that rhythm lies the future of creative exchange. Tokens are mirrors. The question is not whether they can align creators and fans. It is whether we have the discipline to polish the mirror instead of gazing into it.

Data as a commons

In August 2004, in a small office near Clerkenwell, London, Steve Coast launched *OpenStreetMap*. Frustrated by the proprietary stranglehold on geographic data, he began inviting volunteers to upload GPS traces of their local streets. Two decades later, that shared map underpins logistics systems for companies as different as Meta, the UN World Food Programme, and Apple. Coast's principle was disarmingly simple: data gains value when others can build upon it. Each contribution becomes a foundation for the next. The map does not monetise exclusivity; it monetises participation. That is the quiet revolution at the heart of the token economy: shared registries that compound value through openness rather than ownership.

Web3 inherits this insight and encodes it. Tokens can serve not merely as tradable assets but as entries in a common ledger—registries that define provenance, authenticity, and use rights. Yet the commercial instinct to close what was opened remains strong. Many blockchain projects repeat the proprietary logic they claimed to replace. Platforms hoard metadata, restrict APIs, or tie access to premium tokens, mistaking scarcity for strength. The paradox is that data wants depth, not walls. When datasets are shared, they generate ecosystems; when fenced, they decay. The motif here is *the registry as soil*: fertile only when exposed to air and interaction.

The logic of shared metadata is already visible in practice. *Ethereum's ERC-721* standard, introduced in 2018, formalised a structure for non-fungible tokens: each token references metadata—title, image, creator—that can be accessed and extended by third parties. This standardisation enabled interoperability. Platforms like OpenSea, Rarible, and Zora could read the same records without custom integrations. The standard turned a marketplace into a protocol, creating network effects that no single actor could replicate alone. By 2022, over 80% of NFT collections used some variant of ERC-721. The data itself—ownership history, transaction logs, and metadata—became a public commons, powering analytics dashboards, provenance trackers, and fraud detectors. The innovation was not speculative; it was infrastructural.

Consider *Lens Protocol*, launched in 2022 by Aave Companies as a decentralised social graph. Every post, follow, and comment exists as open data, readable by any developer. This allowed independent teams to create companion apps—ranging from analytics tools to moderation filters—without permission. Each new tool strengthened Lens rather than competing with it. The platform's moat came not from exclusion but from extensibility. In economic terms, Lens inverted the platform playbook: instead of locking data behind a single interface, it made the interface optional.

The measurable effects of such openness are profound. When OpenSea began publishing its metadata and event streams in 2020, over thirty independent analytics platforms emerged within a year. One of them, *Dune Analytics*, built a business on querying that public data, attracting over 200,000 users by 2023. OpenSea gained, too:

better visibility, external fraud monitoring, and community trust. Shared data did not dilute value—it multiplied it. The moat was not in secrecy but in the network of interpreters that formed around it.

Contrast that with *NBA Top Shot*, launched by Dapper Labs in 2020. The platform centralised its metadata and gated access to APIs, effectively turning its NFTs into decorative receipts. When a third-party developer attempted to create a trading dashboard, they were denied access. The marketplace peaked within months and then stagnated. By 2023, trading volume had fallen by more than 90%. Its problem was not licensing; it was isolation. Data trapped inside a single interface suffocates. The counter-example reinforces the principle: shared registries are not anti-commercial—they are anti-fragile.

Open data does introduce risks. Exposure invites spam, duplication, and parasitic extraction. Projects like *OpenSea* have struggled with "metadata scrapers" cloning collections to lure buyers. But openness is not the absence of discipline. It requires governance that defines how data can be reused and attributed. The Ethereum Name Service (ENS) provides one model. By encoding rules for naming and renewal into smart contracts, it creates a public utility whose data can be accessed freely but not impersonated. The system works because it defines stewardship, not censorship.

The deeper implication is philosophical. The token economy redefines property not as possession but as participation. A creator's metadata—the title, image, transaction record—becomes a building block for others' creativity. Each reuse reinforces the original through attribution and analytics. This recursive enrichment mirrors the history of other digital commons: the GNU General Public License in software (1989), Creative Commons in culture (2001), and Wikipedia in knowledge (2001). Each movement began as resistance to enclosure and matured into infrastructure. Tokens, properly designed, extend that lineage.

The value of a shared registry can be measured in secondary innovation. Open metadata turns every record into an API. A song NFT that publishes its streaming rights openly invites remixing tools, royalty dashboards, and marketplace integrations. A real-estate token that exposes transaction metadata enables valuation models and risk indices. The ecosystem deepens as each layer reads from the same source of truth. Lock-in becomes obsolete; depth becomes defensibility.

There are limits. Open data does not guarantee equitable participation. Large actors can dominate shared registries through superior infrastructure. In 2022, several analytics firms began selling proprietary dashboards built entirely from public blockchain data, effectively re-enclosing the commons at the interpretive layer. The answer lies not in retreating from openness but in designing reciprocal incentives. Projects like *Ocean Protocol* experiment with data tokens that reward those who contribute verified datasets to a common pool. The lesson: openness needs economics, not charity.

Governance of these commons will define their longevity. The critical design question is how to balance freedom of use with accountability for misuse. Historical analogues suggest the answer lies in stewardship rather than policing. OpenStreetMap relies on a volunteer Data Working Group that mediates disputes without restricting access. Similar models could apply to Web3 registries—councils that audit metadata integrity or flag fraudulent tokens while keeping the base layer permissionless. The ideal is not purity but pragmatism: a commons that self-heals without freezing innovation.

Metrics again expose reality. Ecosystem depth can be quantified by the *derivative-to-original ratio*—how many independent applications or analyses build on a given dataset. Ethereum's open registry supports thousands of such derivatives; closed NFT platforms support none. That ratio is the measure of vitality. The more derivatives, the richer the soil.

The motif of soil returns. Shared data, like soil, thrives under light and use. Each layer of cultivation—indexers, dashboards, marketplaces—adds texture, fertility, and resilience. Lock it away, and it hardens into rock. Web3's competitive edge lies not in owning the field but in tending it.

The unresolved tension is whether capital can coexist with the commons. Venture-backed platforms still crave defensible moats;

open registries resist enclosure. The forward test is this: can a protocol earn profit from participation without closing the gates? The answer will decide whether the next generation of networks grows like forests or fortresses.

Roadmaps users can trust

In September 2022, *Ethereum* executed its long-awaited Merge, transitioning from proof-of-work to proof-of-stake—a technical migration that had been in motion for nearly seven years. The anticipation was immense, the price swings theatrical, yet the event itself passed with calm precision. No major downtime, no chaos, no unkept promises. Vitalik Buterin, Ethereum's co-founder, called it "one of the smoothest large-scale upgrades in crypto history." What made the Merge different from the countless blockchain milestones that collapsed under their own hype was not technological brilliance alone but cadence: a rhythm of shipping, testing, and communicating that built trust layer by layer. Long before the code went live, the community had lived through its rehearsal—testnets, shadow forks, bug bounties, and staged unlocks. The Merge worked because its builders earned credibility through increments.

Web3 is filled with unkept promises. The language of "revolution" comes easily; the discipline of roadmaps does not. Too often, token projects announce sweeping visions without scaffolding them into verifiable steps. When those steps fail to materialise—or worse, when they materialise all at once—the consequence is not merely technical failure but moral erosion. The crash of *TerraUSD* in May 2022 illustrated this brutally. A stablecoin that promised mathematical certainty collapsed in days, erasing $40 billion in value. Beneath the financial architecture lay a simpler flaw: a roadmap that treated confidence as a substitute for contingency.

A trustworthy roadmap is not a marketing artefact. It is a social contract between builders and participants, a declaration of sequencing. Each milestone must represent not aspiration but commitment, each delay not concealment but disclosure. The motif that recurs throughout these disciplined projects is *cadence*: a measured, audible beat that tells participants where they are and what comes next. The best roadmaps build momentum not through promises but through predictability.

Consider *Polkadot's* launch sequence between 2020 and 2021. Rather than releasing a full multi-chain network at once, it staged activation in six phases—first validating governance, then introducing transfers, then parachains. Each phase was tested in public on Kusama, its "canary network," a high-risk environment explicitly designed for failure. By decoupling experimentation from production, Polkadot transformed risk into rehearsal. Each milestone generated evidence, not speculation. The lesson is structural: when the audience can see the scaffolding, trust migrates from personality to process.

Another benchmark came from *Arbitrum*, the layer-two scaling project for Ethereum, which launched its mainnet in August 2021. Before allowing unrestricted use, the team opened a series of test environments where developers could deploy dApps under controlled load. Bugs were rewarded, not punished. When Arbitrum's DAO later voted to unlock governance tokens in 2023, the event passed without the usual "sell-the-news" cliff that has haunted so many launches. Incremental shipping had inoculated expectations. Trust, measured here, took the form of stability: token volatility remained under 5% during the first week post-launch—a rarity in decentralised finance.

By contrast, *EOS*, launched in June 2018 after a $4 billion initial coin offering, exemplified the opposite. Its roadmap promised a decentralised operating system, global throughput, and democratic governance—all at once. Within months, governance froze amid voting cartels and unclear accountability. The network was functional but faith was gone. EOS did not fail because of poor code; it failed because of compressed cadence. When everything is delivered at once, nothing feels earned.

A roadmap users can trust balances transparency with tempo. It must show not only *what* will happen but *when* and *why that order matters*. Incrementalism in blockchain is not bureaucracy—it is epistemology. Each stage validates not just functionality but belief. This is why testnets and pilot programmes carry such symbolic weight: they make progress inspectable. A user who can join a testnet, witness its bugs, and see them resolved internalises confidence. The choreography matters as much as the outcome.

Metrics provide substance. Projects that publish *release-to-test ratios* (number of test deployments preceding each main release) or *uptime reliability post-upgrade* establish track records that outlast rhetoric. Ethereum's Merge, for instance, was preceded by three public testnets—Ropsten, Sepolia, and Goerli—each producing formal audit reports. These iterations were not marketing exercises; they were demonstrations of competence. A roadmap should therefore read less like a brochure and more like a lab notebook: timestamped, versioned, and falsifiable.

Staged unlocks—the gradual release of tokens over time—play an equally crucial role. They convert trust into economic design. Sudden unlocks, often coinciding with headline launches, encourage short-term speculation and sell-offs. Projects like *Optimism*, which began token distribution in May 2022, avoided this trap by tying unlock schedules to proven ecosystem participation rather than arbitrary calendars. Participants earned future allocations by voting, building, or contributing analytics. The result was a rare stability of price and community morale. A roadmap that integrates tokenomics into its cadence communicates continuity through economics as well as code.

Even outside crypto, the principle holds. *Tesla's Master Plan*, first published in 2006, remains a canonical example of staged transparency. Elon Musk outlined a sequence—build a sports car, use proceeds to fund an affordable car, then scale to mass-market models and energy systems. Each milestone was observable and cumulative. The roadmap did not merely inspire; it disciplined both investors and engineers. Web3 projects can learn from this template: narrative becomes credible when it is anchored to milestones that are measurable, not mystical.

Critics of incrementalism argue that it slows innovation. Rapid iteration, they say, is the ethos of software. Yet speed without sequencing collapses into noise. The counter-example is instructive: *Solana*, the high-performance blockchain, gained fame in 2021 for its velocity—thousands of transactions per second. But repeated outages in 2022 and 2023 eroded confidence. Its problem was not scale but synchrony: pushing upgrades without sufficient rehearsal. The reconciliation is clear: cadence is not conservatism; it is choreography. The faster the tempo, the more vital the rhythm.

To design trustworthy roadmaps, transparency must extend beyond progress updates. It includes the humility to mark unknowns—those elements contingent on research, partnerships, or regulatory review. Projects that explicitly label uncertain milestones ("subject to audit", "pending DAO vote") invite collaboration rather than speculation. Such language shifts the relationship between builders and users from persuasion to co-production. When uncertainty is acknowledged, belief becomes resilient rather than fragile.

There is a cultural dividend, too. Incremental development creates rituals of progress—weekly testnet reports, version updates, staged unlocks—that give communities rhythm and identity. These rituals counteract the volatility of token markets by offering continuity through visibility. They transform projects from speculative events into ongoing practices. The motif of *cadence* returns here: a steady beat that users can hear and time themselves against.

The future of trustworthy roadmaps may lie in *programmable transparency*. Smart contracts could publish development milestones directly to the chain—each commit hash linked to a timestamp, each deliverable triggering partial unlocks. This would convert promises into cryptographic artefacts. The roadmap would no longer be a PDF on a website; it would live as code, audited and immutable. Trust would then shift from words to architecture.

The open question is whether communities will accept patience as a feature, not a flaw. Web3's culture, born of velocity and speculation, resists slowness. Yet the projects that endure—Ethereum, Arbitrum, Polkadot—demonstrate that credibility compounds like interest when milestones are earned, not announced. The tension remains between drama and discipline, between hype and habit.

A roadmap users can trust is, in the end, a form of storytelling—one that replaces climax with cadence. The forward test is simple: will the next generation of builders have the courage to ship less, more often?

Chapter 9
What Should Never Be Tokenised

In 2012, a start-up in San Francisco attempted to build what it called "the market for everything." Among its first listings were tokens representing hours of friendship, hugs, and even moments of listening. The company folded within a year, not because of technical failure but moral recoil. When affection is priced, it curdles. The buyers felt awkward; the sellers, exploited. The market had measured what should have remained immeasurable. That experiment, absurd in hindsight, crystallises the question this chapter takes seriously: not *what* can be tokenised, but *what must not.*

The allure of tokenisation lies in its precision. To tokenise something is to make it portable, tradable, measurable—a neat solution to coordination problems that have haunted institutions for centuries. Yet as Michael Sandel warned in *What Money Can't Buy* (2012), the deeper danger of markets is not inequality but corruption of meaning. Price, he wrote, is not neutral; it changes the thing it touches. When tokens enter domains of intimacy, civic trust, or human suffering, they alter the moral temperature of those spaces. The challenge is not technical but ethical: how to draw boundaries around value itself.

Some categories resist commodification because they depend on context, not exchange. Love, care, citizenship, mourning—these are *sacred goods* in the sociological sense: they derive meaning from being insulated from calculation. When blockchain enthusiasts speak of "bringing everything on-chain," they risk dissolving that insulation. A marriage contract recorded immutably may look secure but feels invasive. A trauma survivor rewarded for sharing her story might later wonder whether the telling was healing or transactional. The line between empowerment and exploitation is often the thickness of a coin.

The economist Karl Polanyi described this dynamic as the "double movement" of capitalism: society pushes markets outward, then recoils to protect what markets erode. Tokenisation represents the latest outward surge—a technology capable of wrapping virtually any act or asset in economic logic. Yet the counter-movement has already begun. Communities are drawing red lines: no tokens for organ donation, for personal data without consent, for civic votes disguised as "governance rights." This chapter maps that ethical frontier: where value creation becomes value corrosion.

We begin by examining domains where tokenisation corrodes trust precisely because meaning depends on non-market norms. Intimate relationships lose dignity when performance replaces sincerity. Civic rights become suspect when votes are bundled as assets. Even care work, when gamified through points and badges, risks trivialising compassion into compliance. The sociologist Viviana Zelizer documented such tensions in her study of life insurance's origins in the 19th century: the idea of assigning monetary worth to a spouse's death was once seen as obscene. Only over time, through social reframing, did it become acceptable. The question for Web3 is which reframings we should resist rather than rationalise.

The second section addresses *perverse incentives*: systems that mistake visibility for virtue. When metrics replace meaning, behaviour bends. Consider how social credit systems and engagement scores warp intentions, turning genuine acts of care into competitions for badges. Web3 inherits this danger under a new guise—tokens as reputational capital. The antidote lies in *non-transferable recognition*: credentials that signal participation without inviting speculation. Some call these "soulbound tokens," but the terminology matters less than the principle: decouple identity from liquidity. Recognition should travel, but not trade.

Beyond design lies judgement. No algorithm can anticipate every moral edge case. When an automated system distributes rewards for community care, who decides when care crosses into coercion? When a DAO enforces penalties for "low participation," who interprets absence caused by grief or illness? These are *judgement loops* that require human pause. Mature systems build escalation paths: moments when the process halts and people deliberate. A steward who can suspend an automation preserves not bureaucracy but mercy. The act of review is what keeps technology human.

Threaded through this inquiry is a recurring motif: *the priceless test.* Each section turns on a single question—does tokenising this act increase or diminish its meaning? That test is not sentimental; it is diagnostic. Some domains thrive on exposure to markets. Others depend on remaining partially opaque. The art is discernment. A society that cannot say *this must not be sold* eventually loses the ability to say *this must be protected.*

The stakes extend beyond ethics to design. Web3's credibility depends not only on what it enables but on what it refuses. If decentralisation is to mature into civilisation, it must learn restraint. The most trusted systems of the future will be those that know when not to automate, not to tokenise, not to measure.

The pages ahead offer no moral panic, only precision. We will trace where tokenisation illuminates value and where it extracts it; where quantification clarifies and where it corrupts. The reader will encounter case studies of projects that tried to price compassion, memorialise trauma, or financialise friendship—and what each revealed about the limits of code as culture.

At its core, this chapter is about the boundary between the programmable and the profound. Every generation faces its own temptation to mechanise meaning. For ours, the instrument is the token. The question that follows is simple yet enduring: what parts of human life must remain unpriced for the rest to retain worth?

Sacred, social, sovereign

In 2006, a website called *SnuffedOut* briefly appeared online in California, offering people the chance to bid on "sponsorships" of memorial pages for recently deceased strangers. The listings resembled auctions: the higher the payment, the more prominently the buyer's name appeared beside the digital obituary. Public outrage ended the project within days. Yet its logic—turning mourning into a market—has only deepened in subtler forms since. When a grief support forum sells premium access, or a trauma survivor is paid in tokens for "sharing their story," the same corrosion reappears: the price does not merely assign value; it distorts it.

Some things lose meaning when measured. The token economy's great seduction is that everything *can* be represented—every interaction, every contribution, every trace of emotion—transcribed into units of exchange. But representation is not neutral. The moment a feeling, a civic duty, or a collective memory is priced, it risks becoming performative. The sociologist Viviana Zelizer observed that societies draw moral boundaries between what can and cannot be bought; the boundary moves, but its necessity never disappears. The question, then, is not whether markets belong in human life, but where they stop deserving entry.

Intimacy offers the clearest case. The digital economy has already rehearsed this moral confusion. In 2015, the dating app *The League* introduced an "Elite" tier, charging £300 a month for curated matches and priority visibility. The result was predictable: as exclusivity rose, authenticity fell. Conversations turned transactional; users self-optimised profiles for price justification rather than genuine connection. Economists call this *signal inflation*—when costly signals crowd out intrinsic ones. A similar distortion would occur if affection itself were tokenised. Imagine "relationship tokens" on-chain, transferable and tradeable, representing time spent or promises made. Measurability would masquerade as intimacy. The bond would be preserved in record but dissolved in spirit.

The civic sphere faces its own temptations. Experiments in *quadratic voting* and *governance tokens* promise a democratic upgrade through financial precision. Yet history warns that when civic rights become market assets, participation ceases to be public duty and becomes private strategy. In March 2020, the tokenised governance platform *Compound* launched its COMP token, enabling users to vote on protocol parameters. Within weeks, wealth concentration mirrored the very systems decentralisation had sought to escape: a handful of addresses dominated proposals. The experiment revealed a simple truth—liquidity and legitimacy rarely coexist without friction. When voice can be purchased, equality retreats into theory.

By contrast, consider the municipal experiment in Seoul (2021), where the city issued *MaaS tokens* to citizens who used public transport instead of cars. These tokens could not be traded, only redeemed for local services. Participation rose by 17% in the pilot's first three months. The moral difference was structural: the tokens rewarded behaviour without converting citizenship into a commodity. Their non-transferability preserved the social fabric. The design lesson is subtle but essential: markets can motivate, but they must not define.

Trauma narratives offer a third frontier—perhaps the most ethically perilous. In 2021, several start-ups began selling NFTs representing survivors' personal testimonies, framed as "empowering ownership" of their stories. Critics called it commodified catharsis. One survivor, quoted by *The Guardian* (July 2021), described feeling "like my pain was up for auction." The initiative collapsed, yet its premise persists in projects that conflate compensation with healing. When suffering becomes speculative, empathy turns spectatorship. The token is not an honour; it is an intrusion.

Not all attempts to honour human experience through digital records are misguided. The *Shoah Foundation's Visual History Archive*, established by Steven Spielberg in 1994, digitised over 50,000 Holocaust survivor testimonies. It remains a public, non-commercial archive, governed by scholars and educators. The archive's integrity rests on its *non-exchangeability*: the recordings cannot be owned or monetised. Their preservation serves remembrance, not return. The contrast with tokenised trauma projects could not be starker. When memory is stored as a commodity, it loses its sanctity.

The motif that recurs across these cases is *dignity*. Dignity does not resist technology—it resists reduction. To tokenise an act is to abstract it, to strip context for portability. That abstraction is useful for logistics, deadly for meaning. Markets excel at coordination, but not at care. The invisible work that sustains relationships, communities, and mourning depends on unquantified motives: loyalty, duty, compassion. When those motives are substituted with tokens, they mutate. Volunteers start optimising for visible metrics—badges earned, hours logged—rather than quiet contribution. This is not efficiency; it is erosion disguised as engagement.

Some counter that markets can clarify value where sentiment obscures it. Blood donation schemes, for example, pay donors in certain countries without apparent loss of altruism. Yet the nuance lies in framing. Where payments cover inconvenience, not virtue, the act remains social; where they monetise virtue itself, the act degrades. In 1970, Richard Titmuss's study *The Gift Relationship* compared blood systems in the UK (voluntary) and the US (commercial). He found that paid systems produced not just lower-quality blood but weaker social bonds. The token economy risks repeating this finding at digital scale: efficiency at the cost of empathy.

The sovereignty question—the right of individuals to decide what becomes tradable—complicates the moral picture. Libertarian thinkers argue that consent sanitises markets: if I choose to sell a part of myself, who is harmed? Yet consent operates within cultures that shape its meaning. The philosopher Margaret Radin called certain exchanges "incomplete commodifications"—transactions where willingness does not erase wrongness. Selling one's vote, even voluntarily, erodes democracy not because of coercion but because of contamination. It signals that civic duty is for sale, and thus, potentially, so is every duty.

What should remain sovereign, then, is not the individual's right to tokenise everything, but society's right to withhold tokenisation where collective meaning depends on shared boundaries. The principle is not paternalism but preservation. To refuse tokenisation of intimacy, of grief, of citizenship, is to maintain zones of human experience that cannot be arbitraged. These are not inefficiencies; they are sanctuaries.

Technology's greatest test is not its capacity to include more of life within its reach but its discipline to leave parts untouched. The digital age has already redefined ownership, privacy, and identity; now it must rediscover reverence.

The unresolved question is simple yet difficult: when does quantifying value destroy it? Each generation must redraw its moral frontier. For the builders of the token economy, that frontier lies precisely where code meets conscience—where the ledger ends, and the soul begins.

Perverse incentives

In February 2020, the Chinese city of Wuhan—then under the world's first large-scale COVID-19 lockdown—launched a digital platform to reward community volunteers with "caring points." Each act of service, from delivering groceries to elderly neighbours to sanitising lifts, earned numerical credits exchangeable for small gifts. Within weeks, the points economy had devolved into a race: residents began logging trivial acts, photographing the same bin repeatedly to claim credit, and staging performative cleaning sessions for algorithmic witnesses. The system had turned altruism into optimisation. By April, the platform's administrators quietly suspended the programme. A well-meant incentive had made sincerity unmeasurable.

This story is not an anomaly—it is a parable. Whenever metrics replace meaning, behaviour bends. Token economies, with their programmable incentives and transparent ledgers, amplify this effect with mathematical purity. Every reward mechanism carries a moral hypothesis about what should be valued. When that hypothesis is wrong—or incomplete—the results are not neutral; they are corrosive. The challenge is not to abandon incentives but to design them for integrity, not intensity.

The economist Charles Goodhart captured the dilemma in his famous 1975 dictum: *"When a measure becomes a target, it ceases to be a good measure."* His insight, born in the context of British monetary policy, has since metastasised across sectors. From social media engagement metrics to educational rankings, once qualitative activities become games of compliance when quantified. The same pattern now unfolds in decentralised networks, where "engagement mining" and "activity rewards" promise community growth but often deliver noise. The tragedy is structural: the system gets exactly what it asks for—and loses what it actually needs.

A visible case emerged with *Steemit*, the blockchain-based social media platform launched in 2016. It rewarded users in cryptocurrency for posting and upvoting content. Within months, quality collapsed. Bot networks gamed the algorithm by mass-liking each other's posts, inflating engagement while producing near-identical content. The platform became a self-referential economy of spam. By 2018, Steemit's daily active users had dropped by more than 70%. What began as a radical experiment in value-sharing ended as an exercise in vanity mining. The system paid for participation, not contribution.

The same pathology reappeared in smaller DAOs (Decentralised Autonomous Organisations) that attempted to incentivise "community care." In one well-documented instance—*Friends With Benefits*, a social DAO founded in 2020—members earned governance tokens for moderating chats and welcoming newcomers. Initially, participation was genuine. But as token prices rose, moderation became mechanical; members competed for measurable actions, not meaningful interaction. Leaders intervened by redefining rewards through qualitative peer reviews rather than raw counts. The correction worked briefly but revealed the fragility of numerical trust: once people are paid for virtue, they struggle to do it freely again.

Metrics warp intention by simplifying context. When care is scored, kindness becomes performance. When civic contribution is tokenised, duty becomes speculation. The irony is that token systems, built on ideals of transparency and fairness, often replicate the blindness of bureaucracy—rules so rigid they reward compliance over conscience. Economists studying incentive failures refer to this as *multi-dimensional moral collapse*: people optimise one visible dimension (output) while neglecting the invisible ones (ethics, empathy, nuance).

A striking counterpoint comes from the *Wikipedia* community—an economy without tokens, where contribution is measured socially, not financially. The site's volunteer editors, numbering in the hundreds of thousands, receive no monetary reward, only reputation through edit histories and talk-page respect. Yet its resilience outlasts most paid communities. The crucial design feature is *non-transferability*: reputation cannot be sold, and credit is cumulative but personal. A veteran editor's name carries weight precisely because it cannot be converted into cash. That immutability anchors trust.

This principle—earned, not traded recognition—should guide digital incentive design. Non-transferable badges, akin to academic degrees or professional licences, preserve accountability without commodification. They acknowledge competence while preventing speculation. In blockchain terms, this aligns with the idea of *soulbound tokens*, introduced by Vitalik Buterin and colleagues in 2022, representing identity-linked achievements that cannot be exchanged. The model restores meaning by removing liquidity. Value persists, but it does not drift.

Critics object that illiquidity stifles motivation. Yet evidence suggests the opposite: when recognition cannot be sold, its social capital strengthens. In 2021, *Gitcoin*, a funding platform for open-source projects, ran an experiment granting "contributor badges" for verified community work without monetary payout. Participation rates fell slightly at first but stabilised at a higher quality threshold: fewer tasks completed, more enduring contributors. The absence of tradeability had filtered out opportunism.

Perverse incentives also manifest at scale in algorithmic labour systems. Consider *Amazon Mechanical Turk*, the crowdsourcing platform where workers complete microtasks for pennies. Payment per task leads to quantity obsession; accuracy suffers. A 2019 Stanford study found that when workers received public ratings instead of small bonuses, data quality improved by 25%. Recognition—visible, human, reputation-based—outperformed cash. The experiment confirms a broader truth: meaning motivates longer than money, but only when the system signals respect.

The motif that threads through these examples is distortion—how purity of measurement becomes impurity of motive. Tokenisation magnifies this because it merges economic and social currencies into one ledger. The more total the system, the more total the corruption. As philosopher Michael Sandel warns, "Markets don't only allocate—they express." When we tokenise care, we tell people care is countable. When we score compassion, we say compassion has an exchange rate. The damage lies not in the data but in the declaration.

Still, incentives can be redeemed if they reintroduce humility. A well-designed system need not suppress measurement but surround it with meaning. This might take the form of *decaying rewards*—tokens that lose value unless paired with peer validation—or hybrid models where contribution metrics feed into deliberative review, not direct payment. In short: measure, but let humans interpret.

The counter-example worth reckoning with is *Duolingo*. Its streak system, a gamified metric of daily learning, has been accused of addiction and anxiety. Yet its designers consciously introduced *soft failure*: users can miss a day without penalty if they earn "streak freezes." This small mercy transforms compulsion into continuity. The lesson for token economies is similar: metrics need breathing room. A perfect feedback loop suffocates purpose.

To design for integrity, we must remember that not every signal should be stored, and not every act should be priced. The deeper wisdom lies in knowing which incentives invite virtue and which commodify it. Metrics can inform, but they must never define.

The unresolved question remains: how do we build systems that reward without corrupting, that measure without reducing? As tokens become the grammar of value, the real test is linguistic. Can we speak the language of incentive without forgetting the dialect of meaning?

Human judgment loops

At 13:05 UTC on 12 March 2020, as global markets convulsed under the first pandemic shock, MakerDAO—the decentralised lending protocol based in Copenhagen—entered freefall. Ether prices halved in an hour; automated liquidation bots flooded the network. Collateral auctions, designed to maintain system stability without human bias, malfunctioned. Some bidders exploited a flaw to acquire assets for zero DAI. Within minutes, tens of millions of dollars' worth of collateral vanished. The community convened in emergency calls to do what the algorithm could not: pause. Within forty-eight hours, MakerDAO's human governors voted to suspend liquidations and deploy a patch. That act—an intervention the system was never supposed to need—saved it from collapse. It also revealed a truth that decentralisation prefers to forget: automation requires stewards.

The promise of blockchain is incorruptibility through code. Yet the more flawless the automation, the more fragile its failures. Each "trustless" protocol embeds assumptions about behaviour, liquidity, and latency. When those assumptions crack, no contract clause can heal the breach; only judgment can. A *human judgment loop* is the quiet architecture of fallibility: an escalation path that allows someone, somewhere, to press stop. In financial systems, that button prevents insolvency. In civic ones, it prevents injustice. The irony is profound—automation achieves legitimacy only when people can interrupt it.

MakerDAO's crisis was not unique. In September 2021, the Solana blockchain halted for seventeen hours after a flood of transactions from a decentralised exchange overwhelmed its validators. Engineers debated whether intervening would betray decentralisation's ideals. Eventually, seventy validators coordinated a restart through a private chat channel. The decision restored service but fractured ideology. "The pause was the right call," one validator said, "but we shouldn't have to choose between uptime and integrity." The paradox remains unsolved: a system designed to eliminate discretion depends on it in extremis.

To understand why, we must return to design philosophy. Automated systems excel at rule enforcement but fail at rule interpretation. They are brittle at the edges—the zones of ambiguity that define real life. In a decentralised marketplace, disputes arise not because code miscalculates, but because context shifts faster than consensus. A transaction flagged as "spam" might be activism. A delayed vote might result from illness. Edge cases expose moral geometry: precision without empathy. Without judgment loops, the system cannot distinguish exception from exploitation.

The *DAO hack* of 2016 remains the canonical warning. When an attacker exploited a flaw in the Ethereum-based investment fund, draining 3.6 million Ether, the community split. Purists insisted "code is law": the theft, though unintended, followed the protocol's logic. Others argued for reversal to restore justice. The eventual hard fork—creating Ethereum and Ethereum Classic—was itself an act of human arbitration. What the episode revealed was not the weakness of code, but the necessity of conscience. When every rule is absolute, mercy becomes illegal.

Contrast that rigidity with the deliberate insertion of human judgment in *Aragon Court*, a dispute resolution system launched in 2020 for decentralised organisations. Rather than trust automation alone, Aragon routes contested cases to randomly selected jurors who review evidence and vote. Their verdicts trigger smart contracts, but the decision is human. The process slows automation just enough to restore proportionality. Here, slowness is safety. In network design, the capacity to delay is a form of wisdom.

Corporate governance offers analogues. The *NASDAQ* market's circuit breakers, first implemented in 1988 after the Black Monday crash, allow trading halts during extreme volatility. Each pause buys time for reflection—precisely what blockchains, with their relentless tempo, tend to omit. The idea that time itself is a control mechanism deserves attention in Web3. Every protocol should contain not only self-executing logic but self-questioning intervals. To pause is not to fail; it is to care.

Critics of human intervention warn of centralisation creep. Who appoints the stewards? Who guards the guardians? These are valid fears. In decentralised systems, authority hidden behind the veneer of automation is the most dangerous form of power. The answer lies in transparent escalation design: open criteria for when and how judgment is invoked. For instance, *Optimism*, the Ethereum scaling project, created a "Security Council" whose power to pause the network is limited by multisignature thresholds and public disclosure. The council's existence acknowledges that no system should run faster than its capacity to reason.

A limitation worth facing is human bias itself. Judgment loops can drift from deliberation to discretion, from stewardship to interference. The temptation to intervene prematurely—to rescue markets, protect friends, or manage optics—turns safety into paternalism. The lesson from the *Binance Chain* reorganisation incident of May 2019, where operators considered rolling back transactions after a hack but refrained, is caution. Intervention must be possible but rare. Like a fire alarm, its legitimacy depends on silence most of the time.

The motif of the *pause button* threads through every domain where automation meets uncertainty. In autonomous vehicles, emergency drivers remain seated for the rare but vital moments when algorithms falter. In algorithmic content moderation, escalation to human reviewers is not a failure of scale but an act of repair. The presence of judgment transforms error from catastrophe into conversation. Systems that cannot apologise cannot improve.

Philosophically, judgment loops embody what Hannah Arendt called *the space of appearance*—the moment when humans reveal themselves as moral agents through action, not prediction. When a DAO pauses a contract to review a dispute, it performs precisely this act: it reintroduces visibility into a process that would otherwise hide causality behind code. That reappearance is democratic in the deepest sense. It says: the machine does not own the meaning of justice.

Technically, embedding judgment requires friction. Smart contracts must include conditional triggers—delays, thresholds, and veto rights—governed by accountable humans. Socially, it requires culture: norms that treat reflection as strength, not weakness. The "move fast and break things" ethos that defined early digital innovation cannot survive in systems that hold real value, livelihoods, or civic rights. The Web3 generation must learn a new mantra: *move carefully and fix together.*

There are experiments already pointing the way. *Kleros*, a decentralised arbitration protocol launched in 2018, employs crowdsourced juries to resolve disputes over escrow, freelancing, and DAO operations. Its transparency has helped prevent arbitrary enforcement. Yet even Kleros wrestles with scale: as cases multiply, juror fatigue threatens quality. Human loops, like any organ, tire. The solution may not be fewer humans but better cycles—rotating panels, staggered reviews, and layered oversight that mirrors biological systems' redundancy.

The deeper question is cultural. Can decentralised systems embrace vulnerability without perceiving it as defeat? Trustless architecture aspires to remove the need for faith. But communities, not protocols, sustain continuity when things go wrong. After MakerDAO's Black Thursday, users rebuilt confidence not because the code improved overnight but because humans owned their errors in public. Accountability, unlike automation, cannot be programmed; it must be practised.

The closing tension is this: every system must choose between two forms of failure—rigid collapse or flexible correction. To embed human judgment is to choose the latter. Yet it demands courage: to interrupt momentum, to question outputs, to accept that no line of code can foresee the moral texture of reality.

The test for the token economy's maturity will not be how flawlessly it runs, but how gracefully it pauses.

The priceless test

In June 2014, Facebook quietly conducted an experiment on nearly 700,000 users without their knowledge. For one week, the company filtered emotional content in newsfeeds to study how moods spread online. The findings, later published in the *Proceedings of the National Academy of Sciences*, showed what researchers called "emotional contagion"—that happiness and sadness could be engineered at scale. The cost to participants was never financial. It was consent, trust, and dignity. Public backlash followed not because money had changed hands, but because something *priceless* had been traded without permission. The episode revealed a modern paradox: even when data is free, the self should not be for sale.

This paradox is where the "priceless test" begins. The token economy, with its granular logic of exchange, can price almost anything—attention, affiliation, affection. What it cannot do is decide when the act of pricing corrodes meaning. The difficulty is practical, not poetic. It requires a rubric, a method to tell when to say *no*—not from instinct, but from principle. Just as engineers use stress tests to find a material's breaking point, designers and policymakers need a moral equivalent to locate the boundaries of commodification.

The first dimension of this test is *context*. What does the act mean to those involved, and what does the act become once priced? Sociologist Richard Titmuss made this question famous in *The Gift Relationship* (1970), comparing blood donation in Britain's voluntary system with the paid model in the United States. He found that introducing payment reduced both quantity and quality of supply. The meaning of the act changed; generosity became labour, and virtue became service. Tokenisation risks the same distortion. When a community introduces tradable "gratitude points" or on-chain reputation scores, it converts relational gestures into market signals. The visible transaction overwrites the invisible bond. Context, not technology, determines corruption.

A second dimension is *substitutability*. Can what's being tokenised be replaced by something else of equal kind? If yes, a market may be defensible. If no—if the object carries uniqueness bound to identity or experience—it should remain priceless. Consider the *World Health Organization's* 2010 condemnation of markets in human organs: commodification endangered both donor dignity and equitable access. By contrast, regulated carbon markets, where emissions allowances are designed to be interchangeable, demonstrate how tokenisation can serve justice rather than undermine it. The priceless test hinges on this distinction: replaceable goods may be traded; irreplaceable experiences should not.

Third comes *consent*. Not the perfunctory checkbox variety, but informed and revocable participation. The Cambridge Analytica scandal of March 2018 exposed how token-like profiling—aggregating psychological data for political microtargeting—violated this very premise. The people whose data powered those algorithms were not buyers or sellers; they were raw material. Consent was bypassed through opacity. A true priceless test would demand reversibility: the ability to withdraw one's data, revoke its use, and have that revocation respected as a moral right, not a customer service feature.

The counter-example often cited is the open-source software movement. Developers release code freely, often under permissive licences allowing reuse and monetisation by others. Yet here, consent and context align: contributors know the exchange terms, and the value created accrues socially, not extractively. *Linux*, first released by Linus Torvalds in 1991, endures precisely because it frames openness as contribution, not surrender. The priceless test does not reject markets—it clarifies when participation still honours agency.

Then there is *externality*: what effect does tokenisation have on those not directly involved? A tokenised system that rewards public safety reports, for instance, may encourage vigilance—but also voyeurism, as users record neighbours to earn credits. A 2022 pilot of China's "Digital Civilisation Points" in Suzhou illustrated this duality: residents received tokens for community service, but some began staging good deeds for cameras. When metrics reward visibility over virtue, collective welfare decays into performance. The priceless test asks: who benefits when the measure becomes the motive?

Dignity, the test's core metric, resists quantification yet governs all others. Philosopher Immanuel Kant warned against treating people as means rather than ends. In token design, this translates into a simple diagnostic: if an individual's worth in the system depends solely on output—votes cast, content posted, tokens earned—their humanity has been reduced to function. Dignity requires room for non-performance. It allows silence, refusal, withdrawal. Systems that demand constant expression, participation, or gamified engagement turn personhood into a perpetual audit.

A practical expression of the priceless test can be seen in the *Data Union* experiments launched by Ocean Protocol in 2021. The idea was to let individuals collectively sell access to anonymised data streams. Early adopters discovered a threshold: small, well-defined datasets (for environmental sensors or traffic patterns) could be monetised without moral hazard. But when the model extended to health records, unease spread. The project reframed its structure—participants could choose to donate data to research rather than trade it. What mattered was not the transaction but the framing: *from profit to purpose.* That pivot restored dignity to participation.

One might ask whether every domain needs such restraint. Isn't value recognition a form of justice, especially for unpaid labour? Feminist economists like Marilyn Waring have long argued that invisibility in markets often equals exploitation. Yet the priceless test doesn't deny valuation—it distinguishes between recognising and pricing. Care work, for example, can be acknowledged through pensions, public honour, or service credits, none of which require speculative tradeability. Tokenisation should elevate contributions without turning them into chips on an exchange. When systems collapse care into yield, they reward presence but not purpose.

Still, absolutism is dangerous. Refusing all forms of tokenisation can preserve purity at the cost of progress. A case in point: the *Fairphone* initiative, founded in Amsterdam in 2013, uses blockchain tracing to ensure ethical sourcing of minerals. Each transaction is recorded, not to monetise virtue but to verify accountability. The chain of custody tokenises responsibility, not the humans behind it. Here, measurement protects dignity rather than diluting it. The priceless test's nuance lies in its calibration: what kind of visibility enhances worth without commodifying it?

The motif that threads through every example is *boundaries*. Technology erases them by default; ethics redraws them deliberately. The priceless test is the act of redrawing. It does not ask, "Can this be tokenised?" but, "Should it?" The question forces friction into design—a pause for reflection before translation into code. Just as environmental impact assessments became mandatory in industrial projects, ethical impact assessments should accompany every new token model. Asking *what remains sacred here?* may sound archaic in digital markets, but it is precisely this archaic instinct that preserves civilisation from reductionism.

The test is diagnostic, not doctrinal. It can be applied ex ante (before design) or ex post (after damage). It guides creators to identify not the cost of doing something, but the cost of *doing it wrong*. Its most valuable function is explanatory clarity: the ability to justify refusal without sentimentality. Saying *no* with reasons instead of vibes protects discourse from polarisation. It keeps ethics rational, not tribal.

The risk of not applying it is already visible. As decentralised social networks begin to reward engagement with tradable tokens, users face the same existential trade as those 700,000 unknowing Facebook participants did a decade ago: to be studied, quantified, and optimised. The difference now is awareness. We can choose to design systems that measure contribution without monetising identity, that store memory without extracting selfhood. But doing so requires a habit of questioning—the discipline to run every innovation through the priceless test before it touches a human life.

And so the open question endures: what will we still refuse to price when everything can be measured? The answer, quietly, will define the moral ceiling of the token age.

Chapter 10
The Future of Digital Property

On a quiet morning in 2029, a solar-powered drone in rural Kenya negotiates with a nearby weather sensor for access to its data feed. The sensor quotes a micro-fee, denominated in a stablecoin pegged to local rainfall insurance credits. The drone accepts, streams the data, and adjusts its flight path to avoid a coming storm. No human approves the exchange. No institution records the contract. Yet value changes hands, risk is mitigated, and trust—of a kind—is upheld. This is ownership reimagined: rights and responsibilities not as paperwork or possession, but as programmable flows.

We are entering an age when machines will not merely execute instructions but *hold* assets, pay for access, and negotiate their own dependencies. A camera may license its own footage. A car may rent its unused storage to a nearby device. Media objects—songs, articles, training datasets—will become self-aware of their terms, invoking royalties or restrictions as they move. Property, once a human abstraction built on scarcity, becomes a behavioural pattern embedded in code. This shift is not a matter of speculation but of inevitability: wherever computation meets autonomy, ownership evolves from possession to permission.

Yet the deeper question is not how these systems work, but what they make of us. Property has always defined civilisation's edges: who can build, who can exclude, who can claim the fruits of creation. As digital networks extend those edges into every sensor, satellite, and synthetic voice, the politics of possession must be rewritten. The future of digital property is not a matter of wealth alone—it is a question of agency, accountability, and meaning in a world where everything, and everyone, becomes partially programmable.

To glimpse that future, consider the evolution of value itself. The 19th century industrialised production; the 20th financialised it. The 21st is *encoding* it. When a decentralised storage node charges a fraction of a cent per megabyte, or a digital painting earns royalties from each resale, the line between asset and agent blurs. Programmable value is the connective tissue binding AI, blockchain, and IoT—three technologies often treated separately but destined to converge. Together, they form a network that does not just move information, but allocates rights and responsibilities dynamically. Ownership becomes less a noun than a verb: something enacted, conditional, and continuously negotiated at the edges.

This is what we mean by *programmable value at the edges*. Not an abstract utopia of automation, but a practical architecture of consent among devices and actors. Edge computing distributes intelligence closer to where data is generated. Tokenisation gives that intelligence an economic voice. When combined, they enable what earlier ages could only dream of: systems that transact not for speculation but for coordination. A fleet of solar panels balancing a microgrid, or an autonomous tractor sharing soil data with its neighbours, operates through value-coded reciprocity. Each act of exchange carries the imprint of a right exercised and an obligation fulfilled.

But such systems will not endure by novelty alone. They will require *composability as strategy*—a mindset that prizes interoperability over isolation. The most powerful innovations in finance, from derivatives to decentralised protocols, have thrived because they could plug into others. Culture and identity will soon follow the same rule. A digital credential verifying one's qualifications may interface with a social reputation score or a creative licence, forming composite profiles owned by individuals rather than platforms. The architecture of value will resemble a living library, where assets reference, recombine, and refine each other through open standards. The prize of composability is not speed but synergy; the danger is fragmentation by design.

The temptation of our age is to chase velocity. Startups and protocols race to scale, sacrificing resilience for reach. Yet the most enduring infrastructures of the next decade will be *boring* ones—systems that privilege auditability, upgradeability, and long-term safety over hype. The future of digital property depends on institutions that can withstand volatility, not mimic it. Bitcoin's survival since 2009 is owed less to innovation than to restraint: predictable issuance, transparent rules, slow evolution. Stability is not a failure of imagination; it is the infrastructure of trust.

To build for decades rather than cycles demands humility: an acceptance that not every function should be automated, not every incentive financialised, not every innovation accelerated. The same qualities that made traditional property systems durable—clear titles, enforceable contracts, contextual governance—must be reinterpreted for code. If the Web3 era began with experimentation, the next phase requires responsibility. What we build now will become the default grammar of exchange for generations. To treat that lightly would be to repeat the moral naïveté of the early internet: speed without stewardship, scale without conscience.

That is why this chapter ends not with prediction but with a *builder's oath*: four principles to guide those shaping digital property—clarity, consent, context, and care. **Clarity**, because every token, contract, or AI agent must declare what it represents and how it behaves. **Consent**, because participation must be voluntary, revocable, and informed. **Context**, because no code can replace culture; meaning always resides in the human frame. And **care**, because systems are not only technical artefacts but moral habitats. These are not constraints—they are conditions for endurance.

We are moving from the internet of information to the internet of intent. Each transaction, each token, each machine-to-machine negotiation encodes a fragment of human choice. The future of digital property will test whether we can preserve dignity inside automation, reason within scale, and purpose amid profit.

The work ahead is not to predict which protocol wins or which token appreciates. It is to decide what we are willing to own—and what we refuse to. The next property revolution will not be written in law books or ledgers, but in the everyday ethics of design. And that is where the true frontier lies: not in the code itself, but in the conscience behind it.

Programmable value at the edges

In May 2022, in a warehouse on the outskirts of Hamburg, Siemens engineers demonstrated a factory line that no human directly controlled. Each robotic arm, conveyor belt, and inspection camera negotiated its own access to energy and bandwidth through microtransactions. When a sensor overheated, another unit rented its idle processor to run the diagnostic script. Payment flowed automatically via a local ledger node; the repair was billed in fractions of a euro. To the technicians observing, the event looked unremarkable. But it marked a threshold: a machine, for the first time, had autonomously hired another machine to solve a problem, settled the bill, and logged the event without human approval. Property, labour, and currency had momentarily fused into code.

This is the frontier of *programmable value at the edges*—the migration of economic agency from central platforms to autonomous devices. It is a quiet but radical departure from the client-server model that defined the digital age. Instead of cloud systems dictating behaviour from afar, value now circulates at the periphery: where data is produced, where energy is consumed, and where actions matter. The edge—homes, farms, vehicles, microgrids—is becoming a marketplace of intent. Machines don't just execute; they negotiate. They rent, lease, and reward. Ownership becomes operational, and economics becomes ambient.

To grasp the magnitude of this shift, it helps to trace its lineage. The internet's first act digitised information; the second digitised identity and community; the third, unfolding now, digitises value exchange itself. Bitcoin proved that money could move without banks; Ethereum showed that contracts could execute without courts. The next proof concerns coordination: can devices transact without intermediaries? The answer is not speculative. It is already visible in the architecture of *machine-to-machine (M2M)* payments. In 2023, the IOTA Foundation piloted a network of electric vehicles in Trondheim, Norway, that paid charging stations directly per kilowatt-hour. No central billing, no human invoices. A car topped up its battery, transferred tokens, and drove on. The transaction lasted six seconds and cost less than one euro cent in fees.

The principle behind these systems is deceptively simple: when devices hold wallets, they acquire rights. A sensor that owns its data can sell it. A robot that rents its time can earn it. Economic agency becomes a software primitive, available to any entity capable of cryptographic authentication. This development collapses several distinctions once treated as sacred—between user and producer, owner and operator, object and actor. The effect is not only technical but philosophical: the boundary of "who can own" expands beyond the human.

Yet the technology is not an ideology of automation. Its promise lies in decentralising decision-making where it is most efficient. Consider the case of *FarmBot*, an open-source precision agriculture robot first deployed in 2016. Farmers can configure it to autonomously buy weather data or soil analytics from nearby nodes, using stablecoins or energy credits. Instead of depending on distant servers or middlemen, the device composes its own supply chain. The result: reduced latency, higher resilience, and local accountability. When every node can transact, coordination becomes granular—no longer mediated by hierarchies, but by trust encoded in protocols.

The motif that threads through these examples is *negotiation*. Machines don't merely execute orders—they make offers. A smart irrigation pump may propose a data-sharing deal with a neighbour's moisture sensor. A drone may auction its excess storage to another drone mid-flight. Each transaction embodies a miniature contract, balancing cost, risk, and reciprocity. Economic logic migrates into the texture of the physical world. The edge becomes an agora.

But every market needs norms. The challenge is not whether devices can trade, but whether they should. When AI agents begin exchanging value autonomously, accountability risks dilution. Who is liable if a self-charging car overpays a faulty station? Or if an AI assistant rents copyrighted music for background ambience without human consent? The legal personhood of machines remains contested, but the operational personhood is already here. The design question, therefore, is how to encode constraints: ceilings, permissions, and reversibility. Just as a corporate board sets spending limits, each autonomous agent will require policy scaffolding to protect against runaway behaviour.

There are already attempts to address this. The *Fetch.ai* network, founded in Cambridge in 2017, enables autonomous economic agents—software entities representing devices or users—to interact within defined marketplaces. In a pilot with Deutsche Telekom

(2021), energy meters negotiated prices with charging stations based on real-time grid demand. Each agent operated within a sandbox, bound by smart contract rules that limited exposure. The pattern—*freedom within fences*—is instructive. Programmable value thrives not by removing constraints but by making them transparent.

A useful counterpoint comes from failed automation. In 2019, Walmart attempted to deploy shelf-scanning robots across 500 stores in the United States. Despite their efficiency, the project was abandoned. Human staff and customers found the machines intrusive, unpredictable, even eerie. The robots optimised inventory but eroded trust. The lesson: not every transaction benefits from autonomy. Context and empathy remain currencies machines cannot yet trade. Programmable value, to be legitimate, must coexist with human comfort and comprehension.

The economic implications are profound. When devices pay each other, they generate micro-markets invisible to traditional accounting. Imagine a city where lampposts lease light-spectrum data to advertisers, or traffic sensors sell aggregated flow metrics to logistics firms. Each interaction might be worth pennies, but collectively they form the pulse of an *autonomous economy*. According to a 2023 report by the World Economic Forum, machine-to-machine transactions could exceed 100 billion per day by 2030. Whether that prediction materialises is less important than its direction: value will flow where computation does.

The cultural effects may be subtler but no less significant. Once property becomes programmable, creativity itself changes texture. Media files embedded with smart contracts can remunerate creators automatically each time they are played, remixed, or embedded. The streaming platform Audius (launched 2020) has already experimented with such per-use payments on Ethereum. For musicians, this restores a sense of reciprocity long eroded by opaque intermediaries. For audiences, it reintroduces a quiet ritual: each listen becomes an act of direct patronage. The concept of ownership dissolves into interaction.

Still, the allure of frictionless value hides a paradox. Systems that transact continuously risk losing discernment. When every action carries a micro-fee or credit, relationships can collapse into metrics. The danger is *transactional totality*: a world where attention, affection, and ethics are all priced in tokens. The antidote is intentional friction—the capacity to pause, reflect, and reframe purpose. Designers must ensure that programmable value enhances agency without eroding meaning. Not every exchange deserves to be automated; some should remain conversations, not contracts.

A technical motif recurs across these debates: *the edge as frontier*. In computing, the edge reduces latency. In economics, it redistributes power. But in ethics, it tests the limits of control. When rights and revenues circulate through silicon rather than signatures, our institutions must evolve accordingly. Insurance, taxation, and intellectual property law—all rest on the assumption that ownership is human and centralised. That assumption is ending. Policymakers will need to distinguish between stewardship and surrender: how to grant autonomy without abdicating oversight.

The edge, therefore, is not just a technical topology but a moral topology. It is where design decisions become governance choices. The Siemens demo in Hamburg, the cars in Trondheim, the farms powered by FarmBot—all illustrate a world edging toward self-organising economies. Each transaction may be minuscule, but collectively they challenge centuries of legal, economic, and philosophical inheritance.

The unresolved question is how far we should let autonomy run. Should a device be allowed to accumulate wealth? Can a sensor own intellectual property it helps to generate? Who inherits the wallet of an AI agent when it ceases to operate? These are not science-fiction riddles; they are regulatory drafts waiting to be written. The measure of progress will not be how many machines transact, but how responsibly they do so.

The path ahead demands a new literacy—economic, ethical, and architectural. Programmable value at the edges will not replace human enterprise, but it will redefine its texture. We will move from ownership as possession to ownership as participation, from control to coordination, from scarcity to service. What began in a Hamburg warehouse will extend to every connected object in the world. The challenge is to ensure that, as machines learn to pay and earn, we remember what remains *priceless.*

Composability as strategy

In August 2020, a single developer combined two decentralised finance protocols—Compound and Uniswap—into a new service called *yield farming.* By letting users borrow tokens from one and lend them into the other, the experiment produced overnight returns exceeding 100 per cent annualised. The phenomenon, coded in under a hundred lines, triggered a summer-long surge of experimentation across blockchain networks. It was not the returns that mattered, but the revelation: financial systems, when built as open interfaces, could behave like Lego bricks. A user could stack, remix, and extend existing components without permission. Innovation became combinatorial.

This property—*composability*—is now shaping more than markets. It is a design philosophy that privileges interoperability over ownership, connection over control. In software, it means that one system's output can serve as another's input; in culture, that creation itself becomes modular. As assets become programmable, the logic that made decentralised finance explosively generative is migrating to identity, media, and community. Composability is no longer a technical feature. It is a strategic stance. The systems that thrive will not be those that hoard users, but those that invite contribution.

To understand why, it helps to remember how the opposite—siloed architecture—limited previous digital eras. In 2007, Facebook's API famously allowed developers to build games and tools atop its platform, creating a flourishing ecosystem of apps like *FarmVille.* Yet within three years, the company closed that access. The reason was structural: value was captured through enclosure. The platform profited by limiting interoperability, forcing all flows of attention through its own channels. Composability threatens such models because it displaces power from gatekeepers to participants. The consequence is both liberating and destabilising: openness scales creativity but weakens control.

The motif of *Lego* captures this paradox elegantly. Each piece gains meaning only through connection, yet the standard that enables connection—size, shape, colour—must be agreed in advance. In digital networks, that standard takes the form of *open interfaces*: APIs, smart contract protocols, metadata schemas. These are not technical niceties but governance artefacts. When the *Ethereum* blockchain launched in July 2015, its primary innovation was not cryptocurrency but composability: any developer could deploy a contract that automatically interacted with any other. The outcome was a Cambrian explosion of applications—from decentralised exchanges to NFTs—each inheriting trust and liquidity from the layer beneath. Composability turned infrastructure into a commons.

This principle is now extending into cultural and identity systems. Consider the *Lens Protocol*, launched by Aave Labs in 2022. It allows social profiles, posts, and follows to exist as interoperable NFTs, owned by users rather than platforms. A creator's network is no longer trapped in a single app; their audience can move with them. Developers can build new interfaces—blogs, galleries, feeds—without fragmenting data. The social graph becomes a shared substrate rather than a proprietary moat. The implication is profound: culture itself becomes composable. Each expression can be reused, remixed, and extended without losing attribution or value.

Yet composability is not synonymous with chaos. It demands design discipline. Without clear boundaries, systems risk collapse through unintended interaction. The collapse of *TerraUSD* in May 2022 illustrated this vividly. The algorithmic stablecoin was composed atop several open protocols, each dependent on the others' stability. When one failed, contagion spread instantly. The same property that enabled innovation—instant connectivity—amplified failure. Composability magnifies both creativity and fragility. Like chemistry, it rewards those who understand the reactions they provoke.

The question, then, is how to harness composability as a deliberate *strategy* rather than a side effect. One answer lies in modular governance. Open protocols such as *ENS* (Ethereum Name Service) and *Arweave* structure their communities as layered systems: small autonomous groups maintain discrete modules—naming records, storage layers, indexing services—that together form a coherent whole. This allows experimentation without jeopardising integrity. When one module fails, others persist. The system evolves like an organism, not a monolith.

Composability also reshapes incentives. In traditional corporate hierarchies, value flows vertically: product → user → profit. In composable networks, value circulates laterally. A developer who improves a protocol's component benefits not by ownership but by integration: others build upon their work, driving demand for its use. This model mirrors scientific progress more than industrial production. Its reward is propagation, not possession. It is, in essence, a networked form of capitalism grounded in contribution.

One can see early manifestations in creative industries. The *Zora Protocol* (2021) introduced NFTs with perpetual royalties embedded in code. Artists could define how future resales reward both themselves and previous collectors. These tokens can then interact with third-party applications—exhibitions, auctions, playlists—without renegotiating rights. Each new service layers atop the previous, generating derivative value through interoperability. The result is a self-expanding creative economy where attribution compounds rather than dilutes.

A counterexample reveals the stakes. Major streaming platforms, despite their technological sophistication, remain compositional dead ends. A song on *Spotify* cannot be embedded in a social game, remixed into a VR gallery, or linked to a concert ticketing system without corporate approval. The result is stagnation: despite two decades of digital music, revenue distribution remains skewed and innovation incremental. Composability could reverse that imbalance by treating cultural assets as open primitives, each capable of linking into broader experiences.

The strategic lesson extends beyond art. In digital identity, composability determines portability. A verified credential—say, a university degree represented on-chain—should be readable across employers, governments, and applications without revalidation. Projects such as *Verifiable Credentials* (W3C standard, 2019) and *Soulbound Tokens* (proposed by Vitalik Buterin, May 2022) explore this. Each envisions identity as modular: individuals assemble facets of their reputation from various attestations rather than submitting to a single authority. The benefit is autonomy; the risk is fragmentation if standards diverge. Hence, the architecture of composability must balance freedom with coherence.

The motif of *connection* returns here as both metaphor and mandate. The strength of a network lies not in any node's power but in the quality of its links. Open interfaces are the social contracts of the digital age. They define how systems, institutions, and individuals recognise one another. In this sense, composability is political. It decentralises not only computation but also legitimacy. By distributing authority across interoperable protocols, it challenges the logic of monopoly. The platforms of the past century centralised because connection was expensive; the networks of the next will decentralise because connection is free.

Yet freedom carries a maintenance cost. Interoperable systems require common stewardship—standards bodies, open-source maintainers, ethical review boards. Without such care, composability can descend into incompatibility. The early web, for all its promise, became fragmented by competing browsers and proprietary plugins until the W3C enforced open standards in the late 1990s. The same pattern threatens blockchain ecosystems unless coordination improves. Composability is not self-sustaining; it is a civic duty disguised as code.

What makes composability a strategy, rather than a feature, is its compounding effect. Each new interoperable asset increases the total surface area for further innovation. This is the economic analogue of *network externality* but without central ownership. The system grows more valuable as it grows more open. Conversely, closed systems depreciate: every new feature must be built internally, every improvement reinvents the wheel. The more a protocol exposes clear, stable interfaces, the more resilient and adaptive it becomes.

Perhaps the most striking implication is philosophical. Composability dissolves the binary between creator and consumer, between asset and environment. A digital artefact—be it a dataset, identity, or artwork—no longer ends at its edge; it invites participation. Ownership shifts from exclusivity to inclusion. The frontier of innovation moves from invention to arrangement, from discovery to design.

Yet this openness also confronts us with a tension: how much composability is too much? A fully modular world risks abstraction from meaning. If everything can plug into everything, coherence may dissolve into noise. Strategy, therefore, demands restraint. The most successful systems will define clear interfaces and firm boundaries—enough to invite creativity, not enough to dissolve identity.

That may be the defining challenge of the next decade: to build networks porous enough to evolve, but principled enough to endure. Composability, properly understood, is not about connection for its own sake. It is about constructing shared grammar for innovation—one that lets culture, code, and capital speak the same language without losing their dialects. The measure of progress will not be how many systems connect, but how meaningfully they do. The question that remains is deceptively simple: can we design openness that still remembers where it began?

Resilience over speed

On 11 March 2013, a subtle software mismatch split Bitcoin's ledger into two competing histories. Version 0.8 nodes accepted a block that many 0.7 nodes rejected, causing a fork that briefly threatened the very idea of a single, shared record. Within hours, core developers coordinated a rollback to 0.7 on IRC; miners downgraded; exchanges like Mt. Gox throttled activity; the chain reconverged. No heroics. No new features. Just careful process and a clear pecking order of safety over throughput. The lesson travelled far beyond Bitcoin: robust infrastructure survives because it can step back without breaking. Boring beats brittle over time.

Speed seduces. It flatters founders, delights traders, and feeds charts. But infrastructure that matters—payments, identity, cultural registries, machine coordination—demands a different virtue: reliability under duress. The systems that last are auditable, upgradeable, and, frankly, dull. They keep logs you can trust, change in ways you can prove, and fail in modes you can forecast. They do not wow; they reassure. That steadiness is not anti-innovation. It is the precondition for innovation that compounds rather than combusts.

Show, then name. On 12 March 2020, "Black Thursday" struck Ethereum as markets collapsed and congestion spiked. MakerDAO's collateral auctions malfunctioned; some liquidators won positions for zero DAI; governance called an emergency, then paused mechanisms until a patch deployed. Explain: the protocol's designers had encoded pause capability and a path to human review. Implication: resilience is not a slogan but a set of stored options—circuit breakers, rate limits, manual overrides—prepared before chaos, not invented mid-crisis.

Contrast with a second, checkable example. On 14 September 2021, Solana halted for roughly seventeen hours after a surge of transactions overwhelmed validators. Engineers coordinated a restart. Critics cried centralisation; supporters noted that the coordinated pause prevented deeper corruption of state. Explain: the network's speed profile exposed it to saturation risk; restart protocols, social channels, and validator discipline were the thin red line. Implication: high throughput must pay for guardrails in design, culture, and runbooks. If it cannot, it is not a platform; it is a demo.

A credible counter-example sets the boundary. In May 2022, TerraUSD's algorithmic stablecoin spiralled downwards as redemptions drained reserves and reflexive selling crushed its sister token. There was no credible backstop, no time-locked levers to slow panic, no transparent, pre-agreed contingency plan. Explain: the design privileged speed and capital efficiency over verifiable collateral and change control. Implication: some architectures are resilient in story only; their failure modes are not graceful but total. The reconciliation is hard but clear—if a system cannot survive a sudden stop, it was never infrastructure.

Resilience begins with auditability. Logs must outlive markets. They must be tamper-evident, time-synchronised, and queryable without ceremony. That means hash-linked event trails, stable schemas, and retention policies measured in years. It means deterministic builds and dependency pinning so you can reproduce a binary and prove what ran. It means that every change—parameter, contract, configuration—leaves a signed trace and a ticket that names who, why, and when. In practice, this looks like: versioned deployments with immutable IDs; Merkle proofs for critical state; and public changelogs as first-class artefacts. Trust is a ledger before it is a feeling.

Upgradeability sits next. Fast systems often weld innovation directly into production. Mature systems don't. They stage. They shadow. They can roll back. Concretely: treat upgrades as reversible transactions with *time-locked* execution. Publish the patch; start a countdown; allow watchers to inspect diffs; enable vetoes via multi-signature councils with published thresholds. If no credible objections arise, only then apply. This is dull, yes. It is also dignified. Users deserve the right to see what will change before it changes.

Pacing changes prevents cascade failure. Progressive rollouts—canary deployments, region-by-region enables, feature flags with dynamic kill-switches—turn unknown unknowns into bounded experiments. Pair each feature flag with a measurable invariant: median confirmation time, failed call rate, slippage band, liveness percentage. If the invariant exceeds the guardrail, cut over to the safe path automatically. No debate. No pride. Just thresholds that bite. Metrics should be few and legible. They should answer one question: is the system within its envelope?

Separation of powers is another pattern that endures. Do not let the team that writes code also hold the keys to deploy it and the authority to declare an incident over. Split those roles. Require independent sign-off for material changes. In smart-contract land, that implies multi-signature control with a public, rotating set of signers; in platform land, it implies a release manager distinct from feature owners; in finance land, it implies reconciliation by someone who does not touch execution. Bright lines reduce temptation and error. They also clarify blame, which is how cultures learn.

Rehearse failure. Chaos testing has a place in decentralised systems too. Inject latency. Drop packets. Corrupt a non-critical oracle feed in a testnet. What breaks? Who notices? How fast do dashboards update? If engineers cannot state, without hesitation, the three most likely failure paths and the first two remediation steps for each, the system is not resilient. Tabletop drills should be public where possible—at least the scenario and the playbook—not to perform transparency, but to crowdsource scrutiny. Sunlight is a pre-mortem.

Economise complexity. Minimalism is a safety feature. Every external call, every exotic opcode, every nested dependency is a surface for entropy. Prefer boring libraries that have survived years of production over brilliant ones still in preprint. Prefer a smaller instruction set over a larger one. Prefer explicit configuration over magic defaults. If a component is clever, isolate it. Cleverness belongs in sandboxes, not spines. The shortest path to resilience is often subtraction.

Beware hidden clocks. Speed creeps into systems through unacknowledged timing assumptions: heartbeat intervals, gas dynamics, mempool gossip, cache expiry. A design that assumes millisecond consensus or infinite bandwidth will die loudly. Time is the first adversary. Add slack to every critical path. Double the timeout. Then double it again. Shave throughput to buy cushion. Users remember outages more than microseconds. Markets price downtime, not bragging rights.

Make reversibility a product requirement. This is not only about pause functions. It is about designing *recovery windows* for specific actions: upgrades, parameter changes, mint events, and large liquidations. A 24-hour challenge period for governance proposals; a grace interval for voucher redemptions; a staged release of collateral. Reversibility allows humility. It gives stewards permission to say, "We moved too fast; we are stepping back." That sentence must be cheap to utter.

Align incentives with patience. Fee models can hardwire safety. Penalise bursty usage that risks saturation; reward steady participation with rebates; charge lower fees for batched transactions that reduce load. Auctions can be extended by randomised increments to deter last-second gas wars. Rewards should accrue for behaviour that helps the network's health, not just its headline numbers. Design markets for manners.

Put people into the loop with intent, not embarrassment. "Manual intervention" should be an explicit mode, not an ad hoc rescue. Name the role (guardian, controller, council). Publish its remit and limits. Make its actions cryptographically visible and procedurally dull. The presence of a brake pedal does not mean you drive recklessly. It means you can stop when a child runs into the road. Build the brake. Teach everyone where it is.

Use legal wrappers to turn technical promises into enforceable ones. If a consortium runs a critical oracle, bind uptime and data integrity to contractual penalties. If a security council exists, bind disclosure and conflict-of-interest policies. Boring compliance keeps exciting systems alive. Paper is part of the protocol.

Document the doctrine. Write a *resilience charter*: the invariants you refuse to break; the order of loyalties (integrity over liveness, liveness over throughput, throughput last); the thresholds that flip the switches. Put it in the docs, the code comments, and the governance portal. Do not rely on oral tradition. In a crunch, people grab what is written. Give them the right words.

Now, the limitation. Boredom can calcify. A culture that fetishises stability can miss genuine improvements. Formal verification can seduce teams into believing proofs replace prudence; audit badges can become amulets rather than artefacts. Reconcile this by budgeting for deliberate risk: carve out clear, capped sandboxes where speed is allowed—testnets with real but quarantined incentives; controlled pilots with opt-in users and hard stop dates; feature flags with automatic expiry. Curiosity is healthy when fenced.

Two final patterns outlast hype cycles. First, *small blast radii*. Architect for failure domains: shards, cells, and compartments with hard boundaries. A fault should scorch a room, not the house. Second, *plain exit ramps*. When users want to leave—withdraw funds, migrate assets, export identity—let them. The ability to exit is the measure of trust. Trapping users is a form of fragility; it converts accidents into scandals.

Return to the motif of the dull. The infrastructures we admire—aviation, nuclear power, card payments—earned trust by becoming predictably uneventful. Checklists. Drills. Double-entry. Alarms that chirp before they scream. Web3 and its heirs must embrace that inheritance. Aim for releases that cause no headlines. Celebrate patch notes that read like laundry. Write postmortems that teach, not posture. If it feels exciting, it is probably wrong.

The forward test is blunt: faced with a choice between shipping faster and sleeping better, which do you pick? That decision, repeated weekly, writes the culture into the code. Measure resilience explicitly. Compare incidents per quarter. Commit to mean time to *safety*, not merely mean time to recovery. Treat boredom as a KPI. Then guard it.

A builder's oath

On 16 June 2010, in a secure facility in Culpeper, Virginia, representatives of the Internet Corporation for Assigned Names and Numbers—ICANN—performed a ceremony that looked more like a constitutional ritual than a technical procedure. Smart cards were checked, tamper-evident bags unsealed, hardware security modules powered up. Independent witnesses filmed every step. The goal was simple to state and hard to earn: create cryptographic keys for the Domain Name System that the whole world could trust. Put the keys on camera. By July that year, DNSSEC—the system that signs the internet's phone book—was live at the root. The spectacle mattered. It told billions of strangers that power would be exercised in daylight. The lesson for token architects is plain: before speed, before scale, there is a promise.

An oath is not a feature. It is a constraint we accept in public, so that innovation does not dissolve into appetite. The token economy needs such a constraint. We have seen what happens when code races ahead of consent, when design hides context, when platforms pursue growth without care. By 2018, the Cambridge Analytica scandal revealed how behavioural data could be weaponised under the banner of progress; by 2022, cascading failures across crypto markets showed how brittle systems fracture when clarity and accountability are treated as optional. An oath does not prevent error. It prepares us to own it.

The oath here rests on four words—clarity, consent, context, care. They are not slogans. They are habits that become infrastructure. Each binds ambition to responsibility. Each translates into a behaviour you can measure, a mechanism you can test, and a decision you can defend when the lights are bright and tempers short. Think of the ICANN ceremony as a motif: keys on the table, cameras rolling, roles separated, the public invited to watch. The oath must make that level of daylight routine.

Begin with clarity. Show, then name. In April 2021, Apple released iOS 14.5 with App Tracking Transparency. Overnight, millions of users saw a simple, unavoidable prompt: "Allow [App] to track your activity across other companies' apps and websites?" The sentence was not perfect, but it was intelligible. Explain: clarity turns asymmetry into choice by replacing euphemism with plain language at the decision point, not in a buried policy. Implication: tokens that claim to encode rights must present those rights in words a layperson can repeat to a friend. Clarity is a specification in prose before it is a contract in code. If your "membership token" grants early entry, discounted upgrades, and resale royalties, state those entitlements on the token's face—human-readable, signed, and anchored to a reference that will outlive your website. The test is behavioural: could a user explain their rights after ten seconds, without a glossary? If not, the design fails the oath.

Clarity also demands lineage. Every parameter change, upgrade, and governance decision should leave a paper-trail that anyone can reconstruct. Estonia's digital government shows the form. Since the mid-2000s, the X-Road data exchange has logged cross-agency access with cryptographic proofs that citizens can inspect. Explain: the system enshrines an answerable question—who touched what, when, and under what lawful basis? Implication: token platforms should expose similarly queryable histories for rights and transfers, not just balances. In practice, that means stable metadata schemas, versioned documents, and identifiers that link code paths to public minutes. Clarity is a habit of leaving tracks.

Second, consent. Real consent costs time. It must be informed, specific, and revocable. Show a standard that tried to encode this ethic: the European Union's General Data Protection Regulation (2018). It does not forbid data use; it disciplines it with obligations to inform, to minimise, to delete. Explain: consent is not a checkbox; it is a continuing relationship with the right to change one's mind. Implication: tokenised services should embed *reversal* as a first-class operation—unsubscribe without penalty, de-mint personal data tokens without residual hooks, revoke delegated spending limits in two clicks. Measure it: count the steps from "no more" to "no more, indeed." If the path is labyrinthine, consent is performance, not protection.

A counter-example sharpens the line. In late 2022, several NFT marketplaces quietly toggled creator royalty enforcement off, then on again, then into optional modes as competitors undercut fees. Sellers cheered lower friction; many artists saw a rug. Explain: off-chain policy trumped on-chain expectation because the consent boundary was never explicit. Implication: if a right depends on a platform's mood, it is not a right; it is a favour. Reconcile this by binding consent to code and covenant. If royalties are optional, say so in uppercase on day one and offer alternatives: non-transferable patronage badges, membership tiers with service entitlements, or contracts that route a share to a creator-controlled address that only the creator can change. Consent survives when withdrawal is real and conditions are legible.

Third, context. Rights mean different things in different settings; design that ignores setting corrodes meaning. Consider the NHS COVID-19 app launched in England and Wales in September 2020. After a contested debate, the system adopted a decentralised exposure notification model that minimised central data retention. Explain: designers acknowledged the context—public health under extraordinary pressure—while restricting the system's memory to avoid becoming a surveillance tool. Implication: token builders must specify a use frame and enforce it: a museum pass should not silently become an advertising ID; a co-op voting token should not double as a trading chip outside the co-op's charter. The behaviour to measure is spillover. Where does your token end? If "everywhere," context has already failed.

Context also includes *fit*. Not every domain tolerates price signals. In 1970, Richard Titmuss showed that paying for blood in the United States degraded supply and quality compared to Britain's voluntary model. Explain: some goods are relational, not transactional. Implication: the oath demands a *priceless test* before tokenising a practice that binds trust—caregiving, civic duty, trauma narratives. If a token degrades a role into a tally, walk away. Your north star must include the power to refuse.

Finally, care. This is the least fashionable and the most necessary. Care is a posture of stewardship under uncertainty. Show a scene where care salvaged a system: on 12 March 2020, as crypto markets convulsed, MakerDAO's governors used a pre-designed pause to halt malfunctioning auctions and buy time for a patch. Explain: care was encoded as *reversibility*—a timer, a multisignature, an authority with limits and duties. Implication: your protocol should include a brake pedal with a published remit. Name the stewards, bound their powers, and log their actions in public. Safety is not a private chat; it is a civic performance.

Care extends beyond crisis. It is the daily discipline of maintenance—rotating keys, renewing audits, paying for documentation, refusing cleverness where clarity suffices. In 2015, the Ethereum foundation launched the network with a minimal instruction set and a public roadmap; years later, upgrades continue through testnets, audits, and time-locked releases. Explain: boredom was a feature, not a failure. Implication: if your design boasts velocity without a maintenance plan—no deprecation policy, no end-of-life path, no migration tooling—care is missing. You may grow fast; you will not stand long.

Thread the motif back through: keys on the table. Clarity puts them in sight. Consent lets a participant remove theirs without penalty. Context decides which doors they open. Care checks the hinges and calls a locksmith before they fail. These are not abstractions; they are operational tests. Can a newcomer explain their rights? Can a participant withdraw without bargaining? Can an auditor reconstruct the past in an hour? Can the system pause a bad decision tomorrow? If any answer is no, the oath has been recited but not kept.

Two named examples show the oath at work beyond crypto. First, *Open Banking* in the United Kingdom, mandated by the Competition and Markets Authority in January 2018, forced major banks to provide standardised, permissioned access to account data. Explain: clarity came via uniform APIs; consent via user-initiated authorisations with explicit scopes and expiries; context via limitations on what third parties could do; care via regulated accountability and revocation. Implication: when interfaces are open and obligations enforceable, ecosystems grow without extracting dignity. Second, *ICANN's* root key ceremonies continue, split between Culpeper and El Segundo, California, with public scripts, independent witnesses, and contingency plans. Explain: trust is staged, recorded, and boring by design. Implication: the guardians of root identity treat spectacle as transparency, not as hype. Token builders should learn from that liturgy. It works.

A limitation belongs here. Principles can harden into theatre. Consent prompts can numb. Audit logs can flood. Public ceremonies can fetishise optics. Reconcile this by binding the oath to *outcomes*, not rituals. Measure misunderstanding rates in usability tests. Publish time-to-revoke and keep it under a minute. Cap permission scopes and expire them by default. Track how often stewards exercise emergency powers—and work to reduce that number. The oath must cash out in lived experience or it becomes a catechism.

What, then, is the oath in practice? It is four commitments you can sign with your name. For clarity: "We will write rights in plain English and keep the words stable." For consent: "We will ask before we take, and make leaving easy." For context: "We will define the purpose, bind the token to it, and resist scope creep." For care: "We will design for reversibility, document our duties, and prefer maintenance to novelty." Say them aloud in the room where product decisions are made. Put them at the top of the repo. Tie bonuses to them. Publish breaches against them. If this feels severe, good. Severity, not sentiment, keeps promises.

The oath asks for restraint at the edge of possibility. When a new feature tempts with growth, the four words should slow your hand. Does the language clarify? Does the user truly agree? Does the design respect the setting? Have we prepared for failure and repair? If any answer stumbles, you know what to do: stop, rewrite, rehearse, and only then release. The market may reward speed today. History will reward care tomorrow.

The unresolved question is where you will draw the line when urgency and conscience collide. A partner demands a data firehose; an investor pushes for "frictionless" flows; a competitor ships a feature you worry is unsafe. Do you trim the oath to fit the quarter, or do you let a hyped opportunity pass? That choice, repeated, becomes culture. Culture becomes law. Law becomes the ecosystem other people must live in. When the moment arrives—and it will—remember the keys on the table. Will you keep them there, under the camera's gaze, or will you pocket them for convenience? Your answer will tell users what your tokens are truly worth.

About the Author

Arjun Malhotra writes at the crossroads of technology, markets, and culture, helping readers see how software quietly reshapes everyday value. After years building products and advising founders, he focuses on the human side of digital systems: incentives, governance, and the stories we tell about ownership. He believes tools should serve meaning, not replace it. A lifelong reader of economic history, he draws subtle lessons from eras of standard-setting, from coinage reforms to the printing press, to show how today's token experiments fit a longer arc. His work is practical, sceptical of hype, and optimistic about well-designed institutions.

www.ingramcontent.com/pod-product-compliance
Lightning Source LLC
Chambersburg PA
CBHW031343230926
51848CB00002B/355
* 9 7 8 9 3 7 4 5 9 6 9 9 9 *